ABORTION IN THE SEVENTIES

Proceedings
of the
Western Regional Conference on Abortion
Denver, Colorado February 27-29, 1976

Sponsored by

Abortion Referral and Counseling Service of Colorado
Catholics for a Free Choice
Colorado Department of Health
Colorado National Organization for Women
Colorado Women's Political Caucus
Denver National Organization for Women
National Abortion Rights Action League
Rocky Mountain Planned Parenthood
Zero Population Growth

Edited by

Warren M. Hern, M.D., M.P.H. and Bonnie Andrikopoulos

077317
1977
National Abortion Federation
New York, New York

CI AUG. 2 1 1979

Co-Chairpersons of the Conference

Bonnie Andrikopoulos and Warren M. Hern, M.D., M.P.H.

Conference Coordinator

Lynne Hubanks

Special assistance for this conference was provided by:

Berkeley Bio-Engineering Company
Colorado Department of Health
Institute of Medicine, National Academy of Science
Milex Products, Inc. and Milex Western
Rocky Mountain Planned Parenthood
Searle Laboratories - Professional Education Department
  A Division of G.D. Searle & Co.
The Sunnen Foundation
U.S. Commission on Civil Rights, Washington, D.C.

DEDICATION

This book is dedicated to the memory of
John Asher
a beloved friend and colleague
who cared about people
and lived that way

EDITORS' NOTE

When we began organizing the Western Regional Conference on Abortion in the fall of 1975, we decided that the valuable contributions of the participants should be preserved in the same manner as the 1971 New York Conference on Abortion Techniques and Services. The present volume is the result of actual taped transcripts of the entire conference. The informality and spontaneity of the participants' remarks and discussions are preserved as much as possible.

We wish to thank all those who worked so hard to bring about this conference, especially the speakers presented here. We feel that the WRCA was an important event not only for the sharing of information among those working for abortion rights and better abortion services; it was a great psychological boost at a time when these rights are under concerted attack all over the nation. If there is a certain "scrapbook" quality about this volume, it is because we want the reader to share in an important human event as well as learn the facts which were presented here.

Special thanks go to Sarah Lewit for her invaluable advice. We deeply appreciate the expert assistance of Barbara L. Lindheim and Maureen Cotterill in the final editing and preparation of the manuscript for printing. We are responsible, however, for any editing errors which appear. The Sunnen Foundation has been extraordinarily helpful in bringing about both the conference and the publication of this volume. We are grateful to the National Abortion Federation for its sponsorship of the actual publication.

The texts of the papers have been cleared with the individual authors. The discussions which follow each session have not been cleared, and the presentation is the sole responsibility of the editors.

We hope and believe that this volume will provide valuable assistance for years to come to those engaged in providing abortion services and to those who simply wish to understand the issue better.

Warren M. Hern, M.D., M.P.H.   Bonnie Andrikopoulos

FOREWORD

The right of a woman to terminate her pregnancy remains at issue in our time. Currently, the attendant publicity confuses many people and does little to clarify the real choices, or point toward possible solutions. People on different sides of the questions which have been raised believe that precious values are at stake—moral, religious, legal and Constitutional values.

The proceedings of the Western Regional Conference on Abortion represent the intent of the participants in the conference to cast light on the basic questions relating to abortion. As such, this volume is a welcome addition to the rapidly developing body of knowledge on the subject. Little can be decided for the general good of all people—or of women in particular—in the absence of knowledge of the factual issues.

The order in which the topics are discussed in the book does not reflect the stress the editors place upon particular aspects of problems. Rather, it is clear that *all* of the subjects discussed are crucial. Each participant deserves our thanks for making his or her best effort to speak forthrightly to a wider audience. In this, the contributors are worthy advocates—people with a point of view that merits our attention.

Mary F. Berry
Chancellor
University of Colorado at Boulder

THE WHITE HOUSE

February 24, 1976

Dear Ms. Andrikopoulos
and Dr. Hern:

How much I appreciated your gracious
letter telling of plans for the Western
Regional Conference on Abortion and
inviting me to attend.

Although my upcoming personal and
official commitments will not permit me to
be with you, I am grateful for this opportunity to convey my warmest greetings to
all attending and my hopes for the success
of the Conference.

With gratitude and my warmest regards,

Sincerely,

Betty Ford

Ms. Bonnie Andrikopoulos
Warren M. Hern, M.D.
Western Regional Conference
    on Abortion
1400 Lafayette Street
Denver, Colorado 80218

PARTICIPANTS

BONNIE ANDRIKOPOULOS, Lobbyist, Colorado National Organization for Women, Denver, Colorado.

SARAH SPAGHT BROWN, M.P.H., Professional Associate, National Academy of Sciences, Institute of Medicine, Washington, D.C.

JOHN BERMINGHAM, Former Senator, Colorado State Senate.

CAROL BONOSARO, Director, Women's Rights Program Unit, United States Commission on Civil Rights, Washington, D.C.

ELEANORE BOYD, Colorado Right-to-Life Committee, Pueblo, Colorado.

WILLARD CATES, M.D., M.P.H., Acting Chief, Abortion Surveillance Branch, Family Planning Evaluation Division, Bureau of Epidemiology, Center for Disease Control, Atlanta, Georgia.

IRVIN CUSHNER, M.D., M.P.H., Associate Professor, Obstetrics & Gynecology, School of Medicine; Associate Professor, Public Health, School of Public Health; University of California at Los Angeles, Los Angeles, California.

SAM W. DOWNING, M.D., F.A.C.S., F.A.C.O.G., Chairman, Department of Obstetrics & Gynecology, Mercy Hospital, Denver, Colorado.

MARTY DREW, Catholics for a Free Choice, Denver, Colorado.

WILLIAM DROEGEMUELLER, M.D., F.A.C.O.G., Associate Professor of Obstetrics & Gynecology, University of Colorado School of Medicine, Denver, Colorado.

JEAN DUBOFSKY, Deputy Attorney General of Colorado, Denver, Colorado.

NETTIE FISHER, M.S.W., Associate Professor, University of Denver Graduate School of Social Work, Denver, Colorado.

HELEN GERASH, M.D., Psychiatrist, Denver, Colorado.

JAN GLEASON, President, Catholics for a Free Choice, San Diego, California.

MARLENE GOLD, M.A., Director of Counseling, Boulder Abortion Clinic, Boulder, Colorado.

DAVID GRIMES, M.D., Abortion Surveillance Branch, Family Planning Evaluation Division, Bureau of Epidemiology, Center for Disease Control, Atlanta, Georgia.

WARREN M. HERN, M.D., M.P.H., Director, Boulder Abortion Clinic, Boulder, Colorado.

PEGGY HESS, Parent, Team Leader for the Teen Mothers Program, Jefferson County Public Schools, Lakewood, Colorado.

JANE HODGSON, M.D., F.A.C.O.G., Department of Obstetrics & Gynecology, Ramsey Hospital, St. Paul, Minnesota. Former Medical Director, Preterm Clinic, Washington, D.C.

SHIRLEY HYDE, R.N., Denver General Hospital, Denver, Colorado.

CYNTHIA KAHN, Administrative Assistant, U.S. Representative Patricia Schroeder, Denver, Colorado.

REVEREND PAT KIRTON, Minister, United Methodist Church, Denver, Colorado.

KAREN KOWALSKI, R.N., Director of Ob/Gyn Nursing Services, University of Colorado Medical Center, Denver, Colorado.

RICHARD D. LAMM, Governor of Colorado.

JESSICA LUNA, Community Information Specialist, Latin American Research and Service Agency, Denver, Colorado.

REVEREND ALEX LUKENS, JR., Presbyterian Hospital Center, Denver, Colorado.

CYRIL C. MEANS, JR., Professor, New York Law School, New York, New York.

H. BENJAMIN MUNSON, M.D., F.A.C.O.G., Rapid City, South Dakota.

KAREN MULHAUSER, Executive Director, National Abortion Rights Action League, Washington, D.C.

JEAN PAKTER, M.D., M.P.H., Director, Bureau of Maternity Services and Family Planning, New York City Health Department, New York.

WILLIAM RASHBAUM, M.D., F.A.C.O.G., Assistant Professor of Obstetrics and Gynecology, Albert Einstein Medical Center, New York, New York.

JEANNIE ROSOFF, Director, Planned Parenthood Washington Office; Vice-President, The Alan Guttmacher Institute, Washington, D.C.

MARY BENNETT SCHARF, Former Counselor, East High School, Denver, Colorado.

CAROL SCHNEIDER, Ph.D., Staff Psychologist, Wardenburg Student Health Center, University of Colorado, Boulder, Colorado.

PATRICIA SCHROEDER, Member, United States House of Representatives (District 1, Colorado), Washington, D.C.

DON SHAW, Coordinator for Health Education, Jefferson County Public Schools, Lakewood, Colorado.

LINDA SIMS, University Common Ministry, Laramie, Wyoming.

RUTH STEEL, Englewood, Colorado.

CHRISTOPHER TIETZE, M.D., Senior Consultant, The Population Council, New York, New York.

LOUISE TYRER, M.D., F.A.C.O.G., Vice-President for Medical Affairs, Planned Parenthood Federation of America, New York, New York.

FLORENCE UYEDA, M.D., Pediatrician.

JOHN VANCE, President, Colorado Blue Cross/Blue Shield.

SARAH WEDDINGTON, Member, Texas State House of Representatives; Of Counsel, *Roe v. Wade*; President, National Abortion Rights Action League; Attorney, Austin, Texas.

SIDNEY WERKMAN, M.D., Professor of Psychiatry, University of Colorado School of Medicine, Denver, Colorado.

JUDITH WIDDICOMBE, R.N., Executive Director, Reproductive Health Services, St. Louis, Missouri.

SHIRLEY HILL WITT, Ph.D., Director, Mountain States Regional Office, U.S. Commission on Civil Rights.

RORY ZAHOUREK, R.N., Psychiatric Nurse, Creative Health Services, Denver, Colorado.

WELCOMING REMARKS

Shirley Hill Witt, Ph.D.

Welcome to the Western Regional Conference on Abortion. As Director of the Mountain States Regional Office of the U.S. Commission on Civil Rights, I feel particularly comfortable with the subject matter of this three-day conference. Our Commission is one of the few federal agencies which has publicly pronounced its stand regarding a woman's right to decide whether or not to terminate a pregnancy.

In a 200-page legal study released by the Commission last April, the Commission urged Congress to reject proposed constitutional amendments that would deny or limit a woman's right to terminate a pregnancy. The Commission staff director, John Buggs, stated that "the Commission's sole position is its affirmation and support of each woman's constitutional right as upheld by the Supreme Court to decide whether or not to abort." In addition, the Commission maintained that the proposed amendment threatened the enforcement of other civil rights guaranteed by the Constitution. If these amendments were enacted, a dangerous precedent would be established which would facilitate efforts to nullify other Supreme Court decisions. For the same reason, the Commission opposed a states' rights amendment which would permit each state to decide the legality of abortion.

I am sure that during the past years all of us have gone through a good deal of public discussion concerning private morality and public policy on this controversial issue of abortion. The basic moral question stemming from conflicting religious views about the beginning of life is indeed a personal one. As for America's public policy, the fact is the Supreme Court decided that issue three years ago, in a 7 to 2 decision, in *Roe vs. Wade.* There remains an ever-growing concern about the meaning of that Supreme Court decision, its implementation and its implications not only for women but for men as well. Many of these questions will be aired during this conference. Those of us who are here today recognize the seriousness of this concern, for today, some three years after the Supreme Court decision, there is still a deliberate, selective and insidious attempt to undermine that ruling. Even at this very moment we are steadily returning to a period when only women with money can obtain safe abortions. I know that the next three days will be informative for all of us. More importantly, they will provide us with the kind of forum needed to share information and to become more dedicated to one of the most pressing issues of our age: emancipation from our biology.

CONTENTS

NATIONAL ACADEMY OF SCIENCES REPORT

Sarah Spaght Brown, M.P.H.

Published in May of 1975, *Legalized Abortion and the Public Health* is the report of a committee appointed by the Institute of Medicine to examine the effects of abortion on the health of the public, particularly as abortion moved from being essentially illegal to legal.

In 1971, the Institute of Medicine was created to enlist distinguished scholars from the medical profession and other health disciplines in examining policy matters pertaining to the health of the public. The Academy itself was formed in the middle part of the 19th century under charter of the federal government by President Lincoln, to serve as an expert, impartial, nonfederal source of scientific advice to the government. The Institute has carried that charter forward for issues of health and medicine. We, like our parent organization, do studies at the request of the government, but also initiate some projects on our own and seek private funding. Our activities include projects on such issues as national health insurance, ethical issues in human experimentation, health manpower, and malpractice.

This abortion study was initiated by the Institute rather than in response to a federal request. It was our judgment in the spring of 1973 that the controversy following the Supreme Court decision legalizing abortion could benefit from the infusion of facts to counter the rhetoric. One of the charges being made at that time was that abortion was a hazardous surgical intervention with dreaded risks to both the physical and mental health of a woman who obtained the procedure. We noted these allegations with concern and decided that it might be helpful if we could summarize in one document what was then known about the health effects of abortion. To develop the report, we convened a committee with Mildred Mitchell Bateman, Director of the West Virginia Department of Mental Health, as our Chairperson.* We hoped to speak to an audience of policy makers, physicians, interested lay persons, and of course, the Congress.

---

* Other members of the Committee included Henry Foster, Helen Barnes, Elise Boulding, Robert Cook, Ruth Watson Lubic, Brian MacMahon, Frederick Robbins, Lisbeth Schorr and Christopher Tietze.

We undertook no original research ourselves but reviewed data already collected on the health effects of abortion. With important exceptions, we avoided using data collected abroad, primarily because we felt these data were not always applicable to the U.S. In addition the medical practices and laws surrounding abortion in other parts of the world are not always similar to those in the U.S. The study group made a decision at the outset that we would not enter into the philosophical debates surrounding abortion. The Committee felt that its expertise lay in examining data on medical issues associated with abortion.

It is useful to begin with some background information about abortion. The three methods most commonly used in the U.S. to induce abortion are vacuum aspiration and dilation and curettage for pregnancies in the first three months, and replacement of the amniotic fluid with a concentrated salt solution ("saline abortion") to stimulate labor and delivery in the second trimester. In late 1973, the FDA approved the limited use of prostaglandins as an alternative to second trimester saline abortion. Hysterectomy and hysterotomy, both requiring surgical entry into the abdomen, are also occasionally performed in the U.S. (Figure 1). Figures compiled by the Center for Disease Control (CDC) indicate that in 1971, there were approximately 486,000 legal abortions performed in the U.S., rising to 587,000 abortions in 1972 and approximately 616,000 abortions by 1973.[1] This rise in absolute number of abortions was paralleled by a rise in the abortion ratio—that is, the number of legal abortions per 1,000 live births (Figure 2). Although the increase in the abortion ratio also reflects a decline in the number of births and a replacement of legal for illegal abortions, CDC data also show that of those women obtaining legal abortions in 1973 whose age was known, about a third were less than 20 years old, one-third were between the ages of 20 and 25, and one-third were over the age of 25 (Figure 3). About 30 percent of women who obtained legal abortions in 1973 were married at the time of the procedure.[2]

There is evidence indicating that the rise in the number of legal abortions has been accompanied by a decline in the number of illegal abortions, which are known to be less safe medically. If one is able to document a decline in the number of hospital admissions for septic and incomplete abortions, which often result from illegally induced abortions, a logical conclusion is that illegal abortions are declining as well. Our report noted that the ratio of the number of admissions for incomplete or septic abortions per 1000 births in New York City declined from 234 in 1969 to 133 in 1974 (Table 1). This is only a rough indicator of the decline in illegal abortion, but we believe that it is accurate in indicating a trend. Similar declines have been observed elsewhere. At Grady Hospital in Atlanta (Figure 4), there were 33 admissions for septic or incomplete abortions in the last quarter of 1970, declining to five in the first quarter of 1973. Dr. Christopher Tietze has studied this question and concluded that in New York City, 70 percent of the legal abortions obtained by resident

FIGURE I

Methods of Induced Abortion By Weeks of Pregnancy

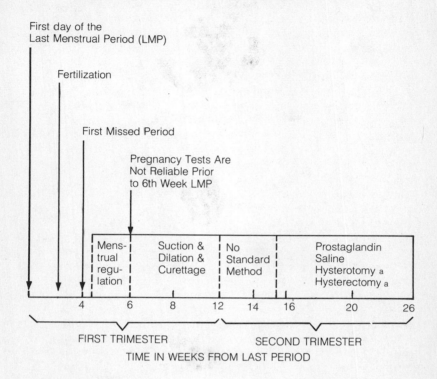

First day of the
Last Menstrual Period (LMP)

Fertilization

First Missed Period

Pregnancy Tests Are
Not Reliable Prior
to 6th Week LMP

| Mens-trual regu-lation | Suction & Dilation & Curettage | No Standard Method | Prostaglandin Saline Hysterotomy a Hysterectomy a |

4   6   8   12   14   16   20   26

FIRST TRIMESTER   SECOND TRIMESTER

TIME IN WEEKS FROM LAST PERIOD

a/ These two methods can also be used in the first trimester.

Source: Adapted from Theresa van der Vlugt, and P. T. Piotrow. "Uterine Aspiration Techniques," *Population Report, Series F*, No. 3, Washington, D.C.: The George Washington University Medical Center, Population Information Programs, June 1973.

women between July 1, 1970 and June 30, 1972, replaced illegal abortions and that the remainder was responsible for about one half of the decline in the live births that occurred in this same period.[3]

Some data suggest that the legalization of abortion has contributed to the birth rate decline documented in recent years. There also seems to be some preliminary evidence that legalization of abortion is related to declining infant mortality rates. Some women, particularly teenagers, who are at high risk of bearing premature or low birth weight infants whose survival chances are relatively poor, are choosing abortion in numbers disproportionate to their representation in the population of childbearing

FIGURE 2

Number of Reported or Estimated Legal Abortions and Abortion Ratios United States, 1970–1973   a/

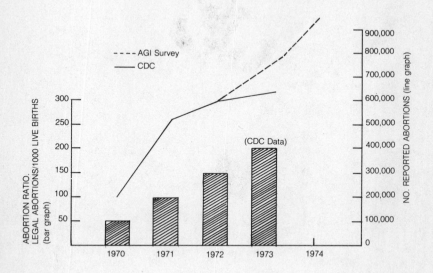

a/ The number of states reporting statewide or partial data to CDC in these years is given below. For those states reporting only partial data to CDC, there are no estimates of how many abortions were performed but were not reported.

1970 — 24 states	1972 — 28 states
1971 — 25 states	1973 — 51 states

Source: U.S. Department of Health, Education, and Welfare, Public Health Service, Center of Disease Control. *Abortion Surveillance: 1972,* issued April 1974; *Abortion Surveillance: 1973,* issued May 1975; and Edward Weinstock, Christopher Tietze, Frederick S. Jaffe, and Joy G. Dryfoos. "Legal Abortions in the United States Since the 1973 Supreme Court Decisions," *Family Planning Perspectives* 7: 25 January/February 1975.

women. Between the years 1968 and 1972, infant mortality rates in the U.S. declined about seven percent (Table 2). In California and New York, two states with an early and dramatic increase in the availability of legal abortions, a decline of nine percent has been recorded. Whether or not this indicates a causal relationship is not clear, but the evidence warrants further study.

Examining the incidence of complications of abortion, the Institute study cited the Ljubljana study conducted in Yugoslavia in 1971 and 1972.[4] This study found that major complications of first trimester abortion are rare and that suction abortion generally seems to have fewer

FIGURE 3

Percent Distribution of Reported Legal Abortions by Age, Selected States, 1973   a/

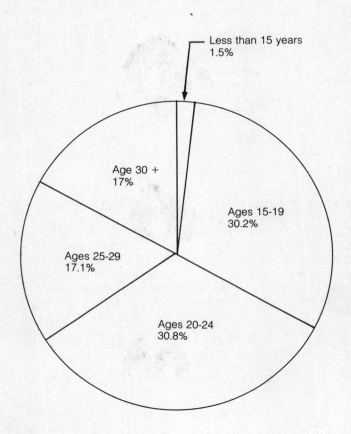

Less than 15 years
1.5%

Age 30 +
17%

Ages 15-19
30.2%

Ages 25-29
17.1%

Ages 20-24
30.8%

a/ There were 489,735 abortions, out of a total of 615,831, for which age was reported. The percentages do not equal 100 because 3.5 percent of the ages were unknown.

Source: U.S. Department of Health, Education, and Welfare. Public Health Service, Center for Disease Control. *Abortion Surveillance: 1973,* issued May 1975.

TABLE 1

Admissions to Municipal Hospitals in New York City for Incomplete Abortions, 1969-1973

Years	Number of Admissions	Number of Births	Incomplete Abortion Admissions per 1,000 Births
1969	6524	27,842	234
1970	5293	31,308	169
1971	3643	27,998	130
1972	3538	24,989	142
1973	3253	24,502	133

Source: Personal communication to Emily Moore-Cavar from Jean Pakter, Director, Bureau of Maternity Services and Family Planning, Department of Health, New York City and published in *International Inventory of Information on Induced Abortion,* New York: International Institute for the Study of Human Reproduction, Columbia University, 1974, p. 642.

complications associated with it than D and C (Table 3). Of course, one of the problems in assessing the complication rates of specific surgical techniques is standardizing the definition of what constitutes a complication and how soon after the procedure it has to occur. The Joint Program for the Study of Abortion (JPSA) study has also collected data on complications (Table 4). The JPSA study, conducted between July 1970 and June 1971, surveyed the mortality and morbidity associated with 73,000 abortions performed in 66 participating institutions. The total

TABLE 2

Infant Mortality Rates for United States and Selected States: 1968-1972
(Deaths per 1,000 Live Births)

Area	1968	1969	1970	1971	1972	Percent Decline 1970-1972
United States a/	22.3	21.2	20.4	19.5	19.0	−6.9
California	19.0	18.3	17.2	16.4	15.6	−9.3
New York	0.9	21.2	19.4	18.3	17.6	−9.3
Washington	19.7	18.9	18.7	18.3	17.1	−8.6

a/ Excludes California, Kansas, New York, and Washington

Source U.S. Department of Health, Education, and Welfare, Public Health Service, National Center for Health Statistics. *U.S. Vital Statistics*, Vol. 1, *Natality,* 1968, 1969. Individual state statistics for 1970-1973 are unpublished.

complication rate, both major and minor, was judged to be between 4.2 and 6.2 per 100 abortions for suction abortion in the first trimester of pregnancy with no concurrent sterilization and with no pre-existing medical problems. The risk of complications increases by week of gestation to a high of about 56.5 to 60.4 for abortion over 13 weeks' gestation with concurrent sterilization and with pre-existing medical problems.[5] Both the Ljubljana study and the JPSA study indicate that abortion is very safe when performed early in pregnancy, and safest of all if performed by suction aspiration.

It is important to add a cautionary note. There is some evidence suggesting that abortion, and especially repeated abortion, may be related to a higher incidence of ectopic pregnancy, miscarriage, prematurity and even sterility in subsequent pregnancies. The data in this

FIGURE 4

Number of Hospital Admissions for Complications due to
Illegal Abortions, Grady Hospital, Atlanta, 1969-1973

NO. OF ADMISSIONS

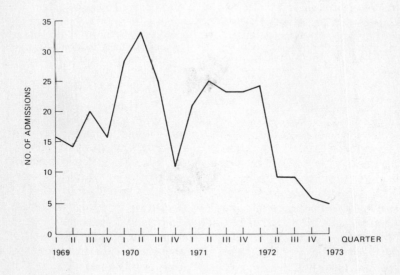

Source: Ronald S. Kahan, Lawrence D. Baker and Malcolm G. Freeman. "The Effect of Legalized Abortion and Morbidity Resulting from Criminal Abortion," *American Journal of Obstetrics and Gynecology* 121:115 January 1, 1975.

TABLE 3

Complications of First Trimester Abortions, Ljubljana, 1971-1972

Type of Complication	Rates per 100 Women Obtaining Abortions	
	Suction	D&C
Perforation of uterus	0.0	0.6
Laceration of cervix	0.7	0.7
Complications of anesthesia	2.9	3.7
Heavy bleeding requiring agents to tighten the uterine walls a/	3.9	6.0
Blood loss exceeding 300 ml b/		
– at abortion	1.9	3.3
– total first 48 hours	5.4	8.9
Post abortion bleeding		
– requiring treatment	9.6	10.0
– requiring hospitalization	1.5	1.9
Retention of tissue	0.9	1.3
Pelvic Infection or fever c/		
during hospitalization	2.0	1.6
– requiring readmission a/	0.7	1.3

a/ Statistically significant differences (P=.01)

b/ These data based on a subsample of 530 cases.

c/ Includes endometritis, salpingitis, temperature rise to 37.6 degrees centigrade for more than two days.

Source: L. Andolsek and M. Owen. "The Operation and the Operator"; L. Andolsek. "Operative Events"; L. Andolsek and M. Owen. "Blood Loss"; and L. Andolsek. "Infection"; in L. Andolsek. *The Ljubljana Abortion Study, 1971-1973,* Bethesda: National Institutes of Health, 1974.

area are incomplete although provocative. The report of a World Health Organization (WHO) study on the long-term complications of abortion will be released in 1977. Until these data are available, the subject of long-term risks cannot be adequately addressed.

An important measure of safety is risk of death. In 1972 there were 20 and in 1973, 22 deaths that were believed to be associated with legal abortion in the United States.[6] Expressed as a mortality ratio (the number of deaths per 100,000 abortions), the mortality ratio is approximately 1.7 in the first trimester and 12.2 in the second trimester. Although these ratios are low, there is a dramatic increase in risk of death associated with abortion by each additional week of gestation, from a mortality ratio of 0.5 for abortion at less than eight weeks of pregnancy to 16.1 for abortion performed at gestations of sixteen weeks or more (Table 5). In addition, the saline method of abortion itself carries a greater risk of death than does suction or D and C.

TABLE 4

Total and Major Postabortal Complications per 100 women Obtaining Abortions by Gestation, Procedure, Pre-existing Complications, and Concurrent Sterilization, Total Patients and Local Patients with Follow-up (FU)
JPSA, July 1, 1970 - June 30, 1971

Type of Abortion	Total Complications		Major Complications	
	Total patients	Local patients with FU	Total patients	Local patients with FU
All patients	Complication Rates Per 100 Women Obtaining Abortions			
12 weeks or less	5.2	7.8	0.6	1.1
13 weeks or more	22.2	26.1	2.2	3.0
Patients *without* pre-existing complications, by procedure				
Suction a/	4.2	6.1	0.4	0.6
D&C a/	6.0	8.2	0.5	0.8
Saline a/	23.4	27.2	1.7	2.4
Hysterotomy b/	33.4	32.9	6.7	6.9
Hysterectomy	49.9	50.9	14.3	15.6
Patients *without* complications *or* sterilization				
12 weeks or less	4.2	6.2	0.4	0.6
13 weeks or more	20.6	26.0	1.6	2.1
Patients *with* pre-existing complications, *without* sterilization				
12 weeks or less	12.7	17.1	1.4	2.0
13 weeks or more	29.9	35.1	4.6	6.7
Patients *without* pre-existing complications, *with* sterilization				
12 weeks or less	25.9	28.0	6.1	7.2
13 weeks or more	35.8	35.4	8.2	8.0
Patients *with* pre-existing complications *and* sterilization				
12 weeks or less	43.0	46.2	14.9	17.1
13 weeks or more	56.5	60.4	13.8	17.4

a/ Without tubal sterilization
b/ With tubal sterilization

Source: Christopher Tietze and Deborah Dawson. "Induced Abortion: A Factbook," *Reports on Population/Family Planning* 14, December 1973.

TABLE 5

Reported Deaths Associated with Legal Abortion in the United States, by weeks of Gestation and Method of Abortion, 1972 and 1973

	Number of Abortions	Number of Deaths	Mortality Ratio (Deaths per 100,000 abortions)
Total	1,202,563	42	3.5
Weeks of Gestation a/			
8 or less	421,896	2	0.5
9-10	361,885	6	1.7
11-12	212,981	9	4.2
13-15	87,573	6	6.9
16 or more	118,228	19	16.1
Method of Abortion			
Suction/D&C	1,065,338	17	1.6
Saline	123,684	19	15.4
Hysterotomy/hys-		5	61.3
terectomy	8,161		
other	5,380	1	18.6

a/ Distribution of abortions based on gestation of pregnancy known for 449,709 abortions reported during 1972 (77 percent of the total for that year) and for 453,535 abortions reported for 1973 (74 percent of the total for that year).

Source: U.S. Department of Health, Education, and Welfare, Public Health Service, Center for Disease Control. *Morbidity and Mortality Weekly Report* 24, January 24, 1975.

Table 6 places the mortality ratio of abortion in perspective by comparing it to the risk of death associated with other commonly performed surgical procedures. These figures show first trimester abortion to be less risky than tonsillectomy, with or without adenoidectomy, and significantly safer than appendectomy or hysterectomy. The mortality ratio for death due to complications of pregnancy and childbirth, excluding abortion, is about 14.1 or 14 deaths to 100,000 live births in 1973.[7]

The decrease in complications related to illegal abortions which have been associated with the legalization of abortion is evidenced in the decline of deaths as well as in the decline in complications measured by septic and incomplete abortions. Figure 5 compares the number of deaths from legal abortions with those from "other" abortions over the past 18 years in the United States. While the "other" category includes miscarriages and abortions of undetermined origin, various observers conclude that most of the deaths included in the "other" category are from illegally induced abortions. For example, of the 47 deaths reported in 1973, 22 were from legal abortions, 16 were from illegal abortions, seven were from spontaneous abortions, and the remaining two deaths were from unknown causes. It is apparent that the decline in deaths from "other abortions" began prior to the legalization of abortion, reflecting in part improved obstetric and gynecological care and general medical procedures.

In assessing the effects of abortion on psychological health, we focused on two questions: the effect of legal abortion on the mental health of the woman obtaining it and the psychological effect of denying a requested abortion on the woman, the resulting child, and the family. The term "psychological" was used to refer in a general way to an individual's emotionaor mental health, and "psychiatric" was used in reference to mental illness or disturbance. A lack of data prevented us from examining such issues as the effects of abortion on marital relationships, family cohesiveness or child abuse. Data on the differential effects of first versus second trimester abortion were also unavailable, although most psychiatric opinion supports the obstetrical judgment that second trimester abortion is more stressful than first trimester abortion.

TABLE 6

Mortality Ratios of Selected
Surgical Procedures
United States, 1969

Operation	Mortality Ratio (Number of Deaths per 100,000 procedures)
Legal Abortion	
First trimester	17a/
Second trimester	12.2a/
Tonsillectomy without Adenoidectomy	3
Tonsillectomy with Adenoidectomy	5
Ligation and Division of Fallopian Tubes	5
Partial Mastectomy	74
Cesarean Section (Low cervical)	111
Abdominal Hysterectomy (not abortion)	204
Appendectomy	352

a/ Based on 1972-1973 data from the Center for Disease Control.

Source: Charles G. Child III. "Surgical Intervention", *Life and Death and Medicine,* San Francisco: W. H. Freeman and Company, 1973, p. 65. this book originally appeared as the September 1973 edition of *Scientific American.*

FIGURE 5

Abortion Deaths By Type of Abortion 1958-1973

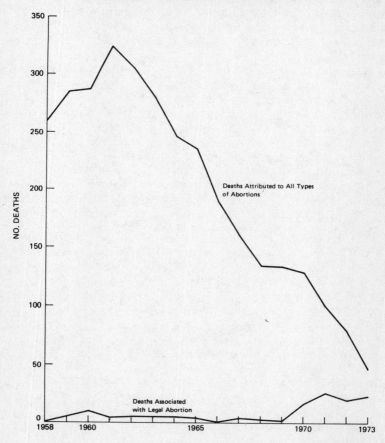

Source: U.S. Department of Health, Education, and Welfare. *Vital Statistics of the United States, Mortality, Part A.;* 1972 and 1973 data are from U.S. Department of Health, Education, and Welfare, Public Health Service, Center for Disease Control. *Morbidity and Mortality Weekly Report* 24: January 24, 1975.

When we began our inquiry into psychological impacts we were struck by the wide range of conflicting findings. After an extensive review of the literature, we concluded that the bulk of the research is marred by both problems of definition and of method. For example, in all studies which have looked at the mental health impact of abortion, terms such as "adverse psychological outcome," or "post-abortion depression" or "abortion-induced grieving" are used. Yet how does one define such terms? If someone is depressed following an abortion, does that qualify as a complication, or do we consider that to be normal, transient depression, similar to "postpartum blues?" Similarly, if a woman visits a psychiatrist following a therapeutic abortion, is that necessarily to be construed as a complication or could it be equally classified as a sign of mental health and maturity? From a methodological point of view, problems include such questions as the selection of an appropriate "control group" to which a group of women undergoing abortions can be compared. Can the psychological health of women choosing induced abortion be compared to that of women who miscarry, who are having a term delivery, or to some other group? These problems in both definition and method probably account for the wide variety of findings on this important subject. In addition many of the studies on the mental health effects of abortion were completed before the Supreme Court ruling, at a time when abortion was still widely illegal.

After taking these methodological issues into account, the study group concluded that there are many methodological problems in abortion research which are serious in the studies conducted prior to the mid-1960s than in later studies. In the early studies, the design shortcomings, in combination with a legal and social climate hostile to objective discussion of the subject, probably account for the wide variety of findings that range from conclusions that abortion has no negative psychological consequences to those suggesting it is an emotionally damaging experience. The more recent studies generally agree that the feelings of guilt, regret, or loss elicited in some women undergoing a legal abortion are usually temporary and appear to be outweighed by positive life changes and feelings of relief. It is likely that there is no psychologically painless way to cope with an unwanted pregnancy, whether it is voluntarily interrupted or carried to term. While an abortion may elicit feelings of guilt, regret or loss, such alternatives as forced marriage, bearing an out-of-wedlock child, giving up a child for adoption, or adding an unwanted child to a family may also be accompanied by psychological problems for the woman, the child, and the family.

The JPSA study mentioned previously collected data on serious psychiatric sequelae of abortion. The study reported a range of between 0.2 and 0.4 psychiatric complications per 1,000 abortions.[8] The complications included two suicides and five depressive reactions associated with major hemorrhage and protracted fever. To put this figure in some perspective, it is useful to compare it with data on the psychiatric complications of childbirth. Fleck reported in 1970 that there are some 4,000 documented post-partum psychoses requiring hospitalization in the U.S. per year.[9] Computed as a rate, this yields a figure of about 1 to 2 per 1,000 deliveries, substantially more than that associated with legal abortion. However, as noted, the issue of proper control groups in assessing the mental health effects of abortion remains problematic, so this comparison of psychiatric sequelae post-abortion and post-delivery

13

must be viewed as suggestive.

Another aspect of assessing the psychiatric consequences of legal abortion is the extent to which denying abortion to a woman requesting such a procedure has adverse effects. Illsley and Hall (1972) surveyed published reports and concluded that "although many women who are refused abortions do adjust to their situation and grow to love the child, about half would still have preferred an abortion, a large minority suffer considerable distress, and a small minority [eventually] develop severe disturbance."[10]

The effects on the child born of an unwanted pregnancy are even more difficult to evaluate than the effects on the mother. One study which looked at this issue was conducted in Sweden by Forssmann and Thuwe (1966).[11] This 20-year follow-up study of 120 children born to Swedish women who were denied abortion showed that in comparison with a matched group of children born at the same time, the "unwanted children" were registered more often with psychiatric services, had engaged in more antisocial and criminal behavior and had received more public assistance. Many more of the unwanted than control children had not had the advantage of a secure family life during childhood. Additional data are available from Prague on a follow-up study of the first seven to nine years of life of approximately 200 children born during 1961-1963 to women denied abortion both on initial request and on subsequent appeal.[12] Preliminary findings suggest that the "unwanted" boys in particular, now entering adolescence, suffer a greater incidence of illness, have poorer grades in school, have more difficulty with peer group relationships and are at seemingly greater risk of future delinquency than a control group of ostensibly "wanted" children.

Based on its research experience, the Institute of Medicine study group established priorities for further research. The most important topics include (1) the long-term complications of abortion, (2) the effects of abortion and denied abortion on the mental health and social welfare of individuals and families, and (3) motivational, behavioral and accessibility factors affecting the use of contraception and abortion.

Discussion

Dr. Mildred Hansen, Obstetrician-Gynecologist, Minneapolis, Minnesota: I'm interested why there has not been any mention of a primary curettage technique between 12 and 20 weeks with dilatation of the cervix being achieved with use of laminaria. I'm wondering if you have any information concerning the technique in the United States or if you're familiar with any information from Ljubjlana, where it's been used for twenty years, on the comparative safety relative to the safety of saline instillation between 12 and 20 weeks.

Dr. Christopher Tietze: The JPSA study which was referred to and which was conducted in the period of 1970-71 did produce some data relating to abortion procedures during the fourth month of pregnancy. The data in that study showed an increase in the complication rate of abortions by suction with period of gestation; the rate was higher in the fourth month than at any earlier time. On the other hand, the complication rate with saline was highest for the earliest procedures and lower in later months. However, the complication rate with suction in the fourth month was lower than with saline at any period of gestation. Obviously it is a technically more difficult procedure to evacuate the uterus from below in the fourth month and there is fair agreement among gynecologists that these late evacuations by suction or by D and C, with or without laminaria, should be done in a hospital setting. More recently, prostaglandins have been added to the methods that can be used and extra-amniotic prostaglandins may be another choice for abortion at that time. The curious thing is that on ethical grounds it has become very difficult to study these questions. If you want to conduct a comparative study you want to assign cases at random. But you cannot assign cases at random if you believe that one method is better than the other. That is true for any field of medicine, not just for pregnancy termination. This ethical consideration is a serious obstacle to the acquisition of knowledge in this important area.

Hansen: When you speak of the long-term effects of abortion are you talking about both the psychological and physical?

Brown: When I made my remarks I was referring specifically to the physical but I would also include the psychological. Dr. Tietze, can you tell us whether or not psychiatric complications are going to be included in the WHO study?

Tietze: The WHO study addresses itself primarily to the question of the effect of a preceding termination of pregnancy and of the method used for that abortion on the outcome of a subsequent pregnancy. A number of studies have been published claiming that premature delivery with all its consequences tends to occur more often after a preceding induced abortion, including legal abortion. Other studies have not been able to establish this. All of the studies to date have been flawed by rather serious statistical errors in their design. We are trying to avoid these errors. As far as psychological effects are concerned, I believe that they are almost unreasearchable. Consider what precedes an abortion. There are at least

15

three decisions the woman has to make: to have or not to have sex, to use or not to use contraception, and to seek or not to seek abortion. If you try to compare the aborters with other women who did not have abortions, who decided to carry their pregnancies to term, or who decided to use effective contraception, or who decided not to have sex in the first place, you have no valid comparison. I consider most of these studies a black art. I don't think that we will learn anything from them.

Unless we standardize very carefully, not only for age, but also for such things as socioeconomic status of the women having subsequent pregnancies, we are not getting to first base. That's exactly what we are doing at WHO and why we need a very large group of women. We expect to have 4,000 women with abortion histories and at least 8,000 controls and that's why it takes so long. Results are expected by late 1977.

REFERENCES

1. U.S. Department of Health, Education and Welfare, Public Health Service, Center for Disease Control. *Abortion Surveillance: 1973,* Atlanta: 1975.
2. *Abortion Surveillance: 1973.*
3. C. Tietze. "Two Years Experience with a Liberal Abortion Law: Its Impact on Fertility Trends in New York City," *Family Planning Perspectives* 5: 39-41, 1973.
4. L. Andolsek, ed. *The Ljubljana Abortion Study 1971-1973,* Bethesda: National Institutes of Health, 1974.
5. C. Tietze and S. Lewit. "Joint Program for the Study of Abortion (JPSA): Early Medical Complications of Legal Abortion," *Studies in Family Planning* 3: 97-122, 1972.
6. U.S. Department of Health, Education and Welfare, Public Health Service, Center for Disease Control. *Morbidity and Mortality Weekly Report* 24, January 24, 1975.
7. U.S. Department of Health, Education and Welfare, Public Health Service, National Center for Health Statistics. "Summary Report, Final Mortality Statistics, 1973," *Monthly Vital Statistics Report* 23: No. 11 (Supplement 2) February 10, 1975, and National Center for Health Statistics. "Summary Report, Final Natality Statistics, 1973," *Monthly Vital Statistics Report* 23: No. 11 (Supplement 2) January 30, 1975.
8. C. Tietze and S. Lewit, p. 107.
9. S. Fleck. "Some Psychiatric Aspects of Abortion," *Journal of Nervous and Mental Disease* 151: 44, 1970.
10. R. Illsley and M.H. Hall. *Psychological Aspects of Abortion: A Review of Issues and Needed Research.* (mimeographed) Aberdeen, Scotland, 1973; and Moore-Cavar. *International Inventory of Information on Induced Abortion,* New York: Columbia University, International Institute for the Study of Human Reproduction, 1974.
11. H. Forssman and L. Thuwe. "One Hundred and Twenty Children Born after Application for Therapeutic Abortion Refused," *Acta Psychiatrica Scandinavia* 42: 70-87, 1966.
12. Z. Dytrych, Z. Matejcek, V. Schuller, H.P. David, and H.L. Friedman. "Children Born to Women Denied Abortion: Initial Findings of a Matched Control Study in Prague, Czechoslovakia," *Family Planning Perspectives* 7: 165-171, 1975.

Medical Aspects of Abortion

First Trimester Abortion

Jane Hodgson, M.D.

At present, one of our biggest problems locally is the possible appointment of an active anti-abortionist as Chairman of Obstetrics and Gynecology at the University of Minnesota. Some of us are appalled at some of the statements that he has made to the press regarding the lack of necessity for any training in first trimester abortions. To quote, he has said, "No special training is needed for performing first trimester abortions. Abortions are a very minor interest, strictly a service. Only a minimum of students are interested in learning to perform abortions." I think that it is pretty obvious to all of us that first trimester abortion is a very important part of medical education. Inasmuch as over a million procedures were performed last year and 85 percent of those were first trimester abortions, its importance would seem fairly obvious.

We have witnessed a real change in the last several years. We have witnessed the evolution of subspecialty. The more I am involved with it, the more I am impressed with its many facets and how complicated this subspecialty can be. I would like to recommend to you a new book published by Williams and Wilkins by Bolognese and Corson from the University of Pennsylvania. It is called *Interruption of Pregnancy–A Total Patient Approach.*[1]

We have witnessed a number of changes in the first trimester abortion. When abortion laws first were liberalized in this country in the late sixties, very few physicians had even used a suction apparatus. It did not take long for the profession to realize that the suction method was far superior to the old D and C method, which had been commonly used in this country. The use of suction has several advantages over the D and C method: speed, decreased bleeding, accommodation to local anesthesia. The completeness of the procedure and the safety rates have definitely improved. One other change that we have seen has been in the use of Pratt dilators over Hegar dilators. The Hegar dilators have been standard equipment in most hospitals in this country. It has been shown that the Pratt dilators require much less work, they are tapered and the dilatation can be performed gradually with less force. Pratt dilators are supplanting the Hegars as standard equipment.

Another new aspect is the use of laminaria. This is becoming very popular, particularly for the mid-trimester procedures. Many are advocating its use in the difficult first trimester procedure where the cervix is very hard to dilate. The desirability of routine use of lami the first trimester may be questionable. We have been using it only in those patients over twelve weeks gestation.

Another change has been the use of clear plastic cannulas instead of the metal cannulas. Another point that has been established is the proper way to apply the tenaculum to the anterior lip of the cervix. Figure 1 shows the difference between the blunt Hegar and the more tapered Pratt dilators. The advantage of plastic cannulas (Figure 2) is that you

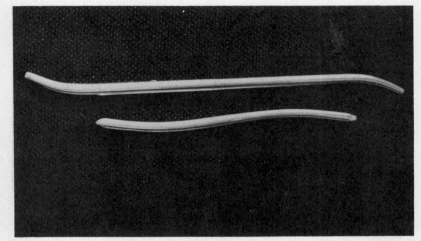

FIGURE 1

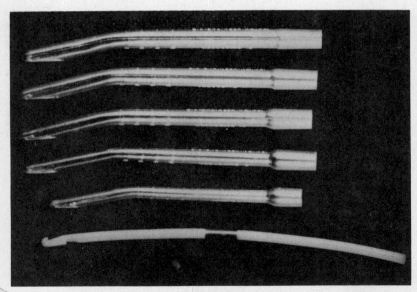

FIGURE 2

can see what's going through the cannula. They are also easier to handle. The Karmann cannula is a soft, flexible cannula only 6 mm. in diameter and is advocated for use during the so-called menstrual extractions or procedures of less than eight menstrual weeks. Figure 3 shows there are two apertures in the end of the Karmann cannula so that there is not as much rotation required. The flexibility and the fact that a minimal amount of dilatation is required are the advantages of the Karmann cannula. However, it is not totally innocuous. I have known of perforations to occur with its use. Another disadvantage is the fact that

FIGURE 3

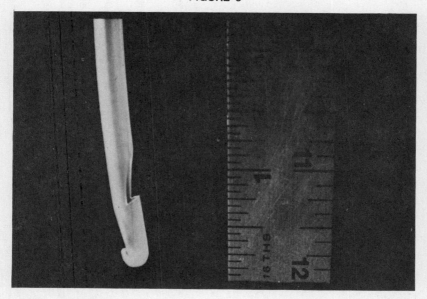

with a small flexible cannula like this, it is very easy to slip over the implantation site. A continuing pregnancy may result. This is a most embarrassing complication. Also, there is a higher instance of retained tissue.

Figure 4 shows the proper way to apply the tenaculum to the anterior

FIGURE 4

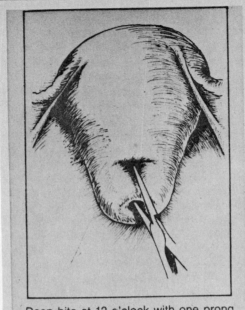

Deep bite at 12 o'clock with one prong actually inside cervical canal minimizes tearing.

lip of the cervix. In their book, Bolognese and Corson fail to mention the fact that it is important to inject the local anesthetic in the anterior lip of the cervix prior to attaching the tenaculum in order to minimize discomfort for the patient.

If you see a patient who has an IUD failure and who is going to have an abortion, do not pull the IUD out the minute you see her. Wait and remove the IUD at the time of the abortion procedure after she has had a paracervical block and a dilatation. You will have a much easier time in removing it. We still see many patients who come in with an IUD that their physician has tried to remove and has been unable to. Either the string is broken or the device has become imbedded in the wall of the uterus. It's best to leave the IUD alone and let the abortionist take it out.

Studies have suggested that less than one vial of Rhogam is necessary to protect the patient against sensitization from the Rh antigen.[2] We have been dividing our dose into three parts. Since the 300 micrograms will protect for up to 30 ccs of transplacental hemorrhage at full term, and since blood volume of the fetus is not over 1 cc at 12 weeks, it would seem logical and adequate to give the patient at 12 weeks gestation 100 micrograms rather than the full dosage in order to protect against sensitization. Hopefully the drug houses will be putting up Rhogam or immunoglobins in smaller doses. This will facilitate the provision of a smaller dose and help to cut down costs.

22

On the subject of prophylactic antibiotics in first trimester abortions, it is very difficult to obtain valid, objective evidence of the efficacy of prophylactic antibiotics in any surgical procedure. The first reason is a matter of sheer numbers. It is hard to get large numbers in any series during relatively short periods and most of the series that have been published have been very small. The second reason is the extreme diversity of the variables. With a ruptured appendix and generalized peritonitis, for instance, some of the variables to measure would be the length of time since rupture, the occurrence of previous attacks, the age and condition of the patient, the skill of the surgeon and the type of incision. All of these things would tend to affect the end result. With respect to the antibiotics themselves there are a number of variables: the dose that is given, the time that it is given, the specific bacterial resistance of the drug, and lowered host-resistance. We recently published a study concerning the incidence of complications in 10,000 consecutive first trimester abortions. The complications were remarkably consistent as well as acceptable and the rate per 1,000 procedures averages 9.1 for major complications and 17.9 for minor complications[3] (Table 1). In this study, the factor of series size is no problem, for over 1,000 procedures a month were done. The complications were fairly consistent, averaging a little under one percent for major complications and a little less than two percent for minor complications. The patients

TABLE I

MONTH	PROCEDURES	COMPLICATIONS	
		Major	Minor
Oct. '72	1,316	13	36
Nov.	1,096	3	20
Dec.	1,247	8	25
Jan. '73	1,451	18	37
Feb.	1,326	13	20
Mar.	1,473	12	21
Apr.	1,283	14	18
May	1,261	15	11

TOTALS   10,453 ———————— 96(0.91%) —— 188(1.8%)

Corrected % (based on 65% follow-up) —— (1.47%) ———— (2.9%)

were all healthy, all female, and their ages varied little. The same procedure, first trimester abortion, was performed, and the setting was uniform. Surgery was performed by equally trained gynecologists, and a uniform method was used in follow-up. The time of the year was between May and September when the incidence of upper respiratory infections was reasonably low.

23

We decided that we would study 4,000 consecutive patients in alternative subgroups of 1,000 each. There were 4 phases of the study. Patients in phases 2 and 4 received prophylactic antibiotics and those in phases 1 and 3 did not. Four thousand procedures were done between May and September. Since a large number came from different parts of the country, we decided that a double blind study was neither justified nor practical. Randomization of 4,000 patients would have imposed insurmountable practical problems. Therefore we designed the study on the basis of randomization by groups of a thousand. Each group that did not receive the antibiotics served as a control for the thousand who did. We used oral tetracycline because this drug is effective against a wide spectrum of bacteria and oral administration was a necessity on an outpatient basis. The regimen was economical. The cost was a total of 38¢ per patient. The particular regimen used was an alternate method of treatment approved by the Center for Disease Control in Atlanta for the treatment of gonorrhea infections in patients who are allergic to penicillin. Since 1.4 percent of our routine cervical cultures revealed evidence of gonorrhea, it seemed logical to provide adequate and immediate therapy for this group. The patients initially received a gram and a half of oral tetracycline. This was two to three hours before the procedure. They then received 500 milligrams every six hours for four days, for a total dose of 9.5 grams. The number of significant drug complications was very small, probably because of the short duration of therapy. As with any oral medication, it is impossible to state with absolute certainty the degree of patient compliance, but we felt that it was satisfactory. These patients are often frightened and insecure and many of them request antibiotics. As far as we can tell, the compliance was acceptable.

We divided our complications into major, minor, and minimal. The major included all instances of hospitalization and fever over 100° for three days or longer. The minor complications consisted of fever over 100° for more than 24 hours but less than 72, accompanied usually by complaints of cramps and bleeding. None of these symptoms warranted hospitalization, but additional professional care was sought by the patient either in an emergency room, a physician's office, or the clinic, thereby interfering with their normal activities. A third type of complication is also reported. This is the so-called minimal type that consisted largely of a reported temperature elevation to 100° or higher but of less than 24 hours in duration and requiring no additional therapy. The minimal complications did not interfere with the usual patient activity, but were reported by telephone, by the patient at the time of her followup visit, or by the physician's followup forms. The on-call personnel noted a prompt reduction in the volume of telephone calls when antibiotics were added to the protocol (Table 2).

In the second and fourth phases, where antibiotics were received, there was a marked reduction in the number of total complications. They

TABLE 2

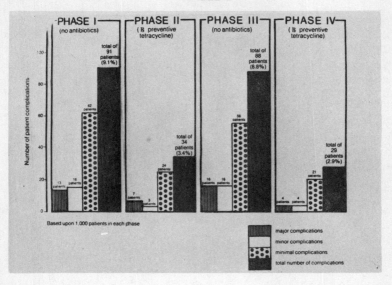

Based upon 1,000 patients in each phase

dropped about 64 percent from 91 patients in phase 1 to 34 in phase 2, and from 88 patients in phase 3 to 29 in phase 4. Table 3 shows the number of patient hospital days in the four groups. These results are comparable. There were 65.5 patient hospital days in phase 1, 14 in phase 2, 62 hospital days in phase 3, and 18 hospital days in phase 4.

TABLE 3

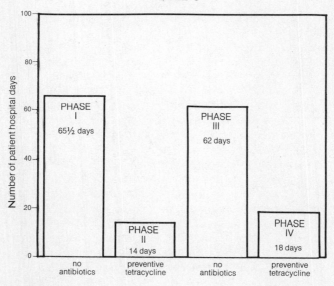

REFERENCES

1. R. J. Bolognese and S. L. Corson. *Interruption of Pregnancy - A Total Patient Approach,* New York, William & Wilkins, 1975.
2. D. Nortman. *First Trimester Abortion and the Need for Rh Immune Globulin,* Newton, Massachusetts: Preterm Institute, 1973.
3. J. E. Hodgson and K. C. Portmann. "Complications of 10,043 Consecutive First Trimester Abortions: A Prospective Study," *American Journal of Obstetrics and Gynecology* 120: 802-807, 1974.

Second Trimester Abortion

William Droegemueller, M.D.

In December 1973, the naturally-occurring prostaglandin $F_2\alpha$ was released by the Food and Drug Administration for use in terminating second trimester pregnancy. In most centers, prostaglandin has become the drug of choice by injection during amniocentesis in second trimester abortion. The misnomer, prostaglandin, would suggest limited functions for this family of hormone-like fatty acids. Various members of this group of lipids alter a wide range of physiologic processes and possess powerful pharmacological action. They are among the basic compounds of man. The scientist's interest in the prostaglandin has focused on three broad functions of this group of fatty acids. They are: 1) activity of smooth muscles, 2) change in blood flow to a specific organ and 3) regulation of internal secretion of glands. The naturally-occurring prostaglandins have a short duration of action because they are rapidly metabolized or inactivated when they enter the systemic circulation. It appears that the cell membrane is the primary site of formation of prostaglandin. Many investigators postulate that their site of action is also in the cell membrane. It is important to emphasize that these compounds are among the most potent of all known biological materials, producing marked effects in extremely small doses. The various cells of the body have abundant supplies of catabolic enzymes that tend to confine and limit the action of prostaglandin to a specific area. Chemically, prostaglandins are 20-carbon, carboxylic acids. Presently there are 14 natural prostaglandins. However, over 1,000 prostaglandin analogs have been synthesized and several are undergoing preliminary clinical studies.

Prostaglandins have a ubiquitous origin and function throughout the body. They have been identified in minute amounts in all tissues from both men and women who have been examined. It is useful to compare prostaglandins with hypertonic saline.

The principal advantage of prostaglandin over hypertonic saline for second trimester abortion is its greater margin of safety. The serious and sometime fatal complications of hyperosmolar coma, hypernatremia, and diffuse intravascular coagulation that have been reported with rapid absorption or faulty injection techniques with saline have not been associated with prostaglandin. The half-life of naturally-occurring prostaglandin $F_2\alpha$ in the general circulation is less than one minute.

Therefore, if inadvertent intravascular injection occurs, the drug will be rapidly metabolized. On such an occasion, the patient will be violently ill and experience severe vomiting, diarrhea, and possibly acute respiratory distress secondary to bronchial constriction, but the duration of this episode will be brief.

The other major benefit of prostaglandin over hypertonic saline is the more rapid injection-to-abortion interval. Data vary from series to series, depending on the abortion patients and the ancillary procedures used to shorten the process. However, the mean injection-to-abortion interval with saline alone is 30 to 36 hours. With prostaglandin alone, it is 18 to 25 hours, and for prostaglandin with laminaria and/or oxytocin, 10 to 15 hours.

The majority of prostaglandin patients' hospital stay is less than 24 hours.They do not have to endure the lengthy period of anxiety between injection and the onset of labor as is observed with hypertonic saline. There are several contraindications for prostaglandin. The package insert lists hypersensitivity to prostaglandin and associated acute pelvic inflammatory disease as absolute contraindications. Allergy to a natural compound and the occurrence of acute pelvic inflammatory disease during the second trimester are both so rare that the warning is relatively academic. It is our opinion that more important contraindications to prostaglandin injection should include a history of bronchial asthma, pulmonary hypertension, glaucoma, epilepsy or hypertensive cardiovascular disease. Any of these medical conditions could be acutely exacerbated by the smooth muscle constriction produced by systemic absorption of prostaglandin.

Candidates for second trimester abortion often experience ambivalence surrounding their request for pregnancy termination. The proper preliminary counseling with a female advocate cannot be overemphasized. She will help the woman to resolve the social and psychiatric problems which accompany the anticipated abortion. This will allow the patient to relieve her anxiety and plan for the future. Second trimester abortion should be performed as an in-patient hospital procedure. It is our policy to routinely insert a thick laminaria into the cervical canal 12 to 16 hours prior to amniocentesis. Generally the insertion of the laminaria is performed as an out-patient procedure in the late afternoon prior to hospital admission the following morning.

Mechanical ripening of the cervix prior to chemical induction of abortion has two distinct advantages. Primarily, this procedure results in a significant shortening of the injection-to-abortion interval. Several investigators have reported that laminaria reduce the interval between injection and abortion by 33 to 50 percent. Secondarily, it has been postulated that laminaria will help to reduce the incidence of cervical-vaginal fistulas. The latter is one of the most serious chronic complications of second trimester abortion. Just prior to amniocentesis, the laminaria is removed. The patient is asked to void. The skin is washed with an antiseptic solution and the skin and subcutaneous tissues are infiltrated with a few ccs of local anesthetic. The amniocentesis is performed with a 22-gauge spinal needle and the site of potential entry into the uterus is usually the mid-line, approximately 3 cm. below the uterine fundus. When correct needle placement has been assured by the free flow of clear amniotic fluid, the depth of penetration should be controlled by an instrument attached to the needle as it punctures the skin or by inserting a small catheter throught the needle Recently, rather than adhere to the rigid 40-milligram suggested dose of prostaglandin, it has been our practice to vary the amount of prostaglandin depending on the fluid volume of the amniotic cavity.

The following is the dosage schedule based on uterine size: at 12 to 15 weeks, 20 mgs; at 16 to 18, 30 mgs; and for greater than 18, 40 mgs. Similar to saline, prostaglandin should not be injected if the amniotic fluid returning via the needle or catheter remains grossly bloody. If following three attempts at needle placement, the fluid continues to be grossly bloody, it is best to stop and obtain an ultrasonic scan for placental localization before proceeding with the abortion.

The first milliliter of prostaglandin should serve as a test dose. One should wait for a minute or two to observe any symptoms of rapid systemic absorption of the drug before injecting the remainder of the total dose. For optimal results, it is important that a small volume of drug be immediately distributed throughout the amniotic fluid. For 10 minutes post-injection, encourage the patient to change position and agitate her abdomen to facilitate the drug coming in contact with the membranes. When this is not done, the injection-to-abortion time is prolonged as much as six to eight hours. The course of the abortion is monitored by serial pelvic exams every three to four hours. Once cervical dilatation begins, the abortion generally occurs within four hours. With spontaneous expulsion of the fetus, the discomfort abruptly diminishes. The patient is taken to an examination room and the placenta removed by traction on the cord. The uterine cavity is routinely explored with ring forceps and the cervix inspected for laceration. When the pregnancy is greater than 16 weeks, curettage is performed for excessive bleeding or suspected retained products of conception. It has been our clinical experience that spontaneous abortion prior to 16 weeks of pregnancy is often incomplete and requires curettage of the uterus.

There are two definite drawbacks with prostaglandin. When used alone for second trimester termination, approximately one-third of patients will require a second injection of prostaglandin at 24 hours to complete the abortion. This percentage can be dramatically reduced by modifying the protocol to include a second injection of prostaglandin at six hours or the addition of oxytocin and/or laminaria. The second major disadvantage is the gastrointestinal toxicity associated with systemic absorption of prostaglandin. Between 50 to 75 percent of patients experience vomiting and 10 to 25 percent have diarrhea following intraamniotic injection of prostaglandin if one uses the full 40 mg. dose. The incidence of side effects can be reduced by adjusting the dose of prostaglandin to the amniotic fluid volume. Many clinicians reduce the severity of the gastrointestinal symptoms by premedicating their patients with drugs such as Lomotil® and Compazine®

What about concomitant drug usage? Aspirin and indomethicin are specific prostaglandin antagonists and will result in prolongation of the injection-to-abortion time interval. D-antigen appears in fetal tissue as early as the 40th day of pregnancy. Therefore, every unsensitized Rh negative woman should receive an injection of anti-D gamma globulin following the abortion.

Basic research has demonstrated the synergistic effect of myometrial contractions when prostaglandin and oxytocin are combined. The package insert recommends that concomitant intraamniotic administration of prostaglandin and intravenous oxytocin be used with caution in the absence of adequate cervical dilatation. This warning is to reduce the incidence of posterior cervical perforation occasionally found in primiparous patients. The national monitoring studies being conducted by the Upjohn Company have shown over 75 percent of patients receive oxytocin prior to the termination of the abortion. When prostaglandin is given intraamniotically, its half-life, as determined by radioimmunoassay, is between three and six hours. Therefore during the initial one to two hours post-injection, the uterus remains in a state of tetany. Oxytocin given intravenously during that period of tetany produced by 40 mgs. of $F_2\alpha$ probably will not facilitate the abortion procedure.

At the present time natural prostaglandin $F_2\alpha$ is the only prostaglandin approved by the FDA. During the next year it is anticipated that prostaglandin E_2 vaginal suppositories will be released by the FDA. The most promising method of using the 20-milligram E_2 suppositories was described by Schulman.[1] He suggests placing the suppository inside of the vaginal diaphragm thus allowing the prostaglandin to exert the local effects on the cervix or lower uterine segment. The combination of the diaphragm and E_2 suppositories resulted in a mean abortion time of approximately 13 hours. Also this method significantly reduced the incidence of gastrointestinal side effects.

The development of prostaglandin analogs has initiated speculation that intrauterine application of chemicals may be eliminated in favor of intramuscular injection. For the past two years we have been studying the intramuscular injection of 15-methyl $F_2\alpha$. The addition of the methyl group to the 15-carbon synthesizes analogs with increased potency and a longer half-life than their apparent natural compounds. In a pilot investigation, the advantage of the 15-methyl intramuscular compound was somnolence. The patients were sleepy after they got over the initial gastrointestinal disturbance and had reduced discomfort during labor. However, the disadvantages include severe gastrointestinal toxicity in the majority of patients and symptoms of acute respiratory distress in two of 20 patients. This latter, more serious, complication will probably, to a great extent, limit the use of the 15-methyl analog of $F^2\alpha$. Because of this problem, we stopped using the 15-methyl compound.

REFERENCES

1. H. Schulman, L. Saldana, T. Tsai, T. Leibman, M. Cunningham, and G. Randolph. "Prostaglandin E_2 Induced Abortion with Vaginal Suppositories in a Contraceptive Diaphragm," *Prostaglandins* 7: 195, 1974.

Complications of Abortion

William Rashbaum, M.D.

Since New York State's liberal abortion law became effective in July 1970, pregnancy terminations have increased and changed dramatically. The suction technique was developed by the Chinese in the 1950s and was adopted by the Eastern Europeans in the 1960s. It was brought to the United States in the late sixties, helping to change completely the provision of early abortions.

Changes in the law and technique transformed a dangerous, expensive, clandestine, illegal, disreputable procedure, previously performed by avaricious criminals, who varied from well-trained physicians to totally unqualified non-professionals, into an inexpensive, safe operative procedure. This procedure is now performed with increasing frequency by well-trained specialists. Through clinical experience, they have garnered a facility and expertise that has minimized the risk of early abortions. The statistical papers dealing with early abortions are well known. In this paper we will try to present some of the clinical factors involved.

Early in 1970, Planned Parenthood of New York City was planning an ambulatory abortion facility. Mr. Henry Villard, then president of the Board of Trustees, suggested that a "superspecialist" in abortion should be created. Over the last several decades, the concept of superspecialist has evolved in many areas of medicine, such as the microcardio-vascular surgeon and the oncologist. The medical advisory committee of Planned Parenthood of New York City felt Villard's suggestion was unnecessary. The operative procedure was so simple that any gynecological specialist, even any resident, could accomplish this satisfactorily. But over the last several years, Mr. Villard's suggestion has become a reality. More and more procedures are performed by a cadre of specialists working in non-hospital facilities and obtaining results that have minimized complications. In January 1975, the Center for Disease Control in Atlanta reported that, "When compared to mortality from full-term pregnancy, abortion in the first trimester is ten fold safer."[1]

Tietze reported in the Joint Program for the Study of Abortion (JPSA) study of complications of early abortion covering the period of 1970 to 1971 that total and major complications decreased by approximately one-half during the course of the study.[2]

General Factors Regarding Complications

Many factors contribute to complications of abortion. In the JPSA study, Tietze suggests that the relatively poor general health of the non-private urban patients contributes to the higher complication rate for this group.

The equipment used plays an important role. In late 1970, we were using suction machines run by foot power and held together by rubber bands. Certainly, the low complication rates of today are in part the result of the better suction machines.

The high rate of cervical injuries reported in the Ljubljana studies, 0.7 percent of all cases, is probably due to Hegar dilators, which most of us in this country have found far more traumatic than the Pratt type dilator.[3]

Out patient abortion tends to be safer than in-hospital. Tietze notes the following factors: the out patient is healthier than her hospital sister, and the skill of the operator in the clinics may be greater because of larger number of procedures performed. Finally, Tietze feels that there may be a greater tendency to under-report complications in out patient cases.

The choice of anesthesia also plays a role. Tietze reported that, contrary to expectation, total complications were higher with local anesthesia and the rate of repeat curettage was about two to three times greater with local anesthesia than with general. It seems reasonable that the discomfort of abortion with local anesthesia is the major factor. While dilatation can be performed relatively painlessly under local anesthesia, suction evacuation and curettage is not completely relieved by para-cervical blocks.

The skill of the operator is unquestionably a factor. This skill is largely a function of experience. If one compares the well-trained ob-gyn specialist who performs one to two cases per week or month with a comparable specialist who devotes much of his professional time to doing large numbers of abortions, the experience factor is obvious.

Andolsek found that operators who performed two hundred to three hundred procedures a year had fewer complications than those who did less than a hundred cases a year. She also noted that complications were higher with operators who performed more than three hundred cases per year, but this was based on only three physicians out of more than twenty-eight for whom data were recorded.

One last factor that should be considered is the structure of the clinic. Most large clinics are staffed by physicians who are regular employees. A few of the clinics work on a "piece-work" basis (payment based on procedures performed). This must to some degree be a negative factor.

Prevention, Diagnosis, and Management of Specific Complications

For the following discussion of specific complications, their prevention, diagnosis, and management, it is useful to classify them by immediate, delayed, and late occurrence.

Immediate Complications

Perforation. Perforation of the uterus is the most dramatic, feared, and significant complication. This condition is under-diagnosed to a great extent. To prevent uterine perforation, the operator should use tapered dilators such as the Pratt or Hawkins Ambler. Never use force either with dilators or with insertion of suction tip or curette. When starting dilatation the direction of the cervical canal may be difficult to find, especially in cases of less than eight weeks LMP. Gently changing the direction of the dilator to account for acute anteversion or retroversion will allow the dilator to "fall into" the proper course. Rarely, the internal os is found to be stenotic. The insertion of dilators progressively larger by only one to two millimeters will allow the operator to go back to the smallest dilator and pass the internal os with ease. If one has difficulty, one should assume that an error is being made and should recheck the position of the uterus. Also, during the course of dilatation one may pass one or more dilators easily and then encounter resistance. This resistance is at the internal os and can be overcome by gentle, steady pressure.

Be certain of the direction of the uterus at all times. What seems to be anterior without anesthesia may actually be posterior or vice versa with traction on the cervix. And after partial evacuation, the uterus can change position because of changes in its density and weight. Ordinarily, one can insert a given size suction tip corresponding to the size of the largest dilator used. If one has dilated to 31 Pratt and has difficulty in inserting a #10 suction tip, suspect a change in the direction of the uterus.

Do not use the uterine sound. Some physicians feel that this instrument is helpful in determining the direction of the fundus. To the contrary, one can perforate easily and be misled. Rather, reexamine the uterus bimanually, including a recto-vaginal exam.

Forswear in-and-out movement with any rigid cannula. This is, in my opinion, the easiest way to perforate a uterus. Rotation of the cannula will be sufficient to evacuate the tissue and frequently will facilitate separation of the placenta. Most important, rotation is safe.

Curette with care. The curette is an excellent instrument with which to perforate the uterus. It is important to check the fundus and both cornuas with a curette. This must be done gently, with force being exerted on the curette only in the outward direction. One can also postulate that on occasion one will encounter either a deeply imbedded pregnancy (precursor to an accreta), a weak spot in the uterine wall caused by scar tissue (myomectomy or cesarean section), congenital weakness, or thinness of the wall as found in a grand multipara.

Anomalies of the uterus. With complete reduplication of the uterus, the direction of the canal is lateral. If this anomaly is not detected perforation can occur easily. (Figure 1)

Diagnosis of Perforation. If perforation is suspected, the cardinal rule is to abandon suction. To determine whether, in fact, the wall of the

35

uterus has been perforated, one can either use a small curette or dilator and gingerly probe in the suspected area. Remember that frequently, in pregnancy, the site of implantation enlarges disproportionately more than other areas of the uterus (Piscacek's Sign). One must ascertain whether or not the continuity of the uterine wall has been breached.

Management. If you discover a definite defect in the uterine wall, every effort should be made to complete the emptying of the uterine cavity. Uterine perforation without injury to other viscera may, when recognized early, be an innocuous event provided that the uterus is completely empty. It is my experience in handling almost all of the complications of New York City's largest ambulatory abortion facility that, given the above circumstances, no further treatment other than observation is required. Substantial hemorrhage almost never occurs with an empty uterus.

Tietze, in the JPSA study, recorded 187 perforations in roughly 53,000 cases for an incidence of 3.5 per thousand. This includes in-hospital and outpatient cases. One must remember that this is an overall figure which was considerably lower at the end of the study. His study corresponds to the start of the provision of legal abortions on a large scale in New York City.

The incidence of perforations at the ParkMed ambulatory clinic has progressively declined from 1.1 per thousand in 1971 to 0.3 per thousand in 1975. The Ljubljana study reported an incidence of 0.9 per thousand, while Planned Parenthood of New York City reported an incidence of 0.3 per thousand in 1974 and 0.0 in 50,000 cases in 1975.[4]

In the JPSA study, over 50 percent of the patients with recognized perforations underwent laparotomy. Experience has taught us that if no visceral damage is detected and the uterus is emptied, the perforation will heal without intervention. The patient must be hospitalized and observed carefully. Frequent monitoring of the vital signs and serial hemoglobin or hematocrit determinations as well as intravenous fluids are necessary. Under these circumstances, most patients recover uneventfully. Some institutions perform laparoscopy routinely, but in my opinion, this is not necessary. Should signs of progressive intra-abdominal bleeding develop, surgery is indicated. Significant bowel injury obviously requires immediate laparotomy.

Cervical Injury. This may be classified as minor or major. Minor cervical injury can occur with either the single-tooth tenaculum or Allis-type tenaculum. This may cause minor or perhaps troublesome bleeding which can usually be controlled with pressure, but it occasionally requires suturing. Major cervical injury usually occurs during dilatation, although it can occur at the time of insertion of the suction tip or forceful insertion of a curette. This laceration can be the opening of an old scar from previous labor or may be a new injury. The former rarely bleeds and frequently does not require treatment. The latter can cause not only external hemorrhage but also bleeding into the broad ligament. Broad ligament hematomas are usually self-contained and

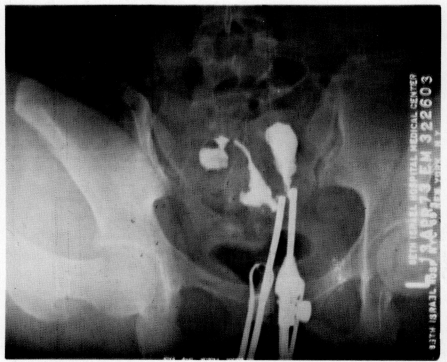

Photo courtesy of William K. Rashbaum, M.D.

Fig. 1. Hysterosalpingogram of double uterus, Pregnant horn on left.

Photo by Susan Perry, courtesy of William K. Rashbaum, M.D.

Fig. 2. Float test of tissue obtained at eight menstrual weeks' pregnancy. Placenta is white tissue above; decidua below.

Photo by Susan Perry, courtesy of William K. Rashbaum, M.D.

Fig. 3. Float test at eight menstrual **weeks**. Placenta above; decidua below.

Fig. 4. Gross appearance of normal tissue at eight menstrual weeks. Placenta is white tissue at lower right.

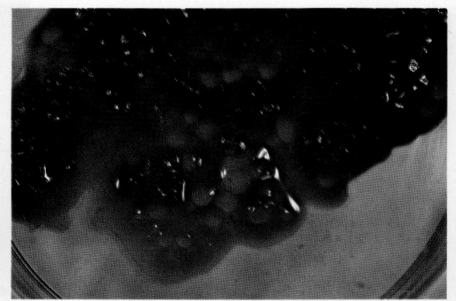

Fig. 5. Gross appearance of hydatidiform mole at eight menstrual weeks.

rarely require operative intervention. I have seen one case of cervical laceration in which arterial bleeding was encountered. This was sutured with great difficulty. Ten days later, bleeding recurred. Some two to three weeks later, there was a third episode of hemorrhage and a hysterectomy was performed.

Difficulty with laminaria tents have been reported. The problem is "dumbbelling" beyond the internal os with difficulty in removal. Dr. Hern feels this problem can be handled by administering a paracervical block and exerting gentle traction on the distal portion of the laminaria.[5]

Water intoxication. This is a rare complication which is the result of the administration of large amounts of pitocin. It can be prevented completely with the concomitant usage of appropriate electrolyte solutions.

Anesthesia complications. Complications from anesthesia, whether it be local or general, are no different from those occurring with any other operative procedure. I think it is important to reiterate that the JPSA study found that there were fewer abortion complications with the use of general anesthesia than with local.

Delayed Complications

Unrecognized perforations. Unrecognized perforations with retained tissue can be disastrous. One of the first mortalities reported by the CDC in Atlanta, which has monitored all abortion mortality, was in this category.[6] The most frequent cause of delayed complications is incomplete emptying of the uterus or retained tissue, resulting in subsequent bleeding or infection or both. Prevention of these sequelae is dependent upon complete evacuation of the products of conception. The Ljubljana double blind study proved that the results with suction and curettage were appreciably better than D and C alone. The study indicates, but does not prove, that suction evacuation with sharp curettage is better than suction alone. Yet in 6.2 percent of the cases which had vacuum aspiration plus curettage, appreciable placental tissue was found.

The treatment of post-operative bleeding, immediate or delayed, is the use of oxytocins and re-curettage when indicated. The treatment of infection requires identification of the organism and treatment with appropriate antibiotics. If the infection is the result of retained tissue, as is usually the case, re-curettage is indicated.

I personally believe that sterile technique is a minor factor if the uterus is completely empty. Sterile technique cannot prevent infection if tissue is left behind. This is a clinical impression which has not been substantiated experimentally.

Careful examination of the tissue removed in every case can frequently prevent the occurrence of post-operative bleeding and/or infection. If the amount of tissue obtained does not correspond with the impression of gestational size, re-evaluation and re-exploration of the uterus is indicated. In cases over 10 or 11 weeks, the entire fetus should be identified. The fetal parts that tend to be retained are the skull and the spine.

Failure to abort. Prevention of this complication can be readily achieved by careful examination of the tissue removed. Failure to abort occurs in the very early pregnancy and also in cases of reduplication of the uterus where the non-pregnant horn is evacuated.

Depression. Tietze in the 1975 abortion factbook states that reliable information on the psychological sequelae of induced abortion is not available.[7] Some psychiatrists have expressed the view that every abortion is a stressful experience involving major risks to mental health. Others believe that most women undergoing abortion continue to lead essentially normal lives and that an adverse psychological reaction to an unwanted birth is far more common and more serious than an adverse reaction to having an abortion.

Late Sequelae

Rh sensitization. Rh sensitization has been shown to occur in the first trimester. This complication is completely preventable in the unsensitized patient by the administration of Rh-immune globulin.

Cervical injury. There are diverse opinions on the increased risk of premature birth, perinatal mortality, and mid-timester spontaneous abortion in subsequent pregnancies as a result of cervical damage at the time of dilatation or too vigorous curettage with damage to the basal layers of the endometrium. Tietze states, "Because the validity of retrospective studies has become questionable due to the finding that women whose pregnancies have ended unfavorably are more likely to admit a prior induced abortion than women with favorable outcome, prospective studies have been initiated by WHO."[8]

Another uncommon late complication we have noted is cervical stenosis. This occurs in patients who bleed little if at all following suction curettage. They usually present one or more months after abortion with a history of amenorrhea and cramps. Diagnosis and cure is achieved by sounding and/or minimal dilatation of the cervix. In the Ljubljana study, they found unexpected synechiae in the cervical canal of 10 percent of the patients who, by chance, had hysterograms. The correlation of this finding to cervical stenosis, if any, is unknown.

Ectopic pregnancy. Andolsek's data does not support the hypothesis that induced abortion leads to an increased risk of subsequent ectopic pregnancy.

One of the rare complications of early abortions is doing a procedure on a patient with an unruptured ectopic pregnancy. The incidence of ectopic pregnancy, according to Hellman and Pritchard, can range from one per 100-200 infants delivered.[9] A certain number of patients who present themselves for early abortion will, in fact, have an ectopic pregnancy. This diagnosis can be strongly suspected, if not proven, by careful gross examination of the tissue removed. Absence of chorionic villi on microscopic examination will certainly increase one's suspicion.

However, careful gross examination can be at least as valuable immediately, without having to wait several days for microscopic sections.

Contrary to most gynecological textbooks, differentiation can be made between decidua and very early villi. Figure 2 shows a specimen dipped in a beaker of water. It has been washed with water immediately after removal. Blood comes out of the placenta more readily; therefore the placenta is lighter in color. The villi are in the lower portion of the small placenta. Both placenta and decidua will float, except that the placenta floats more readily than the decidua (Figure 3).

Summary

Many aspects of prevention, diagnosis, and management of complications of early abortions have been discussed. We have presented clinical experience in conjunction with recent statistics, hoping to enhance the probability of success in clinical work. Increased experience by physicians will decrease the need for surgical intervention for abortion complications. The decrease in complications can be credited to increased clinical experience of the operators involved. Sharing experience in these techniques will help to eliminate complications in pregnancy terminations to the extent possible.

REFERENCES

1. U.S. Department of Health, Education and Welfare, Public Health Service, Center for Disease Control. *Abortion Surveillance: 1973*, Atlanta: 1975.
2. C. Tietze and S. Lewit. "Joint Program for the Study of Abortion (JPSA): Early Medical Complications of Legal Abortion," *Studies in Family Planning* 3:97-122, 1972.
3. L. Andolsek, ed. *The Ljubljana Abortion Study, 1971-1973*, Bethesda: National Institutes of Health, Center for Population Research, 1974.
4. Personal communications.
5. W.M. Hern. "Laminaria in Abortion: Use in 1368 Patients in First Trimester," *Rocky Mountain Medical Journal* 72:380, 1975.
6. S.B. Conger, C.W. Tyler, J. Pakter. "A Cluster of Uterine Perforations Related to Suction Curettage," *Obstetrics & Gynecology* 40:551, 1972.
7. C. Tietze and M.C. Murstein. "Induced Abortion: 1975 Factbook," *Reports on Population/Family Planning,* Number 14, The Population Council, 1975.
8. Tietze, 1972.
9. L.M. Hellman and J.A. Pritchard. *Williams Obstetrics,* 14th ed.,. New York: Appleton-Century-Crofts, 1971, p. 535.

The Joint Program for the Study of Abortion/CDC: A Preliminary Report

David A. Grimes, M.D.
Kenneth F. Schulz, M.B.A.
Willard Cates, Jr., M.D., M.P.H.
Carl W. Tyler, Jr., M.D.

Recognizing the emerging importance of abortion as a public health concern and the virtual absence of statistics, the Family Planning Evaluation Division of the Center for Disease Control initiated national surveillance of abortion in 1969. Our goals are the eradication of all preventable abortion deaths and the control of abortion morbidity. From these goals, our work has developed into four general areas: (1) monitoring the numbers and characteristics of women undergoing abortion in this country each year, (2) studying all abortion-related deaths, (3) studying the early medical complications of abortion, and (4) providing technical assistance and performing special studies of abortion-related health problems. I would like to describe our preliminary data on abortion morbidity derived from the Joint Program for the Study of Abortion under the auspices of CDC (JPSA/CDC). First, I will review briefly the history of JPSA/CDC, describe our methodology, and compare selected demographic characteristics of JPSA/CDC patients with those of the national group of women obtaining abortion; then I will summarize our preliminary analysis.

During 1970 and 1971, the Population Council conducted the Joint Program for the Study of Abortion (JPSA). A multicenter prospective study of the medical complications of early abortion, JPSA encompassed nearly 73,000 patient reports from 66 participating institutions. Its findings were summarized in two publications, one in 1972 and another in 1973.[1][2]

When the first phase of JPSA expired in 1971, the Center for Disease Control assumed responsibility for continuation of the study, and between September 1971 and June 1975, CDC received 80,437 abortion reports from 32 participating institutions. This now constitutes the largest abortion study every assembled.

The methodology of JPSA/CDC was similar to that of the first Joint Program for the Study of Abortion. At each participating institution, trained abstractors transcribed information from the patient's medical chart onto a JPSA/CDC form, initially designed by the Population Council. These reports were then sent in groups to CDC, where the information was coded, key-punched, edited, and then merged onto magnetic tape. We calculated elapsed gestational age for 94 percent of patients by subtracting the date of last menstrual period from the date of abortion. The physician's estimate of gestational age was used for the six percent of patients for whom one or both dates was unknown.

When the 80,437 reports had been collected, we examined the reliability of these data. First, we identified each institution contributing more than two percent of our total number of reports. The resulting 12 institutions together accounted for 86 percent of our data base. We then examined at each of these 12 institutions a one percent systematic random sample of patients' charts. We transcribed selected items from the charts onto blank forms and compared our transcribed data with that originally provided by the contributors.

It is important to have some appreciation of how closely this data base of 80,437 women, encompassing a four-year span, approximates the group of women in the country undergoing abortion each year. As a reference point, let us compare characteristics of JPSA/CDC patients with those of the reported 763,476 women who underwent abortion during 1974.[3]

The age distribution of abortion patients in JPSA/CDC and in the United States in 1974 were similar. Teenagers comprised 32.5 percent and 32.4 percent while 34.4 percent and 31.5 percent were 20 to 24 years old, respectively. It is difficult to draw inferences about racial distributions of these patients because of the large percentage of unknowns in the JPSA/CDC group (16.0 percent). This largely reflects individual institutional policy of not requesting or recording racial or ethnic information. Seventy-four point seven percent of JPSA/CDC patients and 70.9 percent of the national group were unmarried at the time of abortion. Nearly half of the women in each group were primigravidas (46.5 percent and 46.2 percent).

While the two groups are similar, there are several important differences. In the JPSA/CDC group, 31.8 percent of women obtained abortion at eight weeks or less (Table 1), and conversely, 22.4 percent underwent abortion from 13 to 20 weeks. Only 0.6 percent of JPSA/CDC patients had sharp curettage abortions, while 16.3 percent had intrauterine instillation procedures (Table 2). In contrast, in the national group, 41.4 percent obtained abortion at eight weeks or less and only 11.7 percent underwent abortion between 13 and 20 weeks. A much higher proportion had sharp curettage and less than half as many had saline abortions. In addition, approximately 66 percent of JPSA/CDC patients underwent abortions in hospitals and the remainder in private clinics. Approximately 67 percent were categorized as non-private patients.

With this demographic background in mind, let us move to a summary of abortion morbidity findings. There were nearly 100 complications on the reporting form, ranging in severity from breast engorgement after abortion to cardiac arrest, convulsions, or death. The term "total complication rate"

TABLE 1

GESTATIONAL AGE OF ABORTION: PATIENTS:
JPSA/CDC AND UNITED STATES

| Gestational Age | Percent Distribution | |
(weeks from LMP)	JPSA/CDC	United States
– 8	31.8	41.4
9 –10	27.4	27.9
11 –12	15.9	15.0
13 –20	22.4	11.7
– 21	2.3	1.2
Unknown	0.2	2.8
TOTAL	100.0	100.0

Source: Center for Disease Control, Atlanta.

TABLE 2

TYPE OF PROCEDURE OF ABORTION PATIENTS:
JPSA/CDC AND UNITED STATES

| Type of Procedure | Percent Distribution | |
	JPSA/CDC	United States
Curettage	80.2	89.1
Suction	79.6	76.9
Sharp	0.6	12.2
Intrauterine Installation	16.3	7.7
Hysterotomy/Hysterectomy	1.0	0.6
Other	2.5	1.9
Unknown	0.0	0.8
TOTAL	100.0	100.0

Source: Center for Disease Control.

refers to the percentage of women who sustained one or more complications of any variety or severity. On the other hand, the term "major complication rate" denotes the percentage of women sustaining one or more of 15 complications that were defined as major: (1) cardiac arrest, (2) convulsions, (3) death, (4) endotoxic shock, (5) fever for three or more days, (6) hemorrhage necessitating blood transfusion, (7) hypernatremia, (8) injury to bladder, ureter, or intestine (9) pelvic infection with two or more days of fever and a peak of at least 40°C, or with hospitalization for 11 or more days, (10) pneumonia, (11) psychatric hospitalization for 11 or more days, (12) pulmonary embolism or infarction (13) thrombophlebitis, (14) unintended major surgery, and (15) wound disruption after hysterotomy or hysterectomy.

The data collected on complications reaffirmed that abortion remains a safe medical procedure. While approximately 12 percent of patients sustained one or more complications, fewer than one percent sustained a major one (Table 3). Overall, suction curettage was the safest abortion method: only five percent of patients undergoing the procedure sustained one or more complications, while only 0.4 percent sustained a major complication. Instillation patients were approximately eight times more likely to suffer a complication and approximately five times more likely to sustain a major one. The complication rates for hysterotomy and hysterectomy (major abdominal operations) were even greater.

TABLE 3

TOTAL AND MAJOR COMPLICATION RATES BY
TYPE OF PROCEDURE

Type of Procedure	Complications per 100 Abortions	
	Total	Major
Suction Curettage	5.0	0.4
Sharp Curettage	10.6	0.9
Instillation	42.7	1.9
Hysterotomy	49.4	14.9
Hysterectomy	52.9	16.1
TOTAL	12.3	0.8

Source: Center for Disease Control, Atlanta.

Seven to eight weeks was the safest abortion interval (Table 4). From 7.2 percent at six weeks or less, the total complication rate declined to a nadir of 4.7 percent in the seven-to-eight-week interval, corroborating the findings of the initial JPSA report. The rate then increased to a maximum of nearly 40 percent in the 17-to-20-week group and then declined slightly thereafter. The seven-to-eight-week interval also had the lowest major complication rates. Thereafter, the rate climbed steadily to a maximum during the 21-to-24-week interval.

TABLE 4

TOTAL AND MAJOR COMPLICATION RATES BY
GESTATIONAL AGE

Gestational Age (Weeks from LMP)	Complications per 100 Abortions	
	Total	Major
– 6	7.2	0.36
7 –8	4.7	0.27
9 –10	5.6	0.45
11 –12	8.2	0.77
13 –14	17.0	1.37
15 –16	33.1	1.91
17 –20	39.9	2.16
21 –24	36.1	2.26
TOTAL	12.3	0.80

Source: Center for Disease Control, Atlanta.

44

Current tenets in abortion methodology suggest that during the first 12 weeks of pregnancy, suction curettage is the method of choice. The 13-to-15-week interval is commonly considered a "gray zone" in which no method is applicable. Instillation procedures are considered the safest method at 16 weeks and beyond. Among these 80,437 patients, however, suction curettage was not only the safest abortion method during the first trimester but through the 20th week of pregnancy (Table 5). Because these second trimester procedures frequently encompassed other instrumental techniques in addition to suction curettage, the generic term "dilatation and evacuation" may be preferable. The instillations (approximately 12,000) represented predominantly intra-amniotioc saline but included over 1,100 intra-amniotic prostaglandins. The major complication rate of dilatation and evacuation in the second trimester was higher than that of suction curettage performed in the first trimester. Nevertheless, the major complication rate of dilatation and evacuation was lower than that of instillation procedures at each comparable gestational age. The likelihood that these differences in rates could be due to chance alone in the 13-14-week group was less than one in 1,000. The difference in rates remained statistically significant in the 15-to-16-week group at a "p" value of less than 0.05. In the 17-to-20-week group, significance was approached but not attained because of the small number of patients in the dilatation and evacuation group (590).

TABLE 5

NUMBERS OF PATIENTS AND MAJOR COMPLICATION RATES FOR
SUCTION CURETTAGE AND INSTILLATION PROCEDURES
BY WEEKS OF GESTATION

Weeks of Gestation	Suction Curettage		Intrauterine Installation		Significance Tests for Difference Between Rates	
	No. of Patients	Major Complications per 100 Abortions	No. of Patients	Major Complications per 100 Abortions		
– 6	4,659	0.28				
7 –8	19,340	0.23				
9 –10	21,542	0.39				
11 –12	11,956	0.51				
13 –14	4,351	0.71	1,100	2.27	p	.001
15 –16	1,409	0.92	2,542	1.77	p	.05
17 –20	590	0.85	7,004	1.81	p	.10
21 –24			1,572	2.04		

Source: Center for Disease Control, Atlanta.

A number of potentially confounding variables may have contributed to these differences in rates. It is possible, for example, that differential rates of follow-up led to differential rates of ascertainment of major complications. However, deleting from analysis all patients for whom we had no follow-up (45 percent of the 80,437 women), we observed the same pattern. To study the effect of two other potentially confounding variables, we excluded from analysis all women with pre-existing medical conditions or concurrent sterilization (17 percent of the data base). Again, we found the same pattern. Abortion by dilatation and evacuation in the second trimester was significantly safer in terms of major complications than was instillation. Total complication rates, likewise, corroborated these findings, only the differences in rates were even larger.

What are the implications of these preliminary findings? First, let me re-emphasize that this work is preliminary, and further refinement is required. Other potentially important variables await examination. Among these are skill of the operator, use of prophylactic antibiotics, or IUD insertion at the time of abortion. Nevertheless, further study is warranted, perhaps with random assignment of patients to groups undergoing instillation procedures during the second trimester. On the basis of these 80,437 patients, dilatation and evacuation appears to represent a safe and practical alternative in the second trimester.

In summary, JPSA/CDC, an extension of the pioneering work of the Population Council and the largest abortion study yet assembled, has reaffirmed that abortion is a safe procedure. While approximately 12 percent of patients sustained one or more complications, fewer than one percent sustained a major complication. Suction curettage was overall the safest abortion method, and abortion in the 7-to-8-week interval had the lowest complication rates. Contrary to current thinking, among these 80,437 women, dilatation and evacuation proved the safest abortion method through the 20th week of pregnancy.

REFERENCES

1. C. Tietze and S. Lewit. "Joint Program for the Study of Abortion (JPSA): Early Medical Complications of Legal Abortion," *Studies in Family Planning* 3:97-122, 1972.
2. C. Tietze and S. Lewit. "Early Medical Complications of Abortion by Saline: Joint Program for the Study of Abortion (JPSA)," *Studies in Family Planning* 4:133-138, 1973.
3. U.S. Department of Health, Education and Welfare, Public Health Service, Center for Disease Control. *Abortion Surveillance: 1974,* Atlanta: 1976.

Discussion

Tyrer: The first item that I wanted to bring up for discussion was the matter that Dr. Jane Hodgson presented about the importance of training physicans for performing these procedures. Planned Parenthood agrees with this completely. We have had an experience recently where very knowledgeable physicians in obstetrics and gynecology in general but with no specific training in termination technique volunteered to start services in a program. There were no other physicians in the community who would provide the service. It was assumed that, because the physician had used suction technique with incomplete abortions, it would be appropriate to proceed without any further training. Of a considerable number of cases performed, approximately 50 percent were hospitalized with complications. Dr. Grimes mentioned the increased safety of suction abortion up to 20 weeks. There was a variable he didn't mention. These suction procedures from 12 to 20 weeks are usually done only by very experienced operators. If this were started as a general approach for abortion at this gestational age, the data might not reflect the favorable outcome that they now show.

Hodgson: I think there's a great deal of individual variation in the number of procedures that a person has to do in order to become expert. There seems to be great individual variation. I've tried to train a fair number of residents and students. There's no doubt that people in the field of obstetrics and gynecology have some carryover from their other experience and they are more adept than someone who's been trained in general surgery or in another specialty. The idea that this is a procedure that can be done by paramedicals certainly is a false one. In regard to the use of suction in the second trimester, I would like to ask Dr. Grimes if these procedures were done under local or general anesthesia. I think that the type of anesthesia affects the complication rate a good deal. When you are dealing with a uterus under general anesthesia it's much more easy to perforate and to run into problems. It's difficult to do too much damage if your patient is awake because she'll tell you about it. Local anesthesia results in a much safer procedure.

Droegemueller: I think it's very difficult for a physician to quibble with someone else's statistics. However, to make a blanket statement that second trimester suction is better than instillation technique and to compare it to saline as used today is questionable. I don't doubt that a very skilled surgeon can evacuate a uterus between 16 and 20 weeks with minimal morbidity; but if you make this a general procedure, I think the complications will skyrocket. All of us have done this between 12 and 15

47

weeks. After 16 weeks, there are very few of us who will try to use suction curettage without some preliminary drug or mechanical dilatation of the cervix. We certainly have prostaglandin failures in which the cervix is dilated, and it is easy to do it with serial laminaria. However, if one would have to use abrupt mechanical dilatation such as metal dilators and then suction curettage, I think the morbidity would be substantial.

Tyrer: I'd also like you to comment on the number of procedures you think a physician should perform before he is capable of operating on his own.

Droegemueller: When you talk about the acquisition of knowledge, time and numbers should be the variables. You ought to have some pretest and some post-testing. Different people arrive at that end result at different times. A great deal depends on previous experience, so we don't have a specific number. We stay with our residents, test them, and they have to prove themselves. I think the same thing about traditional education. It's ridiculous that medical school is four years. There ought to be a variable time period with knowledge or skills being the constant, and time or numbers being the variable.

Tyrer: You feel that it's an evaluation of the performance of the individual and everyone should be evaluated and their competence determined before they are allowed to proceed on their own. Is that correct?

Rashbaum: When I first started doing abortions, I took my boards in obstetrics and gynecology and therefore I knew I was competent to do it. After I had done my first few hundred I realized how silly I had been in my previous viewpoint. After I had done a thousand I thought I was an expert but by the time I had done 5,000, I realized I was learning a lot. At this point, having done somewhere around 12,000 procedures, I'm beginning to think I'm reasonably competent. You have to realize that in a teaching service, the abortion patient has low priority. Abortion is given to the first year resident and it's really a scut job. I don't think you can train individuals quickly to do careful, adequate pregnancy examinations and procedures in the first trimester. I'm fascinated by what Dr. Grimes has had to say. I'm also terrified. I think that fear is healthy. Yesterday we were talking with the exhibitors about getting the sort of instruments that we would need to make these second trimester procedures much easier. They're afraid to make them. Suction over 12 weeks is a dirty word. They won't do it because the medical convention will get down on them for breaking the rules. Maybe CDC will have a breakthrough for us so that we can change the rules a little. It looks like an exciting change in abortion procedures.

Grimes: I would certainly concur with what you said about the necessity of very good training. The inverse relationship between the level of training and complication rate has been noted for some time.* With regard to the

* B. M. Beric and M. Kupresanin. "Vacuum Aspiration Using Paracervical Block for Legal Abortion as an Outpatient Procedure Up to the 12th Week of Pregnancy," *Lancet* 2:619, 1971; and L. Andolsek and M. Owen. "The Operation and the Operator," *The Ljubljana Abortion Study 1971-1973*, Bethesda: National Institutes of Health, 1974.

several questions that were directed to me about dilatation and evacuation in the second trimester, most of these procedures in our data base were performed under paracervical block, and most were done as outpatients. The largest single center reporting on second trimester dilatation and evacuation used modified Hanks dilators to achieve cervical dilatation. In other parts of the country, it is customary to use laminaria packed the day before. We cannot yet compare complication rates differentially by saline and prostaglandin. However, I think we can draw some inferences about morbidity rates of prostaglandin abortions.* For example, retained placenta persists as a problem, and gastrointestinal side effects are frequent.

Tyrer: There's one other important issue that I want to raise. Dr. Hodgson raised the question as to whether the IUD should be left in place if a patient elects termination.

Droegemueller: I think it's one of these things where you're damned if you do and damned if you don't, especially if the patient changes her mind. It depends upon the interval from the time you've seen her with an IUD in place and the time when the abortion procedure is going to be accomplished. It may be that she will become ambivalent. Then you have a woman who is carrying the pregnancy with an IUD *in situ* and thus has an increased chance of infection. However, if you pull it out, you may stir up some infection which will make a later abortion procedure more morbid.

Rashbaum: In the first trimester abortion patient, don't pull it when you do your first exam prior to the procedure. Process the patient, give the anesthesia, dilate the cervix, and then remove the IUD.

Tyrer: At the present time I'm working with the Food & Drug Administration (FDA) in preparing the summary that will accompany the Battelle report commissioned to update the 1968 IUD data. Also, I have worked with an ACOG task force that has been developing a technical bulletin on the management of the IUDs.** Their recommendations are: Any time a patient who is pregnant is seen with an IUD in place and the IUD can be removed with ease, it should be removed at that moment. Even though she says she may elect termination, she may change her mind. She may not be seen again until she's further along. By then the IUD may have withdrawn to within the uterus. Then it can be a source of serious infection, septic abortion, and even death. I agree that if you see the patient on the table and are preparing to perform the procedure, it's best to anesthetize the patient and then remove the IUD in conjunction with the termination. There's a grave risk involved in leaving the IUD in place on the premise that she will elect termination.

Tietze: Being the father of the original JPSA and hence the grandfather

* J.H. Duenhoelter and N.F. Gant. "Complications Following Prostaglandin F2α-Induced Midtrimester Abortion," *Obstetrics and Gynecology* 46:247, 1975.
** American College of Obstetricians and Gynecologists. Technical Bulletin No. 10, September 1974, *The Intrauterine Device.*

of JPSA/CDC, which I recognize as a lusty infant who has outgrown its parent, I beg your indulgence and will ask three questions or make three comments. The first one is addressed to Dr. Rashbaum. Did I hear you say that according to the Andolsek study from Ljubljana, the women who had suction procedures plus sharp curettage had a higher complication rate than those who had only suction?

Rashbaum: No sir. What I meant to say was that in 6.2 percent of those patients who had suction curettage (suction aspiration plus curettage), appreciable placental tissue was found at the time of the suction curettage. Not the group with a recheck later.

Tietze: The point is that some of the doctors were in the habit of checking when they had the feeling that they had left something behind, so there may be a certain false interpretation of these cases. These data may have biases because of the selection of cases. My second comment relates to the comparison of suction and instillation in the second trimester. This is an observation we made also during the first JPSA study. We found a lower complication rate for the late suctions than for saline at any time. Of course, this was contrary to common opinion. No one paid any attention to it, just as no one paid attention to our observation that there were fewer complications with general anesthesia than with local anesthesia. Now I have some data from the experience in England and Wales where they do quite a lot of both suctions and D and Cs in the second trimester. D and C is the most widely used procedure now. They do very few salines and they still do a great many more hysterotomies than we do. The mortality is very low in the first trimester with both of the vaginal procedures. It is on the order of three per 100,000 in the first trimester and goes up to something like eight or so per 100,000 for second trimester vaginal procedures. It is lower than for any other second trimester procedures. While this is based on several tens of thousands of cases, the number of deaths is still very small. What really interests me is this curious observation which was against our expectations in 1970-71, and I believe against the expectation of my colleagues now, that the earliest abortions carry a somewhat higher complication rate than those done at seven and eight weeks. In light of the data that have come out of North Carolina and some other places, I have come to the conclusion that, at the time when we did JPSA, everybody used rigid instrumentation, even in the earliest procedures. At the time when the International Fertility Research Program at the University of North Carolina analyzed their data, many of the investigators had come to use flexible cannulas for early abortions. That was the reason for the difference between our findings and their findings. Now I see that JPSA/CDC comes forward again and has the same findings as we had. This is a matter of great importance from the public health point of view and I hope that several of the gynecologists on the panel and perhaps those in the audience might react to that.

Tyrer: Dr. Warren Hern's paper on second trimester termination performed by this technique will be part of the scientific program of this year's

Association of Planned Parenthood Physicians meeting and will be open for discussion.*

Sue Ellen Alishouse, Fort Collins, Colorado: I'd like to know how much the abortion technology and contraceptive technology, such as vaginal suppositories with prostaglandins, are being researched on third world women, outside or inside the United States, prior to FDA approval. I'd also like the response of the physicians on the panel as to their feelings concerning the use of third world or non-United States people in testing new procedures that we won't allow in our country.

Droegemueller: I am on a United States government scientific review committee. We are very prone not to fund any research outside the United States that has not been tested first in this country. Because of the difference in regulations between our FDA and other countries', private industry often does test compounds in England, Sweden, and Singapore prior to bringing them into this country. The FDA question is a two-part one. Research with a new drug has to be approved by the FDA so there is no testing prior to its approval. The research has to be approved before the drug is released to the general public. The new prostaglandin analogs in plastic are being tested in this country at the present time. In the prostaglandin field, products like the 15-methyl analogs were tested in this country prior to being tested in Europe. They go with a different analog in Europe. Although your comment has definite validity, I don't think it's as applicable now as it was three or four years ago.

Tyrer: Drug companies have branches in other countries and they abide by the regulations in that particular country so far as research is concerned. The Food and Drug Administration does not accept across-the-board research that is done overseas. It must be completed and carried out in this country to the satisfaction of the FDA prior to approval in this country.

Dr. Lewis Koplik, Albuquerque, New Mexico: I can assure Dr. Droegemueller that there are not many of us who enjoy doing either midtrimester suction curettages or uterine evacuations. It's a distasteful procedure. The compensation I receive is the fact that it seems less traumatic to the woman than putting her through an induced labor procedure. What about the possibility of combining a feticide, something which will produce fetal maceration in the mid-trimester, with uterine evacuation 24 to 48 hours later? The few times I've done this because the woman has not responded to pitocin, the process of evacuation has been extremely easy. I would like to know both from a complication point of view and a technical point of view, would this be possible?

Droegemueller: Sure. I would support that. Whatever you use to

---

* W. M. Hern and A. G. Oakes. "Multiple Laminaria Treatment in Early Outpatient Suction Abortion," *Advances in Planned Parenthood* 12:2, 93-97, 1977.

dehydrate the fetus would also cause some cervical softening and make the suction curettage that much easier. We certainly have performed that. What I am concerned about is the long-term morbidity of rapidly dilating the cervix mechanically in a pregnancy greater than 16 weeks. I have no quarrel at all with suction curettage up to 16 weeks. As we all know, not all 16 week gestations are the same size. I think that Dr. Koplik's suggestion of combining things is an excellent one and is something that all of us have experienced when we have had failures in inducing second trimester abortion. The longer you prolong the procedure, the more cervical softening, the more receptive the cervix will be to dilatation and, therefore I believe, although I can't prove it statistically, the less the long-range harm.

Dr. Mildred Hansen, Minneapolis, Minnesota: I'd like to allude to my own experience with second trimester abortion preceded by the insertion of seaweed laminaria which remains in place for 18 to 24 hours. My experience, including in-patient people who also had laparoscopic tubal sterilization, includes 1,679 cases between 14 and 20 weeks LMP. One thousand of these were between 14 and 16 weeks, 679 were between 16 and 20 weeks. All of these were performed without a single case of uterine perforation. I think the key to safe, effective second trimester abortion is the use of seaweed laminaria inserted prior to the procedure to allow safe, gradual cervical dilatation. I might also mention that when I perform the procedure I usually have a hand on the fundus. The patients are awake except for those done under general anesthesia for laparoscopic tubal at the same time. A hand on the fundus gives me a great deal of reassurance as to where my instruments are. I use nothing special except curved ring forceps with fine serrations and I do curette every patient. I would like to ask the members of the panel if they're aware of the work of American Association of Gynecologic Laparoscopists indicating the amount of post-laparoscopic tubal morbidity when the IUD is not removed prior to the performance of abortion and laparascopic tubal sterilizations?*

Tyrer: Dr. Theodore King, head of the Obstetrics and Gynecology Department at Johns Hopkins University, indicates that every perforation is routinely hospitalized, laparoscoped, and the procedure completed under direct laparoscopic vision at their department. He says that this cuts down tremendously on the retained products of conception. He says they are now appalled by what they are seeing inside when they look at the perforations. Sometimes a knuckle of bowel is stuck in there. Sometimes there is arterial bleeding that requires opening and suturing.

Renee Ward, Minneapolis, Minnesota: I think Dr. Tietze asked something about early menstrual extraction or menstrual regulation. The

---

* J. Phillips, B. Hulka, J. Hulka, D. Keith and L. Keith. "Laparoscopic Procedures, The American Association of Gynecologic Laparoscopists Membership Survey for 1975," presented at the annual meeting of the American Association of Gynecologic Laparoscopists, Atlanta, November 17, 1976.

implications of the data that Dr. Grimes gave were that perhaps one needs to rethink this on a number of grounds. I'd like to know the opinion of both Dr. Rashbaum, and I know Dr. Hodgson has published in this area. I have a concern about menstrual regulation, and I'll define it as getting a negative pregnancy test. Practitioners have the patients come in, and if the patient is positive she is charged one amount. If she is negative, she is charged another. These data suggest to me that perhaps what we need to do is advise our patients to wait for a positive and give some support and not do a procedure without a positive pregnancy test, given the kind of data we heard earlier.

Tyrer: Dr. Rashbaum deferred to me because I editorialized on an article by Dr. Elton Kessel published in *Family Planning Perspectives.* * He finds that if the pregnancy test is negative at the time a patient comes for a menstrual regulation, the overall complications are less if you ask the patient to return in seven to ten days. At that point either she has menstruated or she has a positive pregnancy test. You can then make a definitive diagnosis and institute the appropriate treatment. This certainly goes along with the CDC data as well.

Hodgson: I'm not surprised that the complication rate is a little higher in the very early group. The early procedure is often hard to do. We often run into problems with obstruction of the small cannulas. It's more difficult to dilate the cervix in a very early pregnancy. It's usually much simpler to do the procedure at eight weeks than it is at six. That would certainly explain the difference in the complication rates.

Hern: I agree with Dr. Hodgson and also point out that, whereas laminaria is used sometimes in the early terminations, there are more complications with the laminaria at that stage also.

Tyrer: I would like to suggest to those who are interested in the continued availability of laminaria that you write to the FDA Devices panel. It is reviewing all devices in the field of obstetrics and gynecology and laminaria are among them. The panel is seriously considering putting laminaria in Class 3, which would mean that they would not be able to be used except experimentally until they had proven to be safe and effective. I would encourage you all to write to this panel with your findings concerning the safety and efficacy of this material and try to influence that panel so that they might consider options other than Class 3.

Linda Weber, Boulder, Colorado: What do you say to someone who wants to know the chances of spontaneous abortion if her IUD is removed? She knows she's pregnant, the IUD is in place, and she wants to know whether or not she's going to abort.

Tyrer: The data indicate that her chance of aborting is reduced by half by

---

* E. R. Miller, J. A. Fortney and E. Kessel. "Early Vacuum Aspiration: Minimizing Procedures to Nonpregnant Women," *Family Planning Perspectives* 8: 33-38, 1976.

removing the IUD. It's about 50 percent if the IUD remains in place, if she has it removed it's reduced to about 25 percent.

Weber: Are there studies being done now on the lowered· risk of perforation with the use of laminaria?

Hern: I don't know of any comparative studies but the two largest series in the literature are mine and Dr. Golditch's in California.* Both series had over a thousand cases without any perforations. I think that it's very hard to make a comparison between different techniques and physicians but there are certainly many people who feel that the laminaria reduces the rate of perforation. I don't think that all the evidence is in on that.

Grimes: May I respond also to Ms. Weber's question about the disposition of the IUD and subsequent spontaneous abortion. A recent paper concerning this came from the Philippines.** Among this group of women with Lippes loops, 48 percent with the device left *in situ* had a spontaneous abortion as compared to 30 percent of the women who had the device removed.

* W. M. Hern. "Laminaria in Abortion: Use in 1368 Patients in First Trimester," *Rocky Mountain Medical Journal* 72:390-395, 1975; and I. M. Golditch and M. H. Glasser. "The Use of Laminaria Tents for Cervical Dilatation Prior to Vacuum Aspiration Abortion," *American Journal of Obstetrics and Gynecology* 119:481-485, 1974.
** G. T. Alvior, Jr. "Pregnancy Outcome with Removal of Intrauterine Device," *Obstetrics and Gynecology* 41:894, 1973.

Public Health Aspects of Abortion

Comparative Morbidity and Mortality in Abortion and Contraception

Christopher Tietze, M.D.

Before discussing the specific topic of mortality associated with various types of fertility control and abortion, I would like to refer to several tables relating to the development of abortion statistics over the past year. Table 1 shows the total number of legal abortions yearly in the U.S. The figures for 1970-72 are those compiled by the Center for Disease Control (CDC).

Table 1

Legal abortions: United States, 1970-1974

Year	Abortions* Reported	Rate per 1000 Women, 15–44	Ratio per 1000 Live Births**
1970	193,490	4.5	50
1971	485,820	11.2	125
1972	586,760	13.2	155
1973	742,460	16.5	239
1974	899,850	19.5	317
Increase 1970–74	365 percent	333 percent	534 percent

Sources: *1970 to 1972 Center for Disease Control, Atlanta.
1973 to 1974 The Alan Guttmacher Institute, New York.
**Six months later

Those for 1973 and 1974 were obtained by The Alan Guttmacher Institute, using a survey of providers of abortion services. Table 2 shows the distribution of legal abortions during the first quarters of 1973 to 1975. In 1973, the Middle Atlantic division, which of course means mainly New York State and New York City, reported more than two-fifths of all the legal abortions in this country. The Pacific division, which includes California, reported more than one-fourth. In some of the other divisions the numbers were ridiculously small. By the first quarter of 1974 the situation had improved and in 1975 it has improved even further. The Middle Atlantic division now reports only about one-fourth of all abortions and the Pacific division about one-fifth. The distribution has improved, although it is still far from being perfect.

57

Table 2

Percent Distribution of Legal Abortions Among Census Divisions:
United States, 1973–1975 (first calendar quarters)

Census Division	1973	1974	1975
New England	1.5	4.8	5.0
Middle Atlantic	41.5	27.3	24.6
East No. Central	7.8	14.1	16.6
West No. Central	2.7	5.0	5.2
South Atlantic	15.0	16.0	16.1
East So. Central	0.7	2.7	3.3
West So. Central	1.1	5.0	6.8
Mountain	2.2	2.8	2.9
Pacific	27.5	22.3	19.5
Total	100.0	100.0	100.0

Source: The Alan Guttmacher Institute, New York.

Table 3 shows abortion rates per 1,000 women of reproductive age, 15-44 years, and abortion ratios per 1,000 live births. In the Middle Atlantic division, there has definitely been a decline of both rate and ratio. The data refer to the state where the abortion was performed, not the state of residence of the woman. In the Pacific division there is not much change, but in all the other divisions there are dramatic changes. In 1973, the Southeast Central and Southwest Central regions reported about four abortions per 1,000 women, which was one-seventh or one-eighth of the rates seen in the Pacific and Middle Atlantic divisions. By 1974 these two South Central divisions had about 10 abortions per 1,000 women, which is about one-third of the rates for the Middle Atlantic and Pacific divisions. The pattern of the abortion ratios was quite similar.

Table 3

Legal Abortion Rates and Ratios by Census Division:
United States, 1973–1975

Census Division	Rate per 1000 Women, 15–44		Ratio per 1000 Live Births	
	1973	1974	1973	1974
New England	9.0	17.0	152	297
Middle Atlantic	31.6	28.4	536	484
East No. Central	10.9	14.9	161	220
West No. Central	8.8	13.1	127	184
South Atlantic	16.5	20.2	233	288
East So. Central	4.0	9.7	49	121
West So. Central	4.4	11.0	53	132
Mountain	9.0	13.3	103	147
Pacific	28.4	30.9	440	463
United States	16.5	19.5	239	282

Source: The Alan Guttmacher Institute, New York.

The next few tables are courtesy of Dr. Jean Pakter and the New York City Health Department. Dr. Grimes' paper indicates that early abortions have a lower morbidity. We also know that they have a lower mortality than late abortions. It is therefore very important that abortion be done early. Among residents of New York City, the percentage of second trimester abortion has gone down from 21 percent in 1971 to 14.5 percent in 1974 (Table 4). The nonresidents present an entirely different picture. In the first

Table 4

Legal Abortion Gestation by Residence: New York City, 1971–1974

Residency Status	Gestation Total (%)	12 weeks or less (%)	13 weeks or more (%)
Residents			
1971	100.0	79.3	20.7
1972	100.0	83.9	16.1
1973	100.0	84.9	15.1
1974	100.0	85.5	14.5
Nonresidents			
1971	100.0	81.2	18.8
1972	100.0	81.8	18.2
1973	100.0	74.2	25.8
1974	100.0	74.4	25.6

Source: New York City Department of Health, Bureau of Maternity Services and Family Planning, New York.

two years before the Supreme Court decisions, 18-19 percent of nonresidents had late abortions. After the Supreme Court decisions, 25-26 percent of nonresidents had late abortions. That simply means that, after the decisions were handed down, clinics opened up in the hinterlands very quickly. Women who needed first trimester abortions could get them in their own state, and, if they were lucky, even in their own community. Hospitals have been much slower in developing abortion facilities. Since most second trimester abortions are performed in hospitals, these women still had to come to New York. I think this is a very dramatic indicator that has important policy implications. Table 5 shows the same data for residents only, arranged by age, separately for white women and other women. I would have preferred to show this in terms of some measure of socioeconomic status. However, the data are not available in that form and so I have to use race or ethnicity as proxy. In each of these two groups, the youngest women, those aborted under 15 years of age, had the highest percentage of late abortions and are therefore exposed to extra risks. Among the older teens, the percentage is going down. The adult women know much better how to handle themselves and to obtain abortions early. Even in New York City, the non-white woman is still disadvantaged in terms of the stage at which she obtains her abortion.

Table 5

Resident Legal Abortion, Gestation by Race: New York City, 1974

Race	Gestation Total (%)	12 weeks or less (%)	13 weeks or more (%)
White			
Under 15	100.0	72.9	27.1
15–19	100.0	83.7	16.3
20–34	100.0	88.5	11.5
35 or more	100.0	90.5	9.5
Other			
Under 15	100.0	63.7	36.3
15–19	100.0	75.0	25.0
20–34	100.0	85.5	14.5
35 or more	100.0	87.0	13.0

Source: New York City Department of Health, Bureau of Maternity Services and Family Planning, New York.

Table 6 addresses itself specifically to the question of the youngest women without distinction by ethnicity. In the upper panel, which is based on published statistics, 64 percent had first trimester abortions and 36 percent had second trimester abortions. Consider the case of a woman who is 14 years and 9 months of age when she gets pregnant. If she had a first trimester abortion, she will appear in the under-15-year age group, but if she delays for whatever reason and has her abortion in the second trimester, she will appear in the next higher age group. Dr. Pakter was kind enough to retabulate these data for me by single years of age. We estimated the age at conception, and these very young women are even at a worse disadvantage than the figure of 36 percent suggests. Actually, of those who get pregnant before 15 years of age, 41 percent have a late abortion. By the time they get to the middle teens, 15-17 years, the adjustment has very little effect.

Table 7 also has policy implications. This is based on a rather complicated manipulation of data collected by the National Center for Health Statistics (NCHS) and more recently by the CDC, which has more complete data on abortion than the NCHS. We made efforts to make the data comparable over the entire period from about 1960 to 1974. In 1960, there were almost 300 women annually dying from all types of abortion. That number goes down to less than 160 in 1969. Very few deaths were associated with legal abortions during that period. The decline in mortality was about 7.5 percent per year. After 1969 the number of deaths begins to go down rapidly.

Some of the deaths from illegal abortion have been replaced by deaths from legal abortions, but the total number of deaths is going down rather rapidly at the rate of about 21 percent per year. The number of deaths

Table 6

Resident Legal Abortion, Gestation of Women Under 18 Years: New York City, 1974

Women Obtaining Abortion		Age	
		Under 15 years	15–17 years
By Age at Termination			
	Gestation		
Number:	12 weeks or less	497	4,598
	13 weeks or more	281	1,719
Percent:	12 weeks or less	63.9	72.8
	13 weeks or more	36.1	27.2
By Estimated Age at Conception			
Number:	12 weeks or less	659	5,324
	13 weeks or more	457	2,054
Percent:	12 weeks or less	59.1	72.2
	13 weeks or more	40.9	27.8

Source: New York City Department of Health, Bureau of Maternity Services and Family Planning, New York.

Table 7

Deaths Associated with Abortion, by Type of Abortion: United States, 1958-1974

Year or average*	All Types	Legally Induced	Other than Legal		
			Total	Illegal	Spon-taneous
1958–62	292	5	287	n.a.	n.a.
1963–67	222	4	218	n.a.	n.a.
1968	162	5	157	103	54
1969	158	4	154	113	41
1970	158	30	128	106	22
1971	132	46	86	63	23
1972	88	24	64	41	23
1973	56	26	30	21	9
1974	48	24	24	6	18

Sources:* 1958 to 1967   National Center for Health Statistics, Rockville.
1968 to 1971   Estimates by Christopher Tietze.
1972 to 1974   Center for Disease Control, Atlanta.

associated with other-than-legal abortion, which is mostly, although not exclusively, illegal abortion, is going down at a rate of 31 percent per year. Some people feel that this represents the decline in the number of illegal abortions. I believe that a decline in the number of illegal abortions has been even greater for several reasons. Back in the 1960s, a large proportion of the illegal abortions in the United States were done by physicians, including some very experienced practitioners, at a comparatively low risk. In 1974, the women who still obtained illegal abortions were probably the poorest, the least educated, the most disadvantaged from every conceivable social and economic point of view. Some probably could not obtain legal abortions because of limitations on the period of gestation for which a particular hospital will do abortions. Therefore, I consider it quite possible that the death-to-case ratio of illegal abortions in 1974 was actually higher, not lower, than it was in 1960. If so, the decline in the number of illegal abortions in the United States has been more rapid than suggested by this table.

Why did the decline in abortion mortality start so long before abortions were legalized in any of the states? There are at least two obvious reasons. There had been significant improvement in the treatment of all sorts of obstetrical and gynecological complications, including those associated with abortion. Also, there had been over these years a great expansion in the use of highly effective methods of contraception. There were probably fewer unwanted conceptions and, therefore, probably fewer illegal abortions. It is very difficult not to associate the accelerated decline in the number of deaths after 1969, from 7.5 percent to 21 percent per year, with the legalization of abortion. In 1970, the New York abortion law came into force and, New York City served the nation, doing two-thirds of its abortions on out-of-town women.

Table 8 is designed to kill another bugaboo that has been around a long time and that is the belief that easy access to abortion interferes with the

Table 8

Pregnancy Rates per 1,000 Women:
Residents of New York City

Age of Women (years)		Conception Year*	
	1971	1972	1973
15–19	141.8	140.8	141.6
20–24	221.1	205.0	199.4
25–29	192.9	178.6	168.9
30–34	129.7	122.1	117.1
35–39	68.3	65.1	64.1
40–44	20.6	20.5	20.1
Total 15–44	138.8	131.8	128.4

*April–March

Source: New York City Department of Health, Bureau of Maternity Services and Family Planning, New York.

practice of contraception. Table 8 shows pregnancy rates per 1,000 women, by age, in New York City during the first three years under the abortion law of 1970. Among the adult women 20 years of age and over, there has been a marked decline in the pregnancy rate. In fact, the decline was probably faster. We know from the experience of many countries as well as from the mortality statistics of the United States, that the passage of a law and even the provision of services does not insure the immediate disappearance of all illegal abortions. There were probably some illegal abortions in the first year and it is almost certain that there were fewer in the second and third year. There was a decline of pregnancy rates in all age groups over 20. Among teenagers, there is no statistically significant change. In my opinion, that can mean one of two things. Most of these teenagers, of course, are unmarried. Probably there was little change in either sexual behavior or contraceptive behavior. The alternative would be that there was more sex and better contraception. The third possibility, that there was less sex and worse contraception, I am inclined to reject on the basis of what I am told.

We now come to the main subject of my presentation. My two colleagues, Drs. Bongaarts and Schearer, have tried to compare, in a meaningful way, health risks associated with contraception, with early abortion, and with no control at all. Health risks, of course, are of two kinds. There are deaths associated with the use of certain fertility control methods, such as oral contraceptives, IUDs, and abortion. There are also deaths associated with the failure of the method, with the pregnancy or the birth of the child, or with the abortion which is undertaken to correct the contraceptive failure. What we did first was to construct a model population, a statistical simulation.* It represents the fertility parameters of what we call a developed country such as the United States and most countries in Europe. It would be completely inapplicable to, say, Bangladesh or Indonesia, where the situation is quite different. This limitation also applies to all other parts of the model. We are talking about risks in our own country and countries similar to it.

The first line of Table 9 assumes no fertility control at all. These are women whose coital frequency, as I have phrased it delicately, is comparable to that customary in wedlock. Obviously a woman who has intercourse only when her boyfriend comes back from college might have a much lower risk of conception than is assumed here. There is a rather high birth rate in the first line. Historical statistics from Western Europe suggest birth rates of about 400 per 1,000 married women per year for women from 20 to 35. This table shows about 600. That is due to the fact that we are assuming in this model a rather short period of breastfeeding.

---

* For a more detailed description of the data sources and the simulation model used to produce these estimates, see C. Tietze, J. Bongaarts and B. Shearer. "Mortality Associated with the Control of Fertility," *Family Planning Perspectives* 8:6-14, 1976.

Table 9

Live Births or Estimates of Induced Abortions:
Rates per 1,000 Women per Year, by Age* and Control Method

Fertility Control Method		Age of Women					
		15–19	20–24	25–29	30–34	35–39	40–44
No control	Live Birth	507	614	588	558	472	317
Abortion only	Abortion	995	1331	1318	1227	1068	651
Orals/IUDs	Live Birth	12	19	19	18	14	7
	Abortion	14	22	22	21	16	9
Traditional	Live Birth	103	160	157	146	114	59
Methods	Abortion	137	206	204	196	155	84

*Nonsterile women

In the second line the women are sexually active but they do not want any children at that time. They are aborting all these pregnancies during the first trimester. The number of abortions in all age groups is about twice as high as the number of live births.

Why is it necessary to have two abortions to replace one live birth? The answer is that a woman who gets pregnant and aborts can get pregnant again much earlier than a woman who does not abort. If she does carry the pregnancy to term it will take nine months. Then there is a postpartum period of amenorrhea, during which she does not ovulate. If she aborts at eight or 10 weeks, she can get pregnant again after three months. Therefore, in this model, there are about two abortions required to replace one live birth.

We have two assumptions on contraception. Those with the lowest effectiveness are the traditional methods such as the condom or the diaphragm. We used data on the experience of women who wanted to space children, not to prevent conception entirely. It is a rather relaxed type of contraception with 90 percent effectiveness. A diaphragm and condoms can do much better but we wanted to have a realistic model. The number of abortions here is not twice as high as the number of live births: It is only about one-third higher. We have assumed a 99 percent effectiveness for users of IUDs and oral contraceptives. This is based on the experience of users rather than on the theoretical effectiveness of the pill, which is very close to 100 percent. The number of pregnancies is very low and the number of abortions that would be required to replace live births is only slightly higher than the number of live births. That is the population model.

Table 10 shows rates of mortality per 100,000 events associated with pregnancy and childbirth and with legal abortion in the first trimester. The basic pattern is quite similar, with the minimum mortality experienced by women in their twenties, then going up rather steeply, particularly for births. For this particular model, we chose the abortion mortality in England and Wales for the period 1968-1973. The level of mortality in

Table 10

Estimates of Mortality Due to Pregnancy and Childbirth,
Induced Abortion, and Oral Contraception

Age of Women (years)	Deaths from Pregnancy and Childbirth*	Deaths from Induced Abortion**	Deaths from Oral Contraception***
15–19	10.8	2.3	1.3
20–24	8.5	1.9	1.3
25–29	12.1	1.9	1.3
30–34	25.1	4.2	4.8
35–39	41.0	9.2	6.9
40–44	69.1	10.1	24.5

*Per 100,000 live births
**Per 100,000 first trimester abortions
***Per 100,000 users per year

England and Wales during this period was about twice as high as in the United States. For the mortality associated with the pill, we also used data from England. For the IUD, we had to use rather weak data which are the only data available. We used the same mortality rate of 1.0 per 100,000 for all ages of women on the grounds that many deaths associated with the IUD are actually connected with pregnancy. We know that pregnancy with and without the IUD is more common among younger women. Other deaths probably follow the general increase of human frailty with age so we assumed the same overall level for all ages of women.

Table 11 shows mortality rates associated with pregnancy and childbirth, with legal abortion, and with contraception per 100,000 women per year. The top line represents women who use no fertility control at all. Among the women under 30, about five to seven per 100,000 per year will die. Later, the rate increases to about 22. The second line shows abortion-related deaths. The assumed risk is twice as high as it should be according to American statistics, but it is still lower than the risk of birth-related deaths. The third panel illustrates the situation with regard to oral contraception. Birth-related deaths are very low among the younger women and then go up rather steeply among the older women using oral contraceptives.

Finally we come to the traditional methods. Younger women experience low death rates, reflecting the low level of mortality associated with childbirth. These go up as women get older and childbirth becomes more risky, in spite of the fact that the incidence of pregnancy and childbirth goes down.

Table 11

Estimates of Annual Deaths Associated With Pregnancy/Childbirth and With Legal Abortion, per 100,000 Women

Fertility Control Method	Age of Women					
	15–19	20–24	25–29	30–34	35–39	40–44
No control						
Birth-related	5.5	5.2	7.1	14.0	19.3	21.9
Abortion only						
Abortion-related	2.3	2.5	2.5	5.2	9.8	6.6
Orals only						
Birth-related	0.1	0.2	0.2	0.4	0.6	0.4
Method-related	1.3	1.3	1.3	4.8	6.9	24.5
Total deaths	1.4	1.5	1.5	5.2	7.5	24.9
IUDs only						
Birth-related	0.1	0.2	0.2	0.4	0.6	0.4
Method-related	1.0	1.0	1.0	1.0	1.0	1.0
Total deaths	1.1	1.2	1.2	1.4	1.6	1.4
Traditional methods only						
Birth-related	1.1	1.4	1.9	3.7	4.7	4.0
Traditional methods, plus abortion						
Abortion-related	0.3	0.4	0.4	0.8	1.4	0.8

Let us summarize what we have concluded so far. First, at all ages and with all methods, with the sole exception of pill users aged 40 and over, any method of control has a lower mortality risk than no control at all. The very high level of method-related mortality among women in their forties using oral contraceptives is particularly applicable in a population where a good many cigarettes are being smoked by these women. If we could construct a model for a non-smoking population, there would still be an increase at the higher ages but it would not be nearly so dramatic. At all ages, with this one exception, mortality with any method is always lower than with no method. Secondly, among younger women, each of the methods alone (abortion alone, oral contraceptives alone, IUD alone, diaphragm or condom alone), has about the same level of risk to life: between one and two per 100,000 per year. Therefore, if the woman is otherwise satisfied with whatever she is using, she has no reason to switch to any other of these single methods for fear that she might die as a result of her current practice.

The bottom line shows the traditional methods with abortion backup in the first trimester. I am referring to diaphragm and condoms, but I could have mentioned other methods such as foam. At all ages, without exception, the mortality level is much lower than with any of the single methods.

66

Obviously, risk of mortality is not a perfect measure of health risks, but it is the only method of measuring that we have. The health risks which are or may be associated with pregnancy and delivery, with abortion, with oral contraception, and with IUDs are so different that you cannot compare them. They differ in severity, they differ in character, and they differ in duration. They differ even in relation to the person who is affected, whether it is the woman or her possible offspring. Who can say, except in terms of his own personal feeling or opinion, what is worse: having a pulmonary infarction, being treated on the intensive care unit for three weeks and then going home; or having a severe pelvic infection which leaves a woman fit but sterile? I cannot compare these situations quantitatively. I can only compare them in terms of mortality.

Also, it should be clear that considerations of health and safety are not the only ones that determine a consumer's choice of method. Other considerations are important, such as convenience of use, reversibility, moral considerations in relation to abortion, life style, and cost.

In Table 12, for comparison purposes we have converted the risks of death into percentage of risk with no control, which is indicated by 100 in the top line. The entries in the next four lines, that is, abortion only, orals only, IUD only, and traditional methods only, are more or less the same for women under 30. Traditional methods plus abortion gives the lowest level of risk of death. Only with the pill for women over 40 is there a slightly higher risk than with no method at all.

Table 12

Relative Mortality among Women 15–44
Using Different Fertility Control Methods
(No Control = 100)

Fertility Control Method	Age of Woman					
	15–19	20–24	25–29	30–34	35–39	40–44
No control	100	100	100	100	100	100
Abortion only	42	48	35	37	51	30
Orals only	25	29	21	37	38	114
IUDs only	20	23	17	10	8	6
Traditional methods only	20	27	27	21	24	18
Traditional methods, plus abortion	5	8	6	6	7	4

National Trends in the Health Impact of Abortion

Jean Pakter, M.D., M.P.H.

We know that what occurs in New York City can frequently be interpreted as representative of what is occurring nationally because of the size and diversity of the city's population. I shall attempt to review what impact the liberalization of the abortion law in New York City has had on births, infant mortality, and pregnancy related deaths.

More than five years have elapsed since abortion became legal in New York. We really had no idea how many terminations of pregnancy would be requested. Guesses ran from 20,000 abortions up to 200,000 for the first year. The latter figure was closer to the fact. In the first year following legalization of abortion in July 1970 in New York City, over two-thirds of the abortions performed in New York City were for nonresidents coming from all over the country, as well as from Canada, South America and abroad (Table 1). Since that time, the situation has changed significantly, particu-

TABLE 1

NUMBER OF LEGAL ABORTIONS PERFORMED IN NEW YORK CITY,
JULY 1970 - JUNE 30, 1975 BY RESIDENCY STATUS

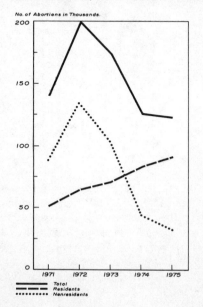

No. of Abortions in Thousands.

Total
Residents
Nonresidents

69

larly since the Supreme Court's decision in January 1973. After that, the proportion of residents and nonresidents receiving abortions in New York City was reversed. At present, about 30 percent of abortions performed are for nonresidents and about 70 percent for residents of New York City. The total number of abortions has decreased from a high of 206,673 in 1971, to 106,317 in 1975. The drop in number is due primarily to the decline in the number of nonresident abortions. As a matter of fact, the number of abortions performed on residents has continued to rise from 1971 to 1974, although the rate of increase is leveling off. The number of resident abortions went from 67,032 in 1971 to 85,898 in 1974 and actually fell slightly in 1975. In the first year, less than one percent were repeaters. Repeat abortions were by definition limited to those performed after July 1, 1970, the time of legalization. In 1972, 13.6 percent of the total number of abortions performed were for women having second or more abortions, increasing in 1973 to 17.8 percent (Table 2). By 1974, the proportion of repeaters was 21.5 percent. However, when the number of repeaters is related to the total number of women who have had a first abortion since July 1970, the rate is 6.6 percent, which represents only a slight increase over previous years. This does not mean that we are complacent about the repeaters. We would like to see the need for repeat abortion minimized as much as possible.

TABLE 2

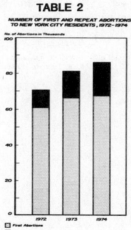

NUMBER OF FIRST AND REPEAT ABORTIONS
TO NEW YORK CITY RESIDENTS, 1972-1974

The question of the impact of abortions on birth rates is frequently asked. Other factors can affect birth rates besides abortions. As a matter of fact, the proportion of the total population in the childbearing age group may have an effect on the birth rate. If the proportion of the population is high for the aged and low for the childbearing age group, this would create a lower birth rate. Therefore, in analyzing our data, we prefer to view them in terms of age-specific birth rates to get a realistic picture of fertility patterns.

In 1964, the birth rate in New York City was 21.2, and in succeeding years it stayed at that level. It was only after 1965 and the advent of contraception on a wide scale that we began to see a decline. In 1968 the birth rate was 18 per 1,000 women aged 15-44. The childbearing population increased in the decade from 1960 to 1970, as did the ethnic group populations (Black and Puerto Rican) with higher fertility rates. It had been predicted by demographers that an unprecedented rise in births would occur in the late '60s and early '70s. As one can see from our data, this did not occur (Table 3). Instead, from 1970 on, we have witnessed a progressive decline in the birth rate. It dropped to 13.8 per 1,000 in 1975, almost breaking the record except for 1936 when it was 13.6. This was the period of the Great Depression.

TABLE 3

NUMBER OF LIVE BIRTHS IN NEW YORK CITY
1945 – 1975

The fertility rates, which are the sums of age-specific birth rates, were tabulated for a succession of years and categorized by ethnic groupings (Table 4). From 1960 to 1974, a progressive decline occurred in the fertility rates for each of the ethnic groups. For the whites, the rate declined from 90.8 per 1,000 in 1969 to 68.9 per 1,000 in 1974. This was the lowest of the three groups. For the nonwhites, the rate declined from 120.5 per 1,000 to 80.6 per 1,000. The fertility rate for the nonwhites is still higher than that of any other groups. The rate for Puerto Rican and other Hispanic groups dropped from 149.4 per 1,000 to 69.3 per 1,000 in 1974. Fertility rates for those aged 15 through 19 show a similar range in fertility by

71

TABLE 4

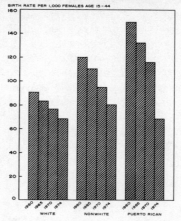

TOTAL FERTILITY RATES BY ETHNIC GROUP
NEW YORK CITY, 1960, 1965, 1970, 1974

ethnic groups, with the white having the lowest fertility rate, the nonwhite highest, and the Puerto Rican rate in between (Table 5). In successive years, the rates declined for the nonwhite and Puerto Rican teenagers but appear to be increasing for the teenage whites from 1960 to 1970. It was only after 1970 that their fertility declined slightly. However, the fertility rate is still the lowest for the white and highest for the nonwhite with the Puerto

TABLE 5

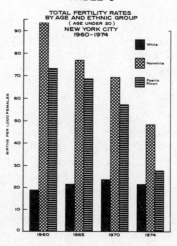

TOTAL FERTILITY RATES
BY AGE AND ETHNIC GROUP
(AGE UNDER 20)
NEW YORK CITY
1960-1974

Rican group second. In comparing the decline in fertility rates, it would appear that family planning services had a much more significant impact on fertility rates for those over 20 than for the young teenagers of 15-17 years (Table 6). After legalized abortions became available, possibly accompanied by better access to family planning services for young teenagers, a distinct drop in their fertility was noted. The older teenage group of 18-19 years are more like the 20-year-olds in terms of their fertility patterns. Although their decline in fertility became evident before 1970, it was not as striking as it was for women in their later twenties (Table 7).

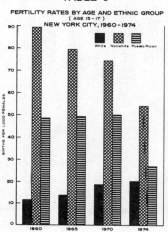

TABLE 6

FERTILITY RATES BY AGE AND ETHNIC GROUP
(AGE 15 - 17)
NEW YORK CITY, 1960 - 1974

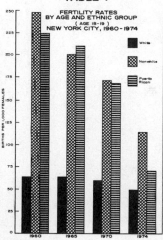

TABLE 7

FERTILITY RATES
BY AGE AND ETHNIC GROUP
(AGE 18 - 19)
NEW YORK CITY, 1960 - 1974

When abortions among residents are combined with live births, one can calculate a so-called "conception rate" (Table 8). The indications are that from 1971 on, this combined rate has stayed at about the same level.

TABLE 8
CONCEPTION RATES
LIVE BIRTHS AND ABORTIONS
PER 1,000 FEMALES
NEW YORK CITY, 1971-1974

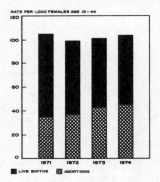

Starting with an infant mortality rate of 26.8 per 1,000 live births in 1964, there was evidence of a decline occurring in the middle '60s followed by a more striking drop (Table 9). By 1975, it was down to 19.6 per 1,000 live births. The ability women now have to plan their pregnancies and have wanted babies has undoubtedly contributed to the decline in infant mortality. The decrease in births to women of high parity and older age groups has also played a role.

TABLE 9

INFANT MORTALITY RATES IN NEW YORK CITY
1945-1975

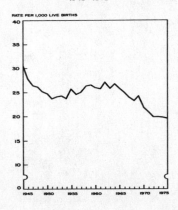

74

One of the most striking consequences of the liberalization of abortion was the elimination of deaths due to illegal abortion, a continued decline in the number of deaths associated with childbirth, and a reduction in deaths following legalized abortion (Table 10). In the last two years, we have not had a single death from illegal abortion, nor have we had a death associated with a termination of pregnancy in the first 12 weeks. In 1975, however, we had three deaths associated with saline terminations. The risks incurred with termination of pregnancy after the first trimester are 10 to 20 times greater than for the early ones.

In 1975, there were 23 deaths in the City of New York associated with childbirth and three with abortion. This is in marked contrast to previous years when deaths due to abortions constituted the leading single cause for pregnancy-related mortality. The mortality rate in 1975 of 2.4 per 10,000 live births was a record low.

As further evidence of the favorable impact of legal abortions, admissions to municipal hospitals for incomplete and septic abortions have declined dramatically. Just the other day, a director of a large municipal hospital told me that a patient had been admitted to the hospital with a diagnosis of "septic abortion." He called his whole resident staff together to see this case since it was a rare event! Ten or fifteen years ago such cases kept the hospital staff very busy. The number of incomplete and septic abortions dropped from a total of 6,524 municipal hospital admissions in 1969 to 3,253 in 1973 and to 2,800 in 1975.

TABLE 10

**PREGNANCY ASSOCIATED DEATHS
TOTAL AND DUE TO ABORTIONS
NEW YORK CITY, 1960-1975**

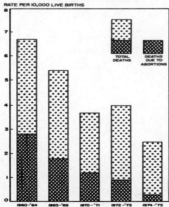

In summary, with the advent of legal abortion, we have witnessed a decline in births, particularly among those of high parity and older age groups, a substantial decline in infant mortality, and a decline in the number of deaths associated with pregnancy.

In the past, deaths following abortions constituted the single leading cause of puerperal deaths, but the picture has changed. Since 1973, there has not been a single death as a result of an illegal abortion. A record low has been established in New York City for infant and maternal mortality.

Surveillance of Abortion Mortality in the United States

Willard Cates, M.D., M.P.H.
David A. Grimes, M.D.
Jack C. Smith, M.S.

Introduction

Induced abortion is among the most commonly performed operations in the United States.[1] Moreover, we probably know more about the epidemiology of abortion than about the epidemiology of any other surgical procedure performed in this country. We have quantified who gets abortions, where they get them, by what method, at what stage of pregnancy, what complications ensue, and finally, who dies as a result of the procedure. We hope that much of the methodology developed for studying abortion can also be applied to studying other surgical procedures. In this way, we can maximize the impact of epidemiology on the quality of medical care in this country.

This report describes the role of the Center for Disease Control (CDC) in documenting abortion-related mortality in the United States. I will first discuss the longitudinal trends in abortion deaths; second, I will discuss the techniques of abortion mortality surveillance used by CDC; and last, I will quantify the risks of mortality a woman faces when she undergoes legal induced abortion.

Longitudinal Trends

Abortion accounted for approximately one of every five maternal deaths in the United States from 1940 to 1974.[2] During these years, the abortion mortality ratio (abortion deaths per one million live births) passed through four main phases (Table 1): 1) between 1940 and 1950 the ratio declined steadily at a mean annual rate of 18 percent; 2) between 1951 and 1965 the rate of decline slowed considerable to a mean annual rate of only 1.7 percent; 3) between 1966 and 1970 the ratio declined at a mean annual rate of 11 percent; and 4) between 1970 and 1974 the rate of decline accelerated to a mean of 30 percent per year. Compared with maternal mortality from other causes, abortion mortality declined faster up to 1950, slower from 1950 through 1965, and faster again after 1965, with the greatest acceleration occurring after 1970.

From 1940 to 1950 the use of antibiotics in maternity hospitals and improvements in obstetrical practice acted simultaneously to decrease

TABLE 1

MATERNAL MORTALITY RATIOS (EXCLUDING ABORTION DEATHS)
AND ABORTION MORTALITY RATIOS , UNITED STATES, 1940-1974

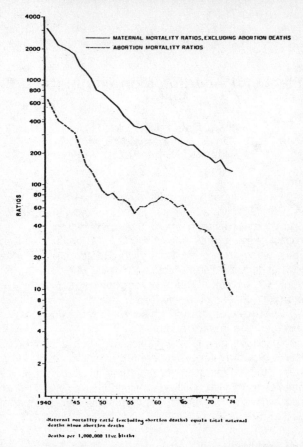

Maternal mortality ratio (excluding abortion deaths) equals total maternal
deaths minus abortion deaths

Deaths per 1,000,000 live births

both abortion mortality and maternal mortality from other causes.[3] Over the next 15 years, however, the leveling off of the rate of decline in abortion mortality may have been related to an increase in the number of illegal abortions. After 1965 the resumption of decline in abortion mortality was probably due to several factors, the most important of which was probably the increased use of contraception and the legalization of abortion.[4]

Techniques of Abortion Mortality Surveillance

Because of the absence of clinical data, vital statistics are of limited use in defining risk factors associated with abortion. In 1972, the CDC began its epidemiologic surveillance of abortion-related mortality. Our aim was to gain more timely and comprehensive information about deaths due to all types of abortion, in order to identify factors to prevent future abortion mortality.

A variety of sources provide the CDC with reports of abortion-related deaths (Table 2). State and local health departments perform continuing reviews of their vital statistics files and prepare regular reports for the CDC on abortion-related deaths. Then, every February we send letters to each central health agency to confirm the number of deaths they have reported to us.

TABLE 2

SURVEILLANCE OF ABORTION-RELATED MORTALITY

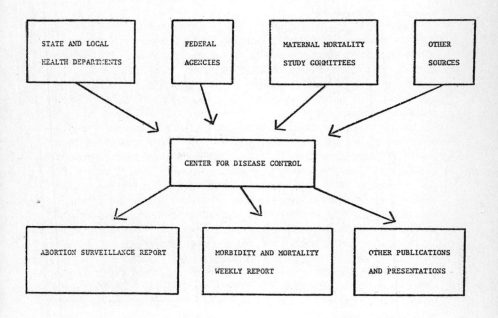

Other federal agencies cooperate in the CDC's surveillance effort. The Food and Drug Administration uncovered three deaths due to spontaneous abortion associated with IUDs during its investigation of IUD morbidity and mortality. The National Center for Health Statistics provides lists of all deaths categorized by the International Classification of Disease code numbers 640-645 (abortion). We compare these lists with reports of deaths already on file and investigate cases of which we were not aware.

The CDC has recently established liaison with maternal mortality study committees in a number of states to determine their methods of reviewing deaths and also to alert them to our interest in receiving information about abortion-related deaths. Finally, we receive individual case reports from private groups (including both pro- and anti-abortion factions) who are aware of our abortion mortality surveillance system and want to ensure that our records are complete.

Once we have been notified of a death, we try to verify that it was actually abortion-related. We call the attending physician, request reports from the coroner, retrieve the hospital case records, and review the clinical details to determine if abortion was in the chain of events leading to death. To date, about one of every six reported deaths associated with an abortion was not caused by the abortion. The primary pathophysiologic event, such as meningitis, usually caused both the abortion and the death.

The Family Planning Evaluation Division staff review data on all deaths after we receive the reports. Our criteria for classifying the abortions as either induced or spontaneous and, if induced, as legal or illegal, have been outlined in a previous CDC publication.[5]

The preventability of these abortion-related deaths is judged by "ideal" standards. This concept involved five assumptions. First, the patient possessed the knowledge and judgment necessary to make an early decision in case of unwanted pregnancy. Second, the community in which the patient lived had family planning and abortion facilities within one hour's travel time. Third, the attending health professionals possessed all the knowledge available on factors involved in the death. Fourth, by experience, all personnel had reached a level of technical ability sufficient to provide abortion services and manage any complications secondary to the procedure. Fifth, the professionals had available all facilities in a well-organized and properly equipped hospital.

This academic approach allows more specific analysis of each case in order to 1) identify areas for continued patient health education, 2) document regions with inadequate family planning/abortion facilities, 3) stimulate instructional aspects of patient management, 4) improve the quality of abortion services, and 5) eventually help reduce the death rate from abortion.

Mortality Risks From Legal Abortion

Forty-eight women died from spontaneous and induced abortion in 1974, compared with 56 in 1973 and 88 in 1972 (Table 3, bottom panel). This decline in the total number of abortion-related deaths has been primarily due to the decreasing number of deaths following illegally induced abortion, from 39 in 1972 to 19 in 1973 to five in 1974 (Table 3, second panel). In contrast, the annual number of deaths due to legal induced abortion remained relatively stable, with 24 in 1974, 26 in 1973, and 24 in 1972 (Table 3, top panel).

TABLE 3

ABORTION-RELATED DEATHS BY CATEGORY AND MONTH, UNITED STATES, JANUARY 1972 - DECEMBER 1974

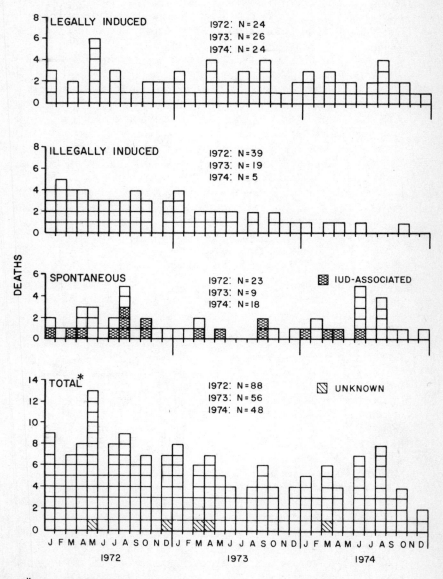

*INCLUDES UNKNOWN

In 1974, a total of 763,476 legal abortions were reported to the CDC. With this figure as the denominator, the death-to-case rate is 3.8 per 100,000 procedures. This is similar to earlier findings reported from New York City, New York State, and California, areas that had previously liberalized their abortion laws.[6, 7, 8] The slight decline in the death-to-case rate to 3.1 in 1974 may reflect the increasing experience with abortion procedures as abortion services became redistributed throughout the United States following the Supreme Court decisions in 1973.

In 1973 The Alan Guttmacher Institute (AGI) reported over 742,000 legal abortions. In 1974 the figure was nearly 900,000 procedures.[9] If these AGI figures are used as denominators, the death-to-case ratios become 3.5 per 100,000 procedures in 1973 and 2.7 in 1974. Thus, the CDC rates of 4.2 and 3.1 per 100,000 procedures probably represent maximum estimates of the death-to-case ratio for legal abortions during those years. In terms of risk of death, legal abortion is a safer surgical procedure than tonsillectomy and appendectomy, which have death-to-case ratios of five and 352 per 100,000 procedures, respectively.[10]

Length of gestation is the most important patient variable associated with mortality from legal induced abortion (Table 4). The risk of death increases directly with length of pregnancy. This finding is consistent with findings from the Joint Program for the Study of Abortion (JPSA) and JPSA/CDC.[11] It underscores the need to educate and counsel women who are pregnant and want to have an abortion not to delay.

Table 4

Death-to-Case Rate for Legal Abortions by Weeks of Gestation
United States, 1972–1974

Gestational* Age	Deaths	Cases**	Rate+	Relative++ Risk
– 8	3	747,550	0.5	1.0
9–10	13	581,002	2.2	5.5
11–12	12	330,537	3.6	9.0
13–15	12	129,536	9.3	23.2
16–20	28	147,160	19.0	47.5
–21	6	30,282	19.8	49.5
TOTAL	74	1,966,067	3.8	—

*Weeks from last menstrual period
**Based on distribution of 1,459,495 abortions (74.2% of total) in which number of weeks of gestation was known
+Deaths per 100,000 abortions
++Relative risk based on index rate for – 8 menstrual weeks' gestation of 0.4 per 100,000 abortions.
Source: Center for Disease Control, Atlanta.

Because abortion is an elective procedure, a woman with an unwanted pregnancy may want to be able to compare the risk of death from abortion with the risk of death associated with continuing the pregnancy to term. From 1972 through 1974, the death-to-case rate of pregnancy and childbirth (exclusive of abortion) was 14.8 deaths per 100,000 live births.[12] The death-to-case rate for abortions induced in the first trimester was 1.7 deaths per 100,000 legal abortions during this same period. Therefore, when compared with fullterm pregnancy, legal abortion in the first trimester is approximately nine times safer.

In summary, abortion mortality has declined faster than maternal mortality since 1965, presumably as a result of increased use of contraception and greater availability of legal abortion. Since 1972, the CDC has been conducting epidemiologic surveillance of abortion-related deaths. The data show that legal induced abortion in the United States is a safe surgical procedure and is, in fact, safer than most other relatively common operations. Our surveillance has determined that *any* delay in seeking abortion is associated with increased risk of death. Therefore, women who are faced with unwanted pregnancy and who want to have an abortion should be urged not to delay the procedure.

REFERENCES

1. E. Weinstock, C. Tietze, F.S. Jaffe and J.G. Dryfoos. "Abortion Need and Services in the United States, 1974-1975," *Family Planning Perspectives* 8: 58, 1976.
2. W. Cates, Jr., R.W. Rochat, J.C. Smith and C.W. Tyler, Jr. "Trends in National Abortion Mortality, United States: 1940-1974. Implications for Prevention of Future Abortion Deaths," *Advances in Planned Parenthood* 11: 106, 1976.
3. L.M. Hellman and J.A. Pritchard. *Williams' Obstetrics,* New York: Appleton-Century Crofts, Inc., 1970, p. 8-10.
4. Cates, et al.
5. U.S. Department of Health, Education and Welfare, Public Health Service, Center for Disease Control. *Abortion Surveillance: 1974,* Atlanta: 1976.
6. C. Tietze, JM Pakter and G.S. Berger. "Mortality with Legal Abortion in New York City, 1970-1972," *Journal of the American Medical Association* 225: 507, 1973.
7. G.S. Berger, C. Tietze, J. Pakter and S. Katz. "Maternal Mortality Associated with Legal Abortion in New York State: July 1, 1970–June 30, 1972," *Obstetrics and Gynecology* 43: 315, 1974.
8. G.K. Stewart, and E.F. Hance. "Legal Abortion: Influence upon Mortality, Morbidity and Population," *Advances in Planned Parenthood* 9: 1, 1974.
9. Weinstock, et al.
10. C.G. Child. "Surgical Intervention," *Scientific American* 229: 90, 1973.
11. Cates, et al.
12. U.S. Department of Health, Education and Welfare, Public Health Service, National Center for Health Statistics. "Summary Report, Final Mortality Statistics," 1972, 1973, 1974, *Monthly Vital Statistics Report* 23 (8): No. 11 (Supplement 2) 1974; 23 (11): No. 18 (Supplement 2) 1975; and 24 (11): No. 20 (Supplement 2) 1976.

Discussion of Public Health Aspects of Abortion in Colorado

Warren M. Hern: Colorado's birth rate has remained relatively stable over the last 15 years, but there has been a steady decline in the infant mortality rate, the maternal mortality rate, and the percentage of low birth weight infants. While it is difficult to point to a causal association, the most dramatic decline in these parameters began in about 1967 when Colorado's reform abortion law was passed.

There were no abortions being reported in Colorado in 1966 and only 140 in 1967. The abortion rate, which is the number of abortions per thousand women of childbearing age, has gone up from 0.2 in 1967 to 14.6 in 1974, an increase of almost 4,000 percent (Table 1). The abortion ratio, which is the number of abortions per 1,000 live births, has gone up about 3,000 percent since then to 231.3 in 1974.

The percentage of low birth weight infants is a very significant indicator of perinatal health and, to some extent, of maternal health. Women with high risk pregnancies generally have a higher percentage of infants born with low birth weight. The percentage of low birth weight infants decreased about 12 percent from the 1963-65 interval (10.5 percent) to the 1972-74 interval (9.2 percent), but almost all the decline has occurred since 1967 (Table 2).

The infant mortality rate in Colorado declined from 22.9 per 1,000 live births in 1967 to 15.7 in 1974, which is a drop of approximately 26 percent. However, two-thirds of the 34 percent decline in the infant mortality rate since the 1963-65 interval has been from the 1966-68 interval to the 1972-74 interval. Maternal mortality rate has declined 20 percent from the 1966-69 interval rate of 17 per 100,000 to the 1972-74 interval average of 13.6 per 100,000 live births.

The numbers are small in Colorado and there are many factors at work, such as improved family planning services. We cannot say that all these rates have declined because abortion was made legal. However, it is a powerful coincidence since, as mentioned by Drs. Tietze, Pakter, and Grimes, women who are at high risk of having problems, such as teenagers, tend to seek abortions for their own reasons. As they remove themselves from the population at risk of problems associated with term pregnancy, they have a proportionately greater impact on the improvement of statistics which reflect these problems.

TABLE 1

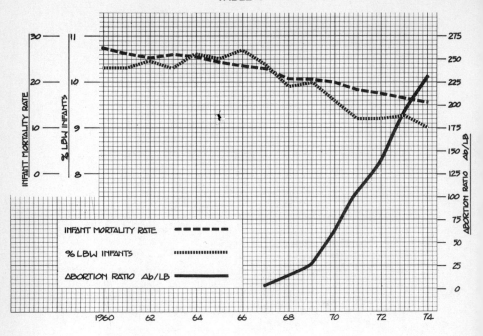

TABLE 2

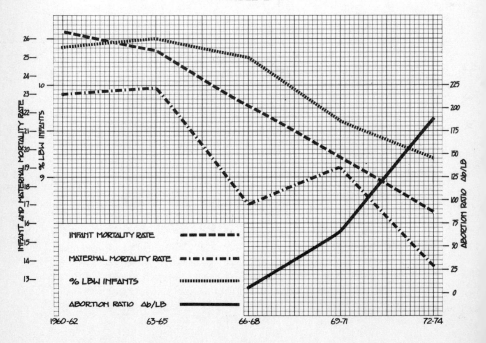

86

Evaluation of Abortion Services

Approaches to Evaluation of Abortion Services

Irvin Cushner, M.D., M.P.H.

I can think of five reasons why programs are evaluated. An abortion program may be evaluated prior to approval for licensure or certification. It might be evaluated prior to referral. This is a worthwhile reason for evaluation if you believe, as I do, that we should not refer until we know that the place to which we are referring is doing good work. A program might have to be evaluated prior to funding and the evaluation could determine whether or not it gets money. The program evaluation may be part of a regular cycle of program surveillance. Finally, there might be a program evaluation in response to some adverse events that become public knowledge.

I would like to address myself to four things: The planning of an evaluation; the setting of objectives for an evaluation and the rank ordering of priorities; how to actually carry it out; and how to arrive at a decision.

Let us talk first about how one plans an evaluation. There are some questions that immediately come to mind. Who is going to do it? By what means? Upon what standards? Standards based on what, where and when? What methods will be used to carry the evaluation out? What will the decision-making process be? In my view, the evaluation team should include a mixture of providers, recipients or their advocates, nonclinical administrators, and when available, professionally trained program evaluators. All of the people involved should have the following characteristics: They must be knowledgeable about abortion, they must be objective, and they should not be related to the program or to the decision-making process. It is my preference that evaluation be entirely external.

What standards would be the basis for the evaluation? At a conference like this, it is easy to lose sight of the fact that in the United States, the entire experience with readily available abortion is less than ten years old. Somebody from another planet could sit in this audience today and think that abortions had been going on for years. Abortion is being evaluated much more intensively than any other medical activity I know, but the whole subject of evaluating health care programs is new. There are some standards for abortion programs that are a matter of public record. Some of us in this room who are somewhat biased are drawn to the "Program Guide for Abortion Services" published by the American Public Health

Association.[1] Our bias is based on the fact that we wrote it. We like it. The National Medical Committee of Planned Parenthood has a set of guidelines which it has recently revised and which Dr. Tyrer is going to discuss with us.[2] The American College of Obstetricians and Gynecologists has a set of guidelines and standards.[3] Perhaps there are others of which I am not aware. An evaluation team might use any one of these, or they might take the best of all and decide on their own standards. Within that framework I would like to leave the subject of published standards and talk about what would be my criteria for the approval of a service program.

I would be willing to vote for approval of an abortion service program if the services provided are safe, if they are readily available and acceptable, if they are humanely delivered; if all three of those characteristics can be documented, based on contemporary findings; and if they are responsive to the local community which that program serves. A standard for Los Angeles may not be appropriate as a standard for New England. Safety comes from people, their clinical skills and the ability of the facility to respond to trouble. Availability and accessibility involves cost and hours, and it comes from policy made by people. Humanism comes from the internal attitudes, values, and beliefs of the people providing the services and the people making the policy. All of this sounds very generic, but this is exactly what a program evaluation is looking for.

Is this service safe? Is it readily available and accessible? Is it delivered in an appropriate way and can this program document that for us? Is that documentation based on yesterday and not five years ago? Is it responsive to this community?

The next thing in planning an evaluation would be how it is going to be done. At the risk of being overly simple, I would say there are two phases to a program evaluation. One is the collection of information and the other is analysis. The information that needs to be collected would come from program information regarding policies and practices that are provided to the team by the facility. The second part of information collecting would be direct observation by the evaluation team of the program, its personnel, and its facilities. When the information is in, the evaluation team would then be responsible for analyzing the clinical program, the program administration and its policies, and patient satisfaction.

When that information has been collected and analyzed, the last step in planning the evaluation would be to consider how the decision-making process is to take place. The first thing you have to do is to define the decision-making group. Who will be able to come to a conclusion and decide whether the program and its evaluation is acceptable? In my view, the most important consideration is that the decision-making group have maximum objectivity. The evaluation team should report to the decision-making group but have no vote. If that is not feasible, the evaluation agency or the persons requesting the evaluation should be in the majority of the decision-making group and not the evaluation team. The team does the work. It does not make decisions. Decisions should be based upon what the evaluation and decision-making group knows about the need for services and the feasibility of producing change in the facility when that is needed to achieve priorities and to meet needs.

How about the evaluation itself? To make you aware of it, I refer you to a document which is not yet published. The document has been put together by Johan Eliot, Mary Beth Moore and Harriette Barber from the University of Michigan School of Public Health.[4] It consists of two checklists. One is a checklist that the facility fills out prior to the arrival of the evaluation team. The second is a checklist the evaluation team fills out when it actually visits the abortion facility. These two documents are the most complete lists of everything that anybody would want to know about an abortion program in order to decide whether it cuts the mustard. It is a beautifully done piece of work.

In the checklist which the facility fills out in advance, the following areas are covered: policy and administration, patient care, emergency care, laboratory and test facilities, counseling, medical records, and the environment. The environment includes public health requirements concerning health care facilities as well as some humanistic dimensions of the environment. The checklist by the evaluation team considers those same areas plus one area that is called general impression. The evaluation team describes what they perceive about the staff and how the staff relates to the woman requesting the abortion. Finally, there is the decision-making process. The evaluation agency should have a committee that is going to make this decision. This committee should be knowledgeable about the reason for the evaluation in the first place. It should review the report of the evaluation team, should be knowledgeable about the needs of the population served, and to what degree that need has been met.

If I were a member of an evaluation committee, I would only be willing to approve an abortion program if the following were revealed in this evaluation. First, there would have to be adequate followup data indicating an acceptable mortality and morbidity experience. If it did not have that, I am not sure I would be willing to go any further. Second, I would want to see documented evidence of appropriate patient management prior to the procedure. That would include an adequate medical history, social history, sexual history; a contraceptive, gynecologic and obstetrical history; a complete physical and pelvic exam; and appropriate routine and indicated laboratory tests. There should be evidence of adequate information and disclosure regarding the techniques, the anticipated experience, the advantages and the risks associated with abortion procedures. There should be an evaluation of the patient's family planning needs including information, services, and supplies. There should be counseling available if requested or indicated. There should be the ability to refer if requested or indicated.

Some of the things that I am including are more easily documented scientifically than others. I am aware that there are different schools of

91

thought about the need for routine counseling. I do not think I would find an abortion program acceptable which did not have counseling and referral services available when they are either requested or seem to be indicated. I am not persuaded that every woman who requests an abortion needs to be counseled; neither am I persuaded that no woman requesting an abortion needs counseling. I think a program needs to document the fact that appropriate procedures are being performed based on the standard community practice. In the community in which I currently work, that program would have to document that its policy and practice limits suction D and C to less than 13 weeks from LMP. I know this is at some variance with some data that have been presented at this conference, but for the moment I am still wed to the notion that suction D and C is appropriate only before the 13th week from LMP. Amnioinfusion, in my view, is the appropriate procedure from the 16th week on. For the gray area between the 13th and the 16th week, there is accumulating data that there may be a role for suction D and C. Perhaps even suction D and C might be more appropriate than amnioinfusion by saline. In my view, that is not yet as well documented as the older standards are. In my own practice and in any program evaluation that I shall participate in, I am going to move slowly before suction D and C becomes the procedure of choice between the 13th and 16th weeks.

In my view, the program policy should restrict abdominal procedures to those in which there is indication for it. The question of combining abortion with voluntary sterilization by intra-abdominal procedure is one which is still controversial. The original Joint Program for the Study of Abortion (JPSA) material indicated that any concomitant sterilization procedure except laparoscopy was associated with a higher morbidity.[5] Voluntary sterilization by hysterectomy is an extremely controversial subject in the family planning and women's health field right now. I am not sure that anybody should be ready to make a policy decision about that yet.

I would require that the facility be adequate for patient emergencies, which would include the technical details of dealing with an acute emergency in the facility as well as documentation of access to hospital services when they are required. I would want to see a contractual affiliation in writing as well as some evidence of the emergency transport system.

An adequate followup service is crucial to any program. I would be looking for evidence that family planning services are provided in a fashion that maximizes protection in the first cycle following the abortion. Ovulation can occur as early as two to three weeks following an early abortion, and any delay in implementing family planning services runs the risk of an early repeat of unwanted pregnancy. I would look for post-procedure history and examination. My bias is for a two-week interval and a post-procedural counseling session if requested or indicated. I would be looking for evidence that services are available at reasonable cost including payment plans and an attempt to recover third party funds. I would look for evidence that the facility is open during hours that are appropriate for patients, appropriate for staff, and appropriate for responding to emergencies. Having a clinic open at three in the morning without enough staff around to take care of a ruptured uterus does not make much sense. I would be looking for minimum waiting time from the first request for the abortion. That is an area in which availability and accessibility touches on safety. An abortion program whose policy does not encourage maximum utilization of first trimester abortion and whose policy engenders delay is, in effect, causing second trimester abortion with its higher risks.

Finally, I would be looking for documented evidence of patient satisfaction by interview or questionnaire. I would want to know that the patients do not perceive the staff as exhibiting negative or indifferent attitudes and behavior. I would be looking for evidence that the program does not manifest indifference toward its patients.

That is the kind of program I would vote for. I am not even sure that my program would meet these criteria right now, but that is the ideal.

What should one do if the program does not meet this ideal? If the program evaluation indicates that the program cannot be scored at the highest level on every single issue, there is some balancing that has to be done. If the abortion needs in that community would be seriously unmet if the clinic closed, one function of an evaluation team and evaluation agency would be to try to induce the changes in the facility that would bring it up to an acceptable level. That is probably one of the most important community services that a program evaluator can do.

References

1. American Public Health Association. "Recommended Program Guide for Abortion Services," "*American Journal of Public Health* 62:1669, 1972."
2. National Medical Committee, Planned Parenthood Federation of America. "Recommended Standards for Evaluation of Abortion Facilities and Procedures for Making Abortion Referrals," memo dated October 15, 1976.
3. American College of Obstetricians and Gynecologists. *Standards for Obstetric-Gynecologic Services,* Chicago, 1974, p. 64–65.
4. J. Eliot, M. B. Moore and H. Barber. *Checklists I and II for the Evaluation of Quality Care in a Freestanding Abortion Clinic,* (mimeographed) Department of Population Planning, School of Public Health, University of Michigan, June 1975.
5. C. Tietze and S. Lewit. "Joint Program for the Study of Abortion (JPSA): Early Medical Complications of Legal Abortion," *Studies in Family Planning* 3:97-122, 1972

National Overview of Quality of Abortion Services

Louise Tyrer, M.D.

The national medical department of Planned Parenthood is in a position to assist the evaluation process to which Dr. Cushner referred. We in the National Medical Committee have been working for some time finalizing recommended standards for evaluation of first trimester abortion facilities, in addition to a recommended format for making abortion referrals. Some of the family planning clinics throughout the country offer abortion services. Those that do not offer the services themselves are a source of counseling for problem pregnancies and referrals. Abortion clinics throughout the country feel that Planned Parenthood has a large patient population to be served with abortion services. We receive calls daily asking for referrals. Planned Parenthood has to make certain that the facilities to which they are referring do meet certain standards and guidelines for the protection of their patients. The same thing is happening to other types of family planning clinics. They are being approached by providers of abortion services and asked for referrals. It is important for them to know how to proceed. We decided that standards for our services would be the type of standards that should be applicable for all services seeking referrals.

Since Planned Parenthood affiliates act as patient advocates when they refer women to another facility for an abortion, their affiliates must be knowledgeable about the total environment and practices of the facility which provides the service to the patient. Furthermore, the referring affiliate has a responsibility for each woman who acts upon its advice. This can aso be a legal responsibility. In some states, the affiliates bear a legal burden if the patient has grounds for redress. These standards will be available to anyone who wishes to write to the national medical department of Planned Parenthood in New York City. They cover standards for endometrial aspiration service, for first trimester abortion service, for making referrals, and for abortion counseling.

We recommend that the review team consist of a trained physician who is knowledgeable in providing abortion services, an administrator, a nurse knowledgeable about abortion procedures, a counselor, a social worker and an experienced volunteer or patient advocate. The evaluation should only be carried out on those facilities that request review voluntarily. Planned Parenthood affiliates should review independent abortion facilities within a reasonable distance. At the present time we do not feel it is necessary to review accredited hospitals.

Before making a visit to a facility requesting review, the facility is supplied with the recommended standards for abortion services. They will have these documents in hand and can bring their facility into conformance prior to the review process. These standards are the criteria used in the review. In addition, the review team looks critically at the written medical guidelines of the independent facility, the performance capability of the physician operators, the liability insurance held by the provider, standing orders for nurses or nurse practitioners, and percentage of contraceptive acceptance by patients. In addition to conformity with the recommended standards, we require proof of current, unencumbered licensure, conformity with the regulations of local health authorities, and adequate liability coverage. We review the personnel, the physical plant, the intake procedures, preoperative management and procedures, operative recovery and discharge procedures, followup, emergency procedures, records, communication with referring agencies and financial practices. Subsequent reviews should be carried out at least every two years or more frequently if there is a change in the medical directorship, substantial change in the administrative practices of the facility, or unduly high complication rates.

The written reports of each visit to a facility are prepared in a form useful both to the referring staff and the provider agency. The reports cover medical practice, and compliance with current recommended standards for pregnancy related services developed by the Planned Parenthood National Medical Committee. These reports serve as the framework of the evaluation.

All facilities used for Planned Parenthood referrals must be willing to report routinely to the reviewing affiliate about the number of abortions performed each month; the number of patients who require hospitalization as an immediate or delayed result of abortion for such reasons as hemorrhage, infection, uterine perforation or ectopic pregnancy; the number of failed abortions and incomplete abortions requiring repeat procedures; any change in the status of licensure or accreditation; any adverse reports from any government or officially certified body; any complaints of malpractice actions, together with copies of the complaints; the legal status of any action; relevant medical records; and any change in the medical directorship.

Each affiliate should prepare an update every six months of a list of approved abortion facilities evaluated for Planned Parenthood referral. The list should be made available to anyone who requests it, and it should be forwarded routinely to the regional and national offices of the organization. The referral list should contain the name, address and telephone number of each approved facility or individual provider within the area served by the affiliate. The list should indicate for each facility the length of gestation accepted, the type of procedure used, and the total cost to the patient. In case of doubt, the propriety of any disclosure of a physician's fee schedule should be checked with local counsel or the staff of the state or local medical society. The list is given to the patient. It includes a disclaimer indicating that Planned Parenthood cannot assume responsibility for this service since there could be a change from the time that program was reviewed until the patient arrived there for the service. It is advisable to obtain prior written approval from the respective providers for the content and circulation of the referral list. It is suggested that the list of approved facilities be drawn up alphabetically within the following categories: For first trimester abortions: (1) clinics, (2) hospitals, (3) private physicians who provide the service in their office, and (4) physicians who provide abortions in the hospital. For second trimester abortions: (1) hospitals where service is available, and (2) private physicians who perform in-hospital procedures. At the present time we do not recommend that second trimester procedures be performed outside of hospitals. Unless it is lengthy the total list should be made available to all patients seeking referrals. In the case of telephone referrals, the affiliate may use a rotating referral system. The rotation system must be documented in the affiliate's records, and whenever possible, each patient should receive the names of a minimum of three providers appropriate to her needs. The reason for this system was complaints from some providers of abortion services that Planned Parenthood was discriminating in providing referral names. We have therefore developed this system for reviewing and evaluating all providers. If they meet the criteria and the standards, they are placed on the referral list so that referrals are made in a fashion that avoids discrimination.

The standards hold that the patient should make her own appointment with the abortion facility. This includes placement of the telephone call. The abortion facility, rather than the affiliate making the referral, should determine the financial status of the patient. Any Planned Parenthood affiliate fee for pregnancy testing, diagnosis or counseling should be billed directly by the affiliate and collected directly from the patient rather than from the provider. No fee shall be charged for telephone information only. No fee should be charged for providing referral information or the referral lists, but the patient may be charged for counseling. No payment of any kind will be accepted from an independent provider. This is to avoid the appearance of a fee-splitting arrangement. In some government contracts, however, the affiliate may bill the government funding agency on behalf of the patient and reimburse the abortion provider. This is required in some states by Title XX Social Services legislation. In each case the patient's right to confidentiality should be observed and her written permission obtained. No Planned Parenthood affiliate may contract formally or informally for abortion referral or provision of abortion services with an independent facility without prior approval from the national office. If any kind of joint venture is contemplated with an independent abortion provider, adequate medical and legal protection must be arranged for the affiliate with approval of the national office. This was included because there were some very unusual contractual arrangements that had developed between abortion providers and the referring agencies.

If a Planned Parenthood affiliate wishes to start an abortion service, it receives copies of the standards and guidelines. It must develop the program according to the standards which I just outlined for you. We have found that it is important to carefully evaluate the performance capabilities of the physicians providing the service. They should have received special training in termination techniques and their technique should be observed to determine that it is appropriate.

I wish to bring to your attention a document prepared by our counsel, Harriet Pilpel. This is a brief discussion of the conditions under which a Planned Parenthood affiliate might incur civil liability in conjunction with abortion referral, and how to avoid it. It is a very worthwhile piece of information that we will share with you if you write to the national office of Planned Parenthood. As you can see, we are very concerned about the care of the patient who comes to Planned Parenthood. We want to make sure that she has the best options from which to choose with regard to her problem pregnancy. If she elects to have an abortion, we want to make sure that she is provided with a safe termination in the appropriate setting, with adequate counseling and postoperative contraceptive care.

Conducting an Evaluation of an Abortion Service

Judy Widdicombe, R.N.

Before you refer any women to a facility, it is imperative that you have seen it. For four years I was the director of a referral agency. At that point we were referring primarily to New York and Washington, D.C., from the St. Louis area. It was my job to monitor site visits. Now I have become a provider, and it has made me put my money where my mouth is. All those things that I thought were important as a referring agency I still feel are very important as a provider. I think that the site visit is very important. Whether or not you are requested to make a site visit, it is important that you see for yourself what is occurring at that facility. One of your responsibilities as a referring group is to provide some support for a woman once she has chosen the option of abortion. Unless you know the service personally and can translate that to your staff, it is impossible for you to help prepare the patient for what she is going to experience once she gets there. Many anxieties stem from fear of the unknown, so it is important to share with the patient a bit of what she is going to experience.

In the days of St. Louis to New York referrals, I would take the plane with a group of women every once in a while. I would leave St. Louis in the morning, traveling with as many as ten women. It gave me an opportunity to sit and chat with the women on their way back and find out just what kind of an experience it was. The feedback from them was very important. For many of them, the anxiety of the procedure was far overshadowed by the fear of getting on an airplane and going to New York City, which sounded like the other end of the world. I do not think we can minimize the individual needs of women who have never been out of their local geographical area. Traveling anyplace can itself be a trauma.

As you look at the facility it is important to know all the things that have been discussed previously. What kind of procedure do they do; what are their limitations; and do they require any documentation? I am glad that Dr. Cushner raised the issue of counseling. I happen to be a counseling advocate. I think this is something that we have to evaluate periodically. Are we providing counseling to meet our own needs or needs that we assume women have? Are we, in fact, letting the women set the tone in establishing what their needs are? This puts the responsibility upon us, whether we are a referral agency or a direct provider of services to develop counseling skills. We must have supervision and staff development of those counselors so that the individual woman's needs can be met. It is important that we do not impose our own anxieties on that patient.

What happens when the patient has been raped? What do you as a provider or as a referral agency do to help a woman who has been raped? What kind of services are provided for her? In our particular agency, for example, we have three counselors who also work with the local rape crisis center. They can assist a woman regardless of when she has been raped and help her work through the anxieties about the problem pregnancy. It is important that we deal with the rape as a separate issue from the decision-making process regarding the pregnancy. That is often very difficult to do.

What do we do with partners or with "significant others?" Do we involve the partners, or the parents, in the counseling? Is this important? Do we see them as part of the decision-making process? Do we see them as part of the woman's anxieties or support system or nonsupport system? Do we allow her the decision as to whether she gets the man involved? What kind of a stand do we take on that? How do we see ourselves functioning in a supportive role? What kind of attitudes do we have about adolescents? We have had one 10-year-old patient. That was a real trauma for all of us, especially those of us who had children 10 years old or older. We have also had a woman who was 52. What kind of attitudes do we have about woman at 52? My heart went out to her. I could not imagine what it would be like to find myself pregnant at 52. What kind of attitudes and what kind of support systems are we willing to provide for those at the extreme ends of the reproduction spectrum?

What about women who come back to a facility for a second or a third procedure? It still continues to be a problem for me. By using the label of "repeater," we set a tone within the facility that singles out women and labels them as special, but it is not always in a positive way. We are doing a study of this and there was a note posted in the telephone room, "Do not forget to ask the woman if she is a repeater." I saw the note and we had a little inservice training about how we could deal with that. The priority question to ask the woman was not, "How are you feeling, what can we do?" but, "Are you a repeater?" We were concerned about getting numbers for the study. We have worked through that problem and now the data are obtained in an indirect way.

What happens with women with delayed menses? Women call who have had unprotected intercourse and may not even have had a delayed menses yet. They are anticipating it or actually are one, two, three or four days late. We have experienced a tremendous amount of frustration dealing with menstrual extraction and menstrual regulation. Unfortunately, my physicians do not feel that it is an optimal procedure. They are concerned about the discomfort. We find that women who are having menstrual extractions without a paracervical block are terribly uncomfortable. This may be because many of them are not pregnant. We have instituted a policy of counseling women with delayed menses. If they are within about 10 days of a missed period, we will give them 100 mg of progesterone in oil and try to induce a bleed. If they do not bleed, we will do an extraction or give them support to wait until they are several weeks further along. This is an important issue because this is where we can really practice preventive medicine. All of us who are involved in the issue are concerned about prevention. We have a moral responsibility to deal with these women in a way that helps them begin to integrate some kind of contraceptive practice into their lives.

Another issue is how the facility deals with contraceptive information. Do they dispense contraception to the women to cover them until they get back to their clinic or physician?

It is important for a referral agency to have a contact person at the facility with whom to share particular problems about patients and for them to have someone in your agency to contact. For example, there should be somebody in the local community to inform that a tissue exam was not compatible with an intrauterine pregnancy. We are concerned that the woman be given information about ectopic pregnancy and that she be told what to expect in case there is a rupture.

An issue that was brought up earlier is reduced fees. I think this is a very important area. What do we do with a woman in a lower socioeconomic class? When we started out seven years ago, 11 percent of our patients were in this group. We are now up to 33 percent. We will not turn anybody away, and more than a third of our fees are less-than-full. This is important if you are an agency evaluating a potential provider. What is the maximum cost? Are there hidden costs? Is everything included? Do they give Rhogam? Do they give prophylactic antibiotics? If the woman is anemic, do they send her home with a prescription for some iron? Do they call her physician? What happens to the welfare of that patient? You need to negotiate with the provider to determine what is a realistic proportion of reduced fee patients that can be seen. It may be one in five, it may be one in ten, or it may be one in eight. There must be an understanding so that that facility knows what it can bear. You know what you can expect from that facility so you do not send all your reduced fee patients to one place. That is not fair. How can we still provide services for the lower socioeconomic group of women?

Physician training and physician backup has been mentioned. I think physician backup on the premises is important. It is rare that we ever function without two physicians in the house. I feel this relates to a number of different things, including good delivery of care. More importantly, if the lone physician has an unusual case and it takes him longer, the whole patient flow stops.

Something that plagues us consistently as providers is patient flow. How do we keep the waiting time for the patient to a minimum? I think it is optimal for the patient to always operate with two doctors in the house. It also gives a doctor in trouble the backup of another pair of hands and another head which might be a little bit calmer than his.

I like to know how the physicians are reimbursed. I do not think it is any of my business to know how much they are reimbursed, but I would like to know whether it is piecework or whether they are paid by the session. What kind of physician coverage is available? Who do the patients call if they have a problem after hours? Assuming that the facility closes at 5:30 or 6 or 7 p.m., what happens if that patient wakes up at midnight and has a problem? Is there an emergency number that she can call? Will she get a response from that number when she does call it? How will those calls be handled? Is the patient referred to an emergency room? Is she dealt with by the physician or by the nurse? What is the policy and protocol that has been developed for that?

Patient feedback is very important and it is important that follow-up be done in two ways. As providers we get patients who are very poorly counseled and very poorly prepared. It makes our job much more difficult in trying to meet their needs in a short time. Follow-up and feedback work in two ways. If you can get criticism on how you are preparing the patients, it is good to know. What are the problems, and how can we continually upgrade our own care?

What about management of complications? Who takes care of them, whether or not the patients are hospitalized, who pays for it? That is always an issue. If it is in fact retained tissue and there are either fetal parts or placental parts, who foots the bill for that? This issue is raised for the most part by a minor who does not want her parents to know, or a married woman who does not want her husband to know. This issue has to be addressed at some time. As far as availability of complication data, my feeling is that complications are underreported. What is complication and how do you deal with it?

Discussion

Hodgson: What has developed within the last six to eight years is a new method of delivery of medical care. The freestanding clinic actually has been on the outside of organized medicine. To many physicians the freestanding clinic is still on the outside and is not accredited.

When I left the private practice of medicine and went to take over as Medical Director of an abortion clinic prior to the Supreme Court decisions, I was definitely on the defensive. Physicians would call and be extremely critical just because we had done the procedure, aside from any possible complications. It was a matter of constantly defending and trying to improve the quality of medical care that was being delivered. These clinics sprang up in response to a definite need. The hospitals defaulted. When abortion was legalized and thousands of women sought the service, the hospitals still defaulted. This is why the freestanding clinics have continued to grow. They have continued to improve. They have demonstrated that they can deliver the services more cheaply and in a more humane manner. They are staffed by people who are dedicated to the idea of service. Consideration for the consumer is far greater in this type of facility than in the ordinary hospital.

What about the future? I would like to ask members of the panel what they think is going to happen. Are the freestanding clinics going to continue to spring up and grow? Are they going to provide other types of medical care? Will they become a comprehensive health facility? Are they going to be completely absorbed into the hospital system? Are they going to become affiliated academically? I would like to see an academic affiliation for them simply because it would help establish good standards. Also, we need to teach medical students and residents. They should be rotated into these clinics.

I'd like to see the facilities used for teaching purposes. On the other hand, I like to protect the patient's privacy. I think many women would resent being used in a teaching facility. One plea I would make is that we not be too arbitrary in our standards because the service is changing rapidly, our techniques are changing, and many of the ideas that we had for standards several years ago have turned out not to be necessary. For example, in our series of over 20,000 procedures, we found that there were only ten patients who required blood transfusions. Only two of those ten occurred during the first week following the abortion. None were given blood during the first 24 hours. This would indicate that the requirement that blood typing and cross-matching be done is unnecessary. The same

103

thing is true about the 13 weeks' limitation for suction curettage. We have to have standards at the present time but I can anticipate that that may change with the use of ultrasound and different mid-trimester techniques. A facility that would provide a complete abortion service would probably be preferable to one that has a definite limit.

Widdicombe: For now, we've made the decision to be a specialty service. In fact, we've turned over many of our educational programs to another corporate entity that does the preventive aspects. We feel that we have a lot of work to do, and in order to do it well, we need to remain specialized. We are working toward a university affiliation. That has been one of my goals for the past three years. I think we will someday be a training facility for the local university hospital. We have an excellent Planned Parenthood and an excellent city Public Health Department that delivers family planning services. I don't want to duplicate. I want to provide services that are not being provided and I want to do it well.

Cushner: The Alan Guttmacher Institute data for 1973 indicated that of 745,000 abortions done in calendar 1973, over 300,000 and perhaps as many as 350,000 were performed in free-standing clinics.* When nearly 50 percent of the services are being provided by a component in the health care system, one can't deal with that lightly. My hope for the free-standing clinics is that they survive stringent program evaluations. I don't have any strong feelings about medical school affiliation. There are days when I would wonder why you would want that. The question you raise about medical school affiliation and the utilization of community-based health facilities for teaching and training comes under a broader umbrella. What will the health care system in the United States be like in the future? Not just abortion care but health care in general. Some of the trends are already clear. There are teams of physicians and non-physician health professionals. The whole trend toward regionalization brings health care closer to one's residence. I can see medical students and residents spending a good deal of their time in community health. Today, I don't see a chance of anything significant like that happening in the majority of medical schools in the United States.

Pakter: In New York City, we felt that we were responsible for seeing that standards would be set up at the highest level possible. In the three months before the law went into effect, we had a number of meetings with our Obstetric Advisory Committee to the Commissioner of Health. From March through the end of June 1970, we developed these recommended standards. The Board of Health then decided to enact these standards

* C. Tietze, F.S. Jaffe, E. Weinstock and J.G. Dryfoos. *Provisional Estimates of Abortion Need and Services in the Year Following the 1973 Supreme Court Decisions*, New York: The Alan Guttmacher Institute, 1975.

into a code so they would become regulations. Before these regulations were enacted, the Board of Health held an open hearing in July. It was an all-day meeting. At that meeting there were people who were opposed to abortions and people who felt that the Health Department had no business regulating the performance of abortions. For several months thereafter the regulations were not enacted, but we had a set of recommended standards. Finally, in October 1970, the regulations incorporating the standards went into effect. Teams of obstetricians, nurses and social workers then visited the various facilities that were performing abortions or planned to do them. These included hospitals as well as freestanding clinics. We concentrated on the hospitals in the beginning because the hospitals were primarily the places where the residents of the city went for their abortions. It was only later that a greater proportion of women began going to the freestanding clinics.

I have heard about abortion patients being admitted to hospital rooms or wards where other kinds of patients were getting care. This should be a matter of concern for all of us. Even though a hospital may be accredited, one should check into the hospital's program for the abortion patients. It should take into consideration the emotional well-being as well as the physical needs of patients.

In the beginning, we had a potentially very serious situation because of a proliferation of commercial referral agencies. We've been talking about referral agencies with regard to the best interests of the patient. Unfortunately, many of the services that were springing up were concerned about their own interests and the welfare of their own financial status. In a short period of time after July 1970, 29 referral agencies were in existence and these were all commercial and profit-making. We finally had to turn to the Attorney General of the State for help in trying to eliminate these agencies. People were often being referred to inferior services rather than the good ones. We still have referral agencies in existence, presumably non-profit in nature. Some are good, some are not good. It's very difficult to eliminate this practice altogether.

All we can say is, let's have informed consumers. We are trying to give more and more emphasis to letting patients know what they should be prepared for when they are going for an abortion. The educated consumer should be knowledgeable about what constitutes an adequate work-up before the abortion. Besides the physical examination and the history, what laboratory tests are going to be done? With the cooperation of our Health Department and Planned Parenthood in New York City, there is a very good little booklet put out recently. It is called *Getting an Abortion in New York City, What You Need To Know*. Although it is tailored for people who are coming to New York City or who are in New York City, the same principles would hold true regardless of locale. It tells the consumer what to expect. From time to time, one sees articles in the press about what one should expect to know about getting an abortion. Unfortunately, there's not enough of that. I think that we need to do a lot more of this kind of thing to get the message across adequately. In our own Health Department, we welcome inquiries and complaints even though we are hard pressed in terms of shortage of staff. The County Medical Society sometimes receives complaints and refers them to us.

When the Supreme Court made its decision, the question immediately arose as to whether we had any rights to have regulations concerning first trimester abortion. There is a difference of legal opinion on this. It has been stated by some lawyers that regulations for first trimester abortions at this time are not legal. Our Commissioner of Health at that time, Dr. Lowell Bellin, did not agree, since in his opinion, with the advice of legal counsel, the New York City regulations are not obstructing service but are designed to enhance standards of care for patients receiving the service. We have similar standards for maternity services. One might regard it as discriminatory not to have standards for abortion services.

Dean Disher, Minneapolis, Minnesota: Dr. Pakter, I'd like you to clarify for me the restrictions placed on the facilities in New York City. I thought, according to the 1973 Supreme Court decision, that it was illegal to place restrictions on first trimester abortions except that they be done by licensed physicians.

Pakter: This is a matter of interpretation. We were not placing restrictions; we were merely spelling out standards. We have them for maternity care and prenatal care. It isn't a matter of telling a hospital or a clinic that they have to have a committee to decide about patients. There is nothing here which interferes in any way with the doctor-patient relationship that the Supreme Court stipulates. It's a matter of determining or deciding whether these regulations are meant to obstruct or whether they are meant to enhance. We choose to interpret this as enhancement, not obstruction.

Dr. Jim Armstrong, Kalispell, Montana: We have heard about how the morbidity and dangers and complications of abortion had been reduced, and the evaluation procedures almost seem as if we are shooting a mosquito with a shotgun. I'm wondering if these evaluation procedures might be more restrictive than the most restrictive of the state abortion laws. Wouldn't it be more productive to put the effort into medical education so that abortion is considered like tonsillectomy, available in a woman's home community without going through all the institutional referral?

Cushner: Your point is well taken. At the risk of sounding flippant, my preference would be for tonsillectomy programs to be evaluated also.

Cates: I was fascinated by Dr. Cushner's matrix of evaluation and applaud that as a first step toward evaluation. My problem with that matrix and also with the APHA guidelines is that they're open-ended. There is no definition of a measurable, specific objective that you can grasp. He mentioned that his first criteria would be to have adequate followup and "acceptable" morbidity and mortality. What's acceptable? You talk about local standards. What is local? What is local in Los Angeles might not be what is local in Colorado. Would you take a census region, or would you take a nation? I think it is important, perhaps, to establish some ideal national standards that are measurable and that are based on the best possible care. Perhaps we should, to hold morbidity and mortality rates up to that type of scrutiny.

Pakter: It becomes very difficult, Dr. Cates, to be specific. In a way, you've answered your own question. It depends on what is considered the best standard in the area. What is considered acceptable at one time will not be acceptable the next time. If you become too specific in spelling out standards, you box yourself into a corner. That's the difficulty of saying what is acceptable followup. If you are concerned about what may happen to this patient after she leaves, and there is no way for this patient to contact the service or doctor, and she is not given both written and verbal instructions, I think these aspects deserve attention. She should get written instructions at the time she is getting her service. If the people who are doing the evaluation exercise this kind of judgment, it would seem to me that they should be able to make an interpretation as to whether the followup is adequate or not. A very knotty problem is the matter of advertising, which has recently been given some attention in the news media in terms of lawyers and doctors advertising. We know some abortion clinics and individual physicians have been advertising. Unfortunately, the problem with advertising is the content and the possibility that it can be misleading. It can lure people who are naive and don't know better to a service which is sub-standard and/or unethical.

Ruth Dolan, Colorado Right-to-Life: I agree with many of the things that the doctors are talking about this afternoon as far as complications are concerned. We recognize these complications and we are very concerned that women are still occasionally dying from abortions. There are many kinds of long-term complications with subsequent pregnancies that we are concerned with. I congratulate this group, particularly, because you are trying to rectify some of the wrongs that we have pointed out all along. You mentioned that there was an anti-abortion group in New York who criticized or violently opposed the health regulations and standards. We have tried in Colorado to get the Department of Health interested in establishing some standards, and I think that these should be established. The least we can do to protect women is to require stringent standards for abortion clinics.

Hern: Thank you very much for your comment. As a matter fact, I testified at a hearing of the State Board of Health which was convened partly because of the efforts of those opposed to abortion. We had a lengthy discussion on this question. The Board of Health concluded that there were serious constitutional questions with these regulations, but I think we all concur that it is important to have very good standards for services. One of the ways we achieve that is by public education and information such as this conference is trying to provide.

Abortion Nursing

Abortion Nursing

Introduction

Rory Zahourek, R.N.

The goal of our panel is to provide insights to abortion nursing in three primary areas: first, the care of the patient and how the abortion patient relates to the nurse; second, nurses' reaction to abortion patients and how nurses experiencing adverse reactions to abortion patients might be assisted; and third, how the team approach relates to nursing care of the abortion patient and whether it helps or hinders that patient.

My abortion nursing experience began in 1967 when Colorado first passed a liberalized abortion law which allowed for abortions in cases of rape, incest or to promote the mental health of the mother. Following that decision, Denver General Hospital was inundated with abortion patients. The staff was ill-prepared to deal with this new kind of patient and had numerous problems. As a psychiatric nurse, I became involved in helping the staff deal with abortion patients as well as working with some patients who had to meet the mental health requirements of the new law. As a result of a pilot project, we defined the role of the therapeutic abortion nurse consultant to include several functions. First, she was a direct caregiver to the patient who acted as a supportive figure and therapist and was always available to explain the procedure and the therapeutic abortion approval process. She served as a coordinator for the approval process and also functioned as a consultant to nursing, medical and social work staff.

The nurse consultants quickly learned that they had to become patient advocates in the numerous situations in which patients were treated punitively or when the nursing staff could not deal with patients adequately. Since at that time very little was known about either abortion or the care of the abortion patient, the nurse consultants became active as community resource people.

The findings of a study of nurses' attitudes toward the abortion patient done in 1974 and reported in *Nursing* in September, 1975 illustrate the problems which were dealt with by the nurse consultant and which are still found in abortion nursing today.[1] The study reported that nurses are deeply divided on both the issue of abortion and what their abortion nursing role should or should not be. Surprisingly, favorable attitudes were inversely related to education. Those nurses who had Associate

Degree preparation were the most favorable, followed by nurses with Bachelor's degrees and those with Master's degrees. However, nurses who were least favorable to caring for abortion patients and to abortion as an issue were licensed practical nurses (LPN's) and students. This point is critical since the majority of patient care is given by LPN's, students and aides. The other group that was most often opposed to abortion and to caring for abortion patients·was the Ob-Gyn nurse. This has implications for current hospital abortion patients since most hospital abortions are done on the Ob-Gyn floor. In spite of these unfavorable attitudes, the majority of nurses who disapproved of abortion for any reason still said that they would take care of the patient, although the data also indicated that the nurses who disapproved of abortion were rarely assigned to the care of abortion patients.

Ambulatory Care Services

Judy Widdicombe, R.N.

My remarks will deal with ambulatory care services outside of the traditional institution, involving an awake-alert patient.

As we look at nursing trends through the years, it is apparent that although the first formal training school was developed only about 100 years ago, we have come a long way from our origins, sweeping floors and cleaning fireplaces, to the point where, in many areas of the country, we are the primary health care providers. This development, the liberalization of abortion and the establishment of more sophisticated delivery systems make it increasingly common for nurses to come in contact with the patient who is in a crisis with a problem pregnancy.

I have been involved with these issues over the past seven years. Having seen in New York and Washington, D.C. that quality health care services could be delivered in a clinic setting, that patients did not have to be hospitalized under general anesthesia, and that the cost could be considerably lessened, we decided to establish an ambulatory care center. Another underlying concern was that we wanted to work outside of the traditional institution, particularly since we were dealing with tremendous numbers of patients who needed expeditious services. We began in 1969 as a counseling and referral service in the state of Missouri, which is crawling backwards on its hands and knees into the twentieth century. Although Missouri is not the least bit ready for sex, we have seen about 50,000 patients with problem pregnancies.

We recognize that traditional nursing care and responsibilities in an ambulatory center involve different problems although there is probably not a nurse in any area of health care delivery, be it a doctor's office, public health agency or hospital, who may not find herself faced with a patient who has a problem pregnancy. However, the nurses in an ambulatory care center are self-selected. In an ambulatory setting that has a specialized delivery system, you are not going to get nurses who have attitude problems and who are opposed to legal abortion. So her attitudes are extremely important and considerable self-assessment is required. First, how does she feel about the issue? Is she committed to women's freedom to choose abortion? I am not pro-abortion; I am not anti-abortion. I am pro-choice. How I feel, and what I would do as an individual is a separate issue from my responsibility as a professional to the women who are seeking services.

How does the nurse feel about her own sexuality? How does she feel about the increasing numbers of adolescents who are sexually active, who are coming to our facility with venereal disease and other problems? In our facility, 15 percent of the women are under 17 years of age. Is she punitive? Is she accepting? Is she nurturing? How has she assessed her own value system and to what extent has she considered how she will respond to patients?

What about the repeater? It is a tremendous problem for all of us who are committed to abortion as a backup method of birth control. There are those women who either consciously or unconsciously, or as the result of the system and the inefficiencies in the system, find themselves faced with more than one problem pregnancy. What is our responsibility as providers of health care for these women when they come in? Should they be treated like other patients or should they be treated differently, since they obviously have not been able to integrate into their behavior the contraceptive information that they received at the time of the first procedure? Should they be treated in a punitive way? I am not sure that I have an answer. We are currently doing a study of women who are consistent nonusers of contraception, using the population of women who are seeking repeat abortion as well as control groups of women who are contraceptors.

At our facility, the nurses have become part of a team effort. We have essentially the same nursing staff that we began with three years ago and the same ten physicians. It is an interesting situation in which the boss is a nurse and the doctor is an employee. The evolution has not been without pain, but the physicians have begun to relax and admit that maybe they do not have all the answers, and respond to what we consider to be the counseling needs of patients.

It is important for the nurse to have an understanding of crisis therapy, crisis theory and crisis intervention. The woman involved in a problem pregnancy is indeed in a crisis. The basic crisis is the fact that she is pregnant, did not plan to be, and perhaps does not want to be. The techniques of dealing with her and with her particular situation are unique. Many times the woman, especially the adolescent, comes in with a pregnancy which is also a symptom of many other things that are occuring. What is our responsibility as professionals in dealing with the other life situations that are there and that are going to be there when the woman leaves the facility? How much of the focus should be on the crisis? It depends on the patient and her specific needs. It requires dealing not only with the abortion decision but also with the issue of contraception. If the patient is an adolescent, her family, especially her parents, may be involved and this is difficult for many parents.

The roles the nurse assumes in an ambulatory center include physician, counselor, and perhaps physician's assistant. She needs to have a broad-based understanding of where the patient is and what her responsibilities are. If the patient still seems ambivalent after having been

114

through the counseling process, the abortion will not be done. If necessary, she will be taken off the table and more time will be spent with her.

A problem that occurs frequently is the refusal of the doctor to do the procedure because the patient is much further along than had been diagnosed. That patient is in a second trauma because she does not meet our criteria and needs the nurse as an advocate and a support. She is extremely important to that patient's well-being. The nurse may also function in the role of manager. There are three nurses in major administrative positions at our clinic: the Executive Director, the Clinic Administrator and the Director of Nursing. I guess you could call us mavericks. We are not involved in the traditional institutional setting.

REFERENCES

1. D. Popoff and *Nursing 75* in collaboration with G. R. Funkhouser. "What Are Your Feelings about Death and Dying, Part II?" Probe Section, *Nursing 75* 5:54-62.

Nursing Staff Problems

Karen Kowalski, R.N.

For four and a half years, I was the head nurse on the labor and delivery unit at the local university teaching hospital. The hospital opened an operating room on our labor and delivery unit which was supposed to provide post-partum tubal ligations. The nursing staff thought that the OR would be used for emergency caesarean sections, which would improve the quality of care for mothers and babies. In reality, the OR was utilized primarily to provide therapeutic abortions, for the most part, suction D and Cs, and a few hysterotomies. As this drama began to unfold, the nursing staff on the unit had varying reactions. Some of the staff were totally unable to resolve their ambivalent feelings regarding their participation in these procedures and subsequent treatment of these patients. There were some who had no qualms and it took a great deal of effort and time through conferences and team meetings to give support to staff with these difficulties so that they could work through some of their feelings.

Nurses who had been employed on the unit at this time could not be compelled to help with procedures. An equitable solution had to be found which would also meet all the specifications of the state personnel service. The state professional organization was called upon to help resolve some of these difficulties. At the convention, the social commission of the organization brought to the floor of the House of Delegates a resolution in the form of a position paper on the rights of abortion patients and the responsibilities and the rights of the nurse. The resolution said that the patient has a right to make the choice and the nurse has a responsibility to care for the patient. If a nurse is morally or ethically opposed to this procedure, that nurse has a responsibility to the institution for which she works to acknowledge her objections and to transfer out of that area. After approval by the state organization, the resolution was adopted for use in the unit in which I worked.[1]

We now have an exhaustive interviewing process for nurses who propose to come to work on the unit, during which it is made quite plain that if they do not feel that they can help with the procedures, if they cannot be supportive to abortion patients, then they are not good candidates for these positions. Nurses are usually able to state their objections to or interest in the unit and to discuss their feelings about abortion.

A source of continuing problems on this unit is that fullfledged labor and delivery obstetrical services are operating simultaneously with abortion services. It has been a real problem to have the recovering suction abortion patient in the same recovery room with recovering postpartum mothers. Frequently the baby and the father are in the recovery room with the mother, at least for the first hour postpartum, which is a problem in terms of how to work with the abortion patient.

There is an inability on the nurse's part to really get to know or understand the patient, what her concerns are and how she feels about the abortion decision. This reflects the fact that the nurse literally has no contact with abortion patient prior to the procedure except for picking them up on their unit, the ten or fifteen minutes they may wait outside of the operating room and an hour post-general anesthesia spent in the recovery room. The patient has usually been premedicated, so when the nurse sees her before the procedure, she is under the effects of drugs, and she is obviously under the effects of general anesthesia afterward. This is a source of a great deal of frustration for the nursing staff because they are very much tuned in to knowing and spending a lot of time with patients.

At the same time it is interesting to see some of the changes in the structural administration of the unit. The operating room and the recovery room are run by a team leader. In the four and a half years that I was there, there have been four different team leaders, while in the labor and delivery side, there have been only two. Not one of these people lasted longer than a year and a half in this position. While trying to determine some of the reasons for the turnover, I began to talk with the different team leaders that have been on the unit. Without exception, every one of them know what was performed in the operating room; they had a theoretical knowledge about abortion, about abortion patients and were very sympathetic and supportive of a woman's right to make a choice about abortion. I watched the ebb and flow of their feelings during the period of time in which they were involved with procedures almost daily. Since about eight or ten procedures a week are performed, the nurses frequently felt that they had to have a break to get out of the room and not be responsible for taking care of patients during the procedures.

Another problem I have noticed is that in university teaching centers where physicians and nurses have a choice whether or not to care for these patients, many physicians opt not to and the responsibility for the performance of abortions falls on a very small percentage of the residency staff. They soon become very angry and feel as though they have been abused. Yet as soon as some of their friends complete their residencies, they go out and perform abortions because there is a great deal of money to be made in private practice. Those who finally agree to perform the procedures feel that the department owes them something because they are willing to take the responsibility, and that they are in some way entitled to run the service in their own way. This has caused some problems in terms of the role of the nurse and patient advocacy. For example, sometimes a physician decides that patients will not obtain counseling through Social Services but will be admitted directly to the service and have the procedure done. This causes conflicts between the nurse, who becomes the patient advocate, and the physician, who wants to run the service in his own way, and who views the nurse as an interference in his relationship with the patient.

In addition to the foregoing problems, there is a conflict for a nurse who cares for delivery patients and makes every effort to save a 600 gm. baby and who also must care for abortion patients. With the neonatal intensive care unit and the technology that that involves there is a real problem in delineating between these roles.

REFERENCES

1. Colorado Nurses Association. Statement on Abortion, June 1973.

Inpatient Services

Shirley Hyde, R.N.

I am a head nurse on a multiservice inpatient unit at Denver General Hospital. Denver General is a city-county hospital. It is an acute care facility serving many of the city's medically indigent patients. My experience with abortion nursing is limited to amnioinstillation. Hysterotomies are rare, and there are a few terminations by hysterectomy but since hysterectomies are not done for sterilization purposes alone, there must be a medical indication. The many patients whose unwanted pregnancies are terminated by instillation come to my 57-bed unit. In addition to the gynecologic patients on the ward, we have orthopedic, neurosurgical and neurological patients, as well as some adolescent patients cared for while the adolescent ward is closed. We also get an overflow of some surgical and medical patients and occasionally we have a postpartum patient on the ward. There is no designated room for abortion patients. Whenever we have an empty four-bed room we assign all abortion patients there, but this is rare, and often we have to mix patients on any of these other services with abortion patients.

In this mixed setting, we run into a variety of roommate reactions to the abortion patient. As Ms. Zahourek mentioned, we were very unsophisticated in abortion nursing skills when Denver General first began to provide services and one of the very first assignments I made for an abortion patient was in a two-bed room with a patient being treated for a fertility problem. Before long, the crying abortion patient came out, followed by the screaming fertility-problem patient, who said, "Get out of my room, you murderer." There have been other reactions based on religious views which were very anti-abortion. Often these are older women, grand multiparas, who want nothing to do with the abortion patient, do not want her in their room and who keep their curtains closed as long as the two are sharing the same room. We occasionally have mothers of stillborn infants who are transferred from the postpartum ward because they are distressed on the OB ward, and these patients do not appreciate having an abortion patient with them. Some of the cancer patients do not like to share a room with therapeutic abortion patients. Recently we had a girl return to her room from the exam room where the procedure was done who found a stack of religious literature on her table. She immediately blamed the staff for placing the literature there. So I talked to her for a few minutes and told her that I thought the young patient next to her had left

121

her the information. She was a 20-year old who had a wicked cancer, had been married a year, had no children, and because of her cancer therapy she would not be having children. She just did not understand what this abortion patient was doing and, in addition, her own death was very much in her mind. Life was very precious to her, even that abortion patient's unborn child. Then we have patients who are in with spontaneous abortions who really want their baby, and they do not care to share a room with an abortion patient. Mixing patients is not ideal, and when we can, we try to anticipate problems and move patients. Sometimes this is not always possible because of bed problems, so we find ourselves later separating patients.

We never see the girl prior to the admission for the procedure. Applications for abortion are all processed in the outpatient department, in accordance with hospital policy which dictates that the patient cannot be over 20 weeks pregnant at the time of the abortion. Instillations are scheduled every Tuesday and Friday, and there are no more than four on each day. The patients go through the regular inpatient admission process, come up to our ward about noon, and go through our ward admission process. She walks into the examining room, the instillation procedure is done under local anesthetic, and she walks back to her room. She is given instructions about what to expect for her management, IV medication, pain medication, labor, activity and diet, and we try to make her as comfortable as possible. That can sometimes be difficult, since if a patient is upset and crying, she does not always hear what we are saying to her. Pitocin is added to the IV, and the patient labors in her room. She aborts in her room in bed and she is taken back to the examining room for a curretage. The cervix is already dilated so that this can be done under Demerol and Valium. If the patient is Rh-negative, she is given Rhogam and is discharged with a scheduled return visit to Family Planning in four weeks. A representative of the Family Planning department visits the patient both while in the hospital and in the outpatient setting. We rarely see the patient afterwards unless she is a repeater.

Among our nursing staff at Denver General Hospital there is almost the same reaction to abortion among the non-professional personnel. Some nurses are very anti-abortion, and they simply cannot work on our ward. They have to transfer to another unit, or to another hospital where abortions are not performed. Some nurses are very comfortable with abortion. They believe in a woman's right to choose and they are able to participate in providing care that the patient needs. Those whose nursing careers predate the abortion law, and I am one, have seen too many septic abortions. These are very sick girls and we have even seen some deaths. We prefer to take care of the abortion patient in the hospital setting where a physician and a nursing staff can give skilled care. We do believe in selective termination of the pregnancy, however, not abortion in lieu of family planning. We help for a while but we need a rest. Others are unable to assist with the procedure itself but can assist in all of the post-injection care. We have had a few nurses who are adoptive mothers and who have been able to assist with the procedure, but they soon realized that if other pregnant girls had terminated their pregnancies, they would not have had babies to adopt, so they find themselves unable to assist with the procedures any further. A number of the single nurses can help, until they get married, get pregnant, and then for some reason that neither they nor I can explain, cannot continue to help with the abortion procedure. Some nurses have experienced a fertility problem and cannot help with the procedure.

Another reaction centers about handling the fetus. This is very distasteful to a number of the nurses, particularly practical nurses and attendants. The girl aborts in bed, the cord is clamped, cut and the fetus is usually carried to the specimen container. When the patient asks about the sex of the fetus, the personnel do not know because they do not look. This situation has not occurred very frequently, so when it does happen we do not handle it very well. Currently the doctor who is doing our instillations tells the patient at the time of injection that many of the nurses are very uncomfortable with the fetus, so if she wants to know the sex, she must ask at the time of her return clinical appointments, and the nurse will look in the chart. This procedure, while not ideal, avoids placing the nurse in a distasteful position, and the patient does find out eventually.

When we first started doing instillations, we were using saline injections. About a year ago we began using prostaglandins. We had been forewarned that there could be a live fetus but we were unprepared for the reality when it did happen. We had a large staff meeting, including the nurses on the ward, the doctors on the gynecologic service, and the Associate Director of nurses. It was decided that pitocin management had not been properly adjusted for prostaglandin therapy. That was readjusted and we have not had any more live fetuses.

There is a great deal of staff reaction to repeaters. The second time a girl has an abortion, she is treated the same as any abortion patient; but when she comes in the third time, the staff pretty much feels that the girl is very irresponsible, and that she should have taken advantage of family planning that has been offered to her in the clinic and in the hospital. Many of the personnel think it is very unfair for a person to come back a third time asking us to abort her. Recently we had a patient back for the fourth time and that really was upsetting to us.

Let me add a couple of words about confidentiality. We try to let patients know that their diagnosis is their own business. If they want to tell someone, that is up to them. We do not reply to a person asking why a patient is in the hospital. We tell them that the patient knows why she is there, and that she is free to discuss or not discuss her diagnosis with anyone. In the same way, she can tell her roommates whatever she wants, but if you have a mixed setting in a four-bed ward and the time comes to abort, it is hard to hide the diagnosis from anybody.

We had a girl the other day whose mother was the only person who knew that she was pregnant. One of her young classmates was in our attendant training program. She met her friend and found out why she was in, went to some of their mutual friends and said: "Guess who is in Denver General having an abortion?"

The personnel in general are not really happy to be involved in abortion nursing. We were not asked and were given no choice when the abortion service was transferred from the Ob-Gyn ward to this unit. So, in a way both we and the patients are captive. We feel that some segregated ward, or even a hospital, with nurses who are dedicated to abortion nursing, is something that we should look for in the future. It is very uncomfortable for nurses and for patients in this mixed setting, even for those of us who really want to help the abortion patient. I think we would have much happier personnel and happier patients if we had segregated settings.

Discussion

Dr. Louis Koplik, Abortion & Pregnancy Testing Clinic, Albuquerque, New Mexico: What did you do when you found out that a patient's confidence had been violated by another individual? My reaction would have been to have that woman kicked out of school. What was your reaction?

Hyde: This particular girl was in the attendant training program. Her instructor and the team leader talked with her and she was advised that she had no place in the nursing service at Denver General. She is no longer with us.

Tietze: I have some statistics on the subject of live-born fetuses. For what it is worth, there are some published statistics that go back to the early days of abortion. During the first six months of this period, second half of 1970, 28 live births were reported associated with abortions, which presented only four hundredths of one percent of all abortions during this period. Twenty-two of these infants weighed more than 600 grams and eight weighed more than 1000 grams, about two pounds. All but one of 1100 grams died within three days, including only two who lived longer than 24 hours. Subsequently, the proportion of live births has declined as more experience with second trimester abortions was accumulated. In other words, a live birth after an abortion procedure is a very rare phenomenon. Certainly it is stressful for all concerned and the best way to avoid these occurrences is to educate women to get their abortions early and to educate the medical services delivery system to reorganize it and develop it in such a way that abortions can be obtained early.

Dr. Mildred Hansen, Minneapolis, Minnesota: I would like to make a remark about revealing to the patients the sex of the fetus. I don't think it's right to discuss with the patient the sex of the fetus or a multiple pregnancy. We're very specific with our staff and I specifically forbid this discussion of fetal sex or multiple pregnancy with the patients. If there is any discussion, I talk to the patient myself. I just feel that it is already a painful experience. This is important for the patient's future sense of well-being, especially in the event that that patient, in later life, becomes infertile. I don't want her to think about the twins she might have had Also, in a subsequent marriage, if she has three girls, I don't want her to ruminate about the boy that she aborted.

Zahourek: I would like to react briefly to the business of seeing the fetus or not. Ms. Kowalski and I are working on a research project right now in relation to stillborns as to whether it is helpful or not to see the stillborn infant or to touch and hold the stillborn infant. There is some theoretical knowledge about seeing and holding the product of conception, the fetus or whatever, that I think is at least helpful for you all to think about. That is, when a person loses an object, having a well-defined object in his or her mind to grieve over tends to aid the grief process toward resolution. I don't know what is right; I don't know what is most therapeutic or most beneficial for the patient, but I would like you to at least consider that as another possibility in terms of whether or not we allow or encourage or refuse to allow patients to see the fetus after an abortion. I think it's important that we not discount the fact that there are those women who do make a decision that is very difficult and that they feel that they have indeed lost something. They consider the potentiality that would never come to pass; that the grieving process is important. It is an easy decision for some women, but there are those women who need and want to grieve. This process can help them resolve the decision and not have to live with it so that eight years later they have a psychiatric hospitalization.

Maggie Myers, San Diego, California: I think it's interesting to talk about the patients' bill of rights and compassionate medical care and the patient getting to make the decision about which procedure to have. But I think it's just as important that if a patient wants to see the fetus, if the patient wants to know the sex of the fetus, if the patient wants to know if it was twins, whether the nurse or the doctor thinks that's a good idea or not, I think it's the patient's right. It's not the right of the nurse or doctor involved; it's not their pregnancy and I don't think it should be their decision.

Alana Gillies, Loretta Heights College Health Service, Denver, Colorado: I have a question for any member of the panel. Has a patient or student ever asked you, "What would you do with an unwanted pregnancy, and what is your feeling about abortion?" I had this with a very upset, hostile student. Would you then throw it back to her or not, give her your feeling or just spend the time to try to talk with her?

Widdicombe: There are some new counseling tapes that have been developed by Preterm Institute in Boston which address this question in dealing with a woman with religious ambivalence. The woman's question to the counselor is "Do you feel it's murder?" And the counselor's response was "I feel it's an ending. And that then after that is a beginning. What I feel is not really as important as how you feel." I think we need to expose a bit of ourselves—but not to the point where the patient uses us as her reason or as her endorsement. I think that they do need to know how we feel.

Counseling and Psychological Aspects of Abortion

Review of Psychological Literature

Carol Schneider, Ph.D.

Many of the studies which have been done by psychological researchers examining the major consequences of abortion are not very good.[1] Since they are often quoted, I will review them and demonstrate with an emphasis on why some of the findings might be misleading.

Early studies in the 1950's by such analysts as Helene Deutsch concluded that there were grave after-effects of abortion.[2] However, the findings were based on anecdotal case material rather than systematic data, so general conclusions were unwarranted. It is important to be aware of anecdotal studies which are not based on reported data. It is also necessary to check that researchers have not drawn unwarranted conclusions from the data. For example, Wilson and Caine had six cases reporting problems among a sample of 220 subjects.[3] They went beyond their data to conclude that abortion has lasting psychological effects which may be serious.

Another problem is that prior to 1970, legal abortions in the U.S. were often obtained by women with real or alleged psychiatric indications. It is not valid to generalize these nationwide study findings to the population of women obtaining abortion under legalization. Despite similar problems of comparability, a well-designed Swedish study by Ekblad found at follow-up that 65 percent of the women felt no guilt, another 10 percent experienced no guilt but found the procedure unpleasant, mild guilt was reported by 14 percent and serious guilt and regret by only 11 percent. Gebhart's study of women obtaining illegal abortions suggest that there were no major negative after-effects, even in the groups which had illegal abortions.[4]

By the late 1960's the studies began to improve. A study of 50 women by Peck and Parcus in 1966, half of whom had abortions for psychiatric reasons, found only one case of acute negative reaction which was quickly relieved, and mild, short-lived guilt was reported by 20 percent.[5] Other research has corroborated that roughly between 10 and 20 percent of abortion patients experienced mild temporary adverse reactions and guilt. This is a group to whom counseling in the short term would be very useful. Fully 98 percent in Peck and Parcus's 1966 study said they would in similar circumstances seek an abortion again. Similar findings are reported in a 1967 study of abortion patients by Niswander and Patterson in Iowa, which found no negative phsychological effects in the group one, two, and five years later.[6, 7] Of a group of 116 women studied in New York in 1967, few had many regrets, and none reported any eight months later.[8] In 1971, a study using the Minnesota Multiphasic Personality Inventory (MMPI) found rapid improvements in neurotic signs after the abortion was performed.[9] Other studies done at this time showed elevated or abnormal MMPIs for women getting abortions compared to pregnant women who were not aborting.[10] However, these studies are contaminated by the fact that many women were only able to obtain abortion for psychiatric indications. It is clear, however, that the MMPI scores look much better after the abortion is over. It is possible that the stress involved in making a decision to abort is an anxiety-creating situation and that the abortion itself does reduce this anxiety.

Follow-up data on women in studies done in the 1960s are characterized by only a "one-third" return rate. The other two-thirds do not come back and are lost to the study. Unless these women are pursued it is impossible to generalize about the study population. Although facilities offering a follow-up medical exam will often get a larger return, the no-show rate is usually high. In fact, the highest percentage of women coming back that I have heard about is over 80 percent, but that is unusual.[11]

In 1973, a study done by Osofsky surveyed 500 patients. Seventy-three percent reported feelings of moderate to much relief immediately after the abortion.[12] After four weeks, 98 percent were functioning well and were happy with their decision. Less than two percent of the population had serious guilt or regrets. A 1974 study compared women with continued problems post-abortion with a group reporting no problems.[13] It was found that reactions were more positive when the male partner or parents were supportive. Those experiencing the worst reactions were alone throughout the whole process.

Another study found a significant correlation between high self-esteem and the least stressful reactions to abortion.[14] In 1974 a follow-up study of a group of over 900 women was able to elicit only 250 returnees.[15] Five percent of those who returned reported guilt or ambivalence. One percent actually attended one or two group counseling sessions to resolve their problems.

A recent review of the literature supports these trends, indicating that women who have good coping strengths before they have an unwanted pregnancy can make a relatively good adjustment after the pregnancy.[16] Mild depression occurs in between 10 and 20 percent, depending on whether the sample is college or non-college. Only between one and two percent have serious problems and those can usually be resolved with therapy.

One group who seem to have trouble resolving an unwanted pregnancy are those with pre-existing mental disease. A number of Scandinavian studies found 11 percent of abortion patients in a psychiatrically disturbed population had regrets. However, they might well have had persistent difficulty coping with a child and the question of whether or not to raise the child themselves. Concluding that these women have trouble with abortion does not mean they would not have had trouble with any resolution of an unwanted pregnancy.

Those who become pregnant under the age of 18 are also a vulnerable group.[17, 18] Their lack of defined personal and sexual identity may make the choices which they must make especially difficult, but this problem is inherent in the problem pregnancy. There is evidence, however, that for some, carrying to term and having to give up the baby is extremely difficult. A Berkeley study reported that 13 percent of the sample of young women giving up their infants attempted suicide within two years.[19] There is much evidence that carrying to term and giving up for adoption may result in more serious problems for young women than terminating the pregnancy. A comment from a student who had carried to term and had given up the infant and who was obtaining a subsequent abortion illustrates this point, "An abortion is no experience I would wish on any girl, but if one becomes pregnant, I believe an abortion is better than carrying it to term and not keeping it. It was sad for those at the home who didn't keep their babies because it was an abrupt end to happiness. I don't feel guilty about the abortion because it really didn't seem to exist that much in my life as the baby did. People who are against abortion can never feel the anxiety that a girl is going through and can never imagine the emotional pain she has. A girl may feel guilty but there's a shorter time of helplessness in an abortion than in full term. In carrying a child you develop responsibilities that make you realize that to bring a child into the world without parents is the greatest wrong you can do to that child. It may sound terrible when I say this but at least I know where the child is. I worry about the other one and I wonder if he's happy and secure. Does he wonder where I am? When he gets old enough will his adoptive parents tell him the truth, or will they say that I died or something? I did die that last day I saw him. I wonder when he's old enough to understand, will he?"

We consistently see in our clinic that women who carry to term have much more severe problems. These are most severe for women forced to carry to term. This is a subject particularly relevant in view of agitation for limitations on the availability of legal abortion. Work in Sweden found that of 160 women not granted an abortion, 20 committed suicide or obtained illegal abortions.[20] Serious developmental, emotional, and physical problems occurred in two-thirds of the children born to these women forced to carry to term, many more than in a control group of wanted children. Ten years later, 20 percent of those mothers said that the original pregnancy should have been terminated. This is a measure of serious rejection.

Hook studied 240 women who were refused abortions seven to 11 years after the refusal.[21] Half of those who were forced to carry to term had serious emotional problems for at least a year after delivery. One quarter

131

still had serious psychological problems. Of the 14 percent who had obtained illegal abortions, none had any psychological problems.

An unpublished study we did in Boulder is relevant to these issues. Of 182 women in the study, only one-third responded to our request to return after six weeks. Older women, those from higher socioeconomic classes and those who used contraceptives were all more likely to return. Apartment dwellers were more likely to return than dorm dwellers. If their parents were upset they were more likely to return than if the parents were supportive before the abortion. The same conclusion emerges: the more stable the social context, the less likely the girls are to return to see us after their abortion. Our guess is that they are doing pretty well or they probably would come back. Of those who did return six weeks after the abortion, only 10 percent complained of depression or loneliness. Only three of the 62 were sufficiently troubled to request another appointment after the follow-up visit. Group therapy was offered at one point but no women were interested. Only five of the group have had more than one clinic contact in the three years since the data was gathered. Another counseling agency on campus reported that none of the study group had requested help there. The five women who had significant problems had all reported difficulties prior to the abortion.

Over the past three years I have seen six patients for whom the reaction to abortion was the precipitating factor for seeking treatment. These women generally had not received any counseling before the abortion; they flew out to New York alone and came back alone.

Conservative religious backgrounds often contribute to the problem of resolving an abortion. Problems with the man involved are often present. If he rejects and will not take any responsibility there is a double loss. Some women have trouble resolving conflicts arising from their wish to be pregnant. A woman told me last week that she felt guilty about being pregnant, even though she used an IUD, because she had wanted so badly to be pregnant that that probably overcame the effects of the IUD.

REFERENCES

1. N.M. Simon and A.C. Senturia. "Psychiatric Sequelae of Abortion: Review of the Literature, 1935-1964," *Archives of General Psychiatry* 15:378, 1965.
2. H. Deutsch. *The Psychology of Women: A Psychoanalytic Interpretation.* New York: Grune & Stratton, Inc. 1945, Vol. 2, p. 179.
3. D.C. Wilson and B.L. Caine. "The Psychiatric Implications of Therapeutic Abortions," *Neuropsychiatry* 1:22, 1951.
4. N. Ekblad. "Induced Abortion on Psychiatric Grounds," *Acta Psychiatry Scandanavia* Suppl. 99:1, 1955.
5. A. Peck and H. Parcus. "Psychiatric Sequelae of Therapeutic Interruption of Pregnancy," *Journal of Nervous and Mental Disease* 143:417, 1966.
6. K. Niswander and R. Patterson. "Psychological Reaction to Therapeutic Abortion," *Obstetrics and Gynecology* 29:702, 1967.
7. K. Niswander, J. Singer and M. Singer. "Psychological Reaction to Therapeutic Abortion II. Objective Response," *American Journal of Obstetrics and Gynecology* 114:29, 1972.
8. R. Kretzchmar and A. Norris. "Psychiatric Implications of Therapeutic Abortion," *American Journal of Obstetrics and Gynecology* 198:368, 1967.
9. H. Brody, S. Meikle and R. Gerritse, "Therapeutic Abortions: A Prospective Study," *American Journal of Obstetrics and Gynecology* 109:347, 1971.
10. D. Ford, P. Castelnuovo-Tedesco, and K. Long. "Women Who Seek Therapeutic Abortion: A Comparison with Women Who Complete Their Pregnancies," *American Journal of Psychiatry* 129:546, 1973.
11. W.M. Hern. "Laminaria in Abortion: Use in 1368 Patients in First Trimester," *Rocky Mountain Medical Journal* 72:380, 1975.
12. J.D. Osofsky, H.J. Osofsky and R. Rajan. "Psychological Effects of Abortion: With Emphasis upon Immediate Reactions and Follow-up," in H.J. Osofsky and J.D. Osofsky (eds.), *The Abortion Experience: Psychological and Medical Impact,* New York: Harper & Row, 1973.
13. M.B. Bracken, M. Hachamovitch, and G. Grossman. "The Decision to Abortion and Psychological Sequelae," *Journal of Nervous and Mental Disease* 158:154, 1974.
14. R. Athanasiou, W. Oppel, L. Michelson, T. Unger and M. Yager. "Psychiatric Sequelae to Term Birth and Induced Early and Late Abortion: a Longitudinal Study," *Family Planning Perspectives* 5:227, 1973.
15. G. Burnell, W. Dworsky and R. Harrington. "Post-abortion Group Therapy," *American Journal of Psychiatry* 129:134, 1972.
16. S. Plattner, unpublished doctoral thesis, Psychology Department, University of Colorado, Boulder, Colorado.
17. S. Goldsmith, M.O. Gabrielson, V. Mathews and L. Potts. "Teenagers, Sex and Contraception," *Family Planning Perspectives* 4:32, 1972.
18. J.J. Kane and P.A. Lachenbrauch. "Adolescent Pregnancy: Aborters vs. Nonaborters," *American Journal of Orthospsychiatry* 43:796, 1973.
19. L. Potts. "Counseling Women with Unwanted Pregnancies," Paper presented at Annual Meeting of Planned Parenthood/World Population, San Francisco, 1971.
20. H. Forssman and I. Thuwe. "One Hundred and Twenty Children Born after Application for Therapeutic Abortion Refused," *Acta Psychiatrica Scandinavia* 42:71, 1966.
21. K. Hook. "Refused Abortion," *Acta Psychiatrica Scandinavia* Suppl. 168, 39:1, 1963.

The Social Context of Abortion

Nettie Fisher, M.S.W.

I am in the process of completing my dissertation on aspects of
abortion.[1] I did a comparative study of two public hospitals, Colorado
General and Denver General Hospital (DGH), which have very different
counseling service delivery systems. DGH has a group information
service. The doctor explains the procedure, the Planned Parenthood
nurse talks about contraceptives, and the social worker indicates that she
is available. They explain to the younger girls that they need parental
consent and to the married women that they need their husbands'
consent. The patients at Colorado General had individual problem
counseling prior to any decision to actually have an abortion. It is
interesting that at DGH my interviews ranged anywhere from an hour and
a half to two and a half hours, as compared to 35 minutes to 45 minutes
at Colorado General. Some of the difference reflects the needs
expressed by one girl: "I needed someone to talk to, to understand me,
understand my particular situation and why I'm doing this."

Since both hospitals make concerted efforts to serve low income
people, my sample has the distinction of being half Catholic and half
minority, making it less representative of the general population. It does,
however, contradict those who believe that people who have moral and
religious conflicts automatically screen themselves out of this alternative.
The majority of the people that I saw were in some conflict. It might
involve differences in opinion between the male partner and the woman,
parental pressure to have or not to have an abortion and the degree to
which there was personal support. Most of the people that I interviewed
came from multiproblem families. For example, one 15-year-old young
lady decided to have an abortion because her 13-year-old sister had
a baby two months ago, her 14-year-old sister had one a month prior
to this, and she felt that otherwise she could not finish school. She was
very opposed to abortion, and she was Spanish-American and Catholic.
Yet she felt that there was no other alternative for her. She was also from
a family of 17 children in which the father was absent. This is just one
example of the complexity of problems that the counselor may be called
upon to deal with when helping a person with an abortion.

Often the abortion is just a complicating factor in a complicated life.
This makes the counselor's role critical. Study participants at Colorado
General who had had counseling, identified the counselor as the most

135

significant person during the abortion. Patients at Denver General identified a variety of personnel in terms of importance. However, they consistently noted the lack of counseling services. Patients expressed this need in different ways. "I need to dump on someone." "I needed someone to help me make my decision." A counselor may not help women make that decision but can help them feel comfortable with the decision they do make. This was the thread which ran through every interview. Some said, "Well, I don't really feel like I have real bad problems but it's good to talk to someone. It's good to know that others are in the same bind. Misery loves company." These were the attitudes of the patients who had been in the group experience.

Myths about abortion were very prevalent among the lower socioeconomic groups. Many of the interviewed women had tried some type of medicinal method of aborting themselves—castor oil, turpentine, quinine, and cold tablets which they took in massive doses. There were several people who did not even realize that abortions were legal. This says something about our information delivery systems, especially for lower socioeconomic groups.

Many people have unfortunately encouraged women to have an abortion because of their own pro-abortion attitudes. This should be avoided as much as anti-abortion attitudes. Counselors can get very concerned and maternalistic, expecially with the teenage girls. A 13-year-old comes in and we think, "My God, what would she do with a baby? She's a baby herself." Instead of dealing with the fact that she's having an unwanted or an undesired pregnancy, helping her understand the alternatives and come to a decision, we unconsciously move them in the direction of abortion.

Psychiatric Aspects

Helen Gerash, M.D.

I want to make sure that everyone understands that the examples given of post-abortion problems and complications are limited to about two to five percent of all abortions. When one considers the emotional and physical trauma abortion involves for most women and the low incidence of serious post-abortion effects, one wonders what is unique about abortion as a surgical procedure. It is a medical invasion of the body. Back in 1973, there were a few studies which were saying there are perhaps 10 percent of abortion patients who have some significant, serious, or moderate adjustment difficulty. Even assuming 10 percent, a higher incidence of psychological reactions is seen in almost any kind of surgery. Abortion patients have inner resources that are fantastic. They are able to handle something that in our culture is looked upon as an extremely explosive emotional, and controversial issue. It is much more controversial than having your appendix out. Six weeks later your appendix patients are still going to be telling you a little bit about the details of what their stomach ache was like beforehand and what their stitches are still feeling like and that they still cannot go skiing and how awful that is. You really do not hear this from the majority of post-abortion women. I just want to emphasize that when we talk about the women who have problems after an abortion, we are only focusing on the tiny two to 10 percent. I am not, however, discounting their importance. Anybody who hurts is important and if there is any way of helping them it should be done.

The other panelists seem to have been working in the context of a clinic setup or a system of physicians and nurses and counseling personnel. This is in striking contrast to the private sector of medicine. In the private sector, there is an abysmal lack of counseling. There is a lack of counseling and a real isolation for the women who are "fortunate" enough to have the money to go to a private doctor, have the abortion done in a private hospital with presumably top-notch medical care. The private patients who get perhaps a bit more personal attention from their doctors are getting next to nothing as far as counseling. Family practitioners, gynecologists, and surgeons may do abortions, however, they are not sending their patients to psychiatrists, social workers, psychologists, or lay abortion counselors. There are a few who are excellent counselors and they really will take time, but I suspect their numbers are very small. One of the things that this conference may want to address itself to is the private sector and what can be done either to raise the consciousness of the doctor or to raise the consciousness of the women to really start demanding as consumers that they have somebody to whom they can talk. They need to know it really would help just to talk about it.

As a psychiatrist, I previously had to see women to help them through the red tape of getting an abortion. I think a lot of the feelings got exaggerated because these women's chances of getting an abortion were on the line. Even discounting some of the exaggeration, one of the things that I was most impressed with was that making a decision to have an abortion, even among the most liberated women, is not an easy decision. It is an agonizing decision even if they have previously decided that under no circumstances will they go through with the pregnancy at this period in their lives. This is true even for those who have used excellent contraception. They agonize over it inside. Many women feel a sense of shame in letting their friends know that they are agonizing over it.

It's important to keep this in mind in view of a recent article by Dr. Bernard Nathanson.[1] He was formerly one of the leaders in the abortion reform movement and later directed one of the largest abortion clinics in New York. Dr. Nathanson asserts that, in his experience, the women having abortions felt no sadness, only relief. It should be noted that he was primarily an administrator and perhaps did not talk to the women very much. It seems that he missed the sadness and the sorrow and the difficulty many women experience in having an abortion.

REFERENCES

1. B.N. Nathanson. "Sounding Board—Deeper Into Abortion," *New England Journal of Medicine* 291: 1189-1190, 1974.

Components of Abortion Counseling

Marlene R. Gold, M.A.

Research shows us that women obtaining abortions are not suffering many bad, long-term psychological effects. This is good and it is very encouraging, but it also leaves us with the question of why we are doing counseling. If the women who are having long-term problems had pre-existing problems there is a question of our proper role. I think there are a tremendous range of needs that abortion patients have that we really can and should be meeting. I think it is good that abortions are much more available now and are medically safer. This in itself answers some of the need. Even if a woman does not have problems after an abortion, when she needs an abortion she has a problem. Whether it is because she did not plan the pregnancy or whether she planned it and has changed her mind, she has a problem that needs a solution. The range of solutions that may be appropriate for her varies. For some, this may be a crisis among crises and this may be a time to begin to cope with them. A counselor can help with this process. She can say, "What else is going on? Is there a way that things can change for you after this?"

We discussed earlier the problem of what to call women who have had more than one abortion. Somebody suggested that if we eliminated that need we would not need a name for them. One thing we can do with counseling is to talk to women about birth control. Not all patients getting abortions are getting adequate birth control information.

No matter what we teach anybody there are going to be people who will not use contraception and sometimes contraception will fail. I do not think we are going to eliminate the need for abortion in the near future. However, we have an obligation to go overboard in making sure that patients have all the information and access that they need. It is easy to assume that birth control information is available because we know where to get it. But that is not true for everyone, and if a woman needs an abortion, there is no better time to make sure that that need is met.

Another thing that counseling can do is to reduce the fear and anxiety about abortion procedures. Dr. Gerash said people have depressions after other kinds of surgery, but I do not think there is the kind of fear and the kind of mythology about other kinds of surgery as there is about abortion. We need to speak to that before a woman can have an abortion. It may be that her decision is made and it was not a difficult decision, or even if it was a difficult decision, that it is resolved by the time she walks in and requests an abortion. Nevertheless, she may not have any concept of what exactly the abortion is medically, or what is going to happen to her physically. These things are terrifying. One thing we can do in a counseling program is to make sure that she knows what is going on. Then if she suffers the same kinds of convalescent ailments that other surgical patients do, she can anticipate them better.

It is going to take a long time to educate people adequately so that they will understand that abortions are not the ugly, back-alley things that they used to be. I see counseling as being able to meet different needs that different people will have. It helps just to have someone to talk to. A woman's friends may be so in favor of the abortion that she has not had a chance to think that it might be a sad thing for her. I suspect the doctor who did not see any sadness did not ask the patients how they were feeling, because it is often there. Just giving a woman the chance to express herself, to reconfirm her decision, or to express doubts, or to back out if she wants to, is absolutely essential for her before having the abortion. A counselor can focus on the patient and her psychological needs and her immediate physical needs. She can give a kind of attention that the nurse cannot give and that the doctor cannot give. I think that is tremendously important and I think it is missed very much when it is not available. Continuity of care is also important. If someone is talking to the woman before, during, and after the procedure, it is ideal.

Dr. Gerash brought up the problem of the private sector and doctors who do a few abortions for their private patients. It is feasible to have counseling, even on a very small scale. Counselors could be called upon to work in a doctor's office on a part-time basis. It does not need to be expensive. The other option is group counseling; this can be effective for information-giving. Individual attention to the individual problem is not possible but birth control information and information about the procedure can be communicated in a group setting. I do see counseling as absolutely essential because this is a crisis time in the woman's life. From what we heard, how well she will cope with it depends a lot on what her mental health was before. Nevertheless, I think even the most healthy woman has many needs during a pregnancy which she is considering terminating that must be met. If we are talking about caring for that woman, then we must be meeting these needs as well as the medical ones.

Discussion

Hern: I would just like to make some observations as someone who's involved in providing these services and who has been working with them for some time. I have an impression that is shared by many other people in the field that one of the most important things in the psychological outcome for the patient is whether the environment for the patient, for the woman who is having the abortion, is supportive, or whether it is judgmental or nonjudgmental. The other day I was talking with a woman who had two children and wanted to have an abortion. She loved children and she was really looking forward to having another one someday but this was a bad time for her. She said that she'd called her family gynecologist and had talked to him about having an abortion. He said, "Oh, now, why don't you come on in and we'll pick out a name for the baby." At the doctor's office when she was told the results of her pregnancy test, she started to cry. The nurse immediately started berating her about wanting to have an abortion. I think that these are the kinds of things which are very difficult for women and have to be recognized. It's an intensely personal choice and I think that individual or group counseling can be tremendously helpful to women. In fact, I really think that that is an absolutely essential part of the whole process.

A sociologist named Rosengren found that the woman's definition of whether or not the pregnancy was an illness was far more important in terms of the outcome of the pregnancy than the doctor's perception.* I think that points out the biosocial nature of pregnancy as a condition. That is why it is necessary to take into account these various factors.

The third observation I'd just like to make briefly is that, while we are most concerned with the sequelae and the psychological aspects for the woman who is having the abortion, there are a number of other people involved, one of whom is the man who helped her get pregnant. That is a very significant question which is really not much addressed by any of the literature. Also, what are the effects of providing abortion services for those who are doing it? One of the things that was mentioned earlier was that it is frequently necessary for those who work in the service to take a

---

* W.R. Rosengren. "Social Sources of Pregnancy as Illness or Normality," *Social Forces* 39:260, 1961; and "Social Instability and Attitudes Toward Pregnancy," *Social Problems,* 9:371, 1952.

break, to stop doing it for awhile, even though they may not be against abortion. This is one of the things we see in outpatient abortion also. It's a very intense emotional experience, particularly for the counselors, who really spend most of the time with the patient, but I think it's also a pretty intense experience for the doctor. This is really dependent upon how much you are involved with the patients as people. If you're working in a factory situation, such as a clinic in New York City which does 150 to 200 abortions a day, it does not lend itself to individual contact between the doctor and the patient. The doctor is much less likely to be affected by the emotional situation the patient is going through. However, if the doctor is in a situation where he or she has the opportunity to really talk to the patients, the doctor is much more likely to be emotionally involved. This becomes an emotionally exhausting experience. The closer you are to this, the more impressed you are with the kind of difficulty that patients have in going through this and the kinds of effects that they do experience afterwards. One of the real limitations of later abortion procedures is not necessarily the technology of doing the abortion, but what it does emotionally to people. This is one of the most difficult things for the doctors, the counselors, and the nurses to cope with. One of the things we have to figure out is how we help people cope with these kinds of reactions so that they can give high quality and effective personal care to the women.

Gold: One of our jobs as counselors or people working with a woman having an abortion is having to undo a lot of what's already been done to her, perhaps from the moment she found out that she was pregnant. Perhaps she had a counselor who told her what to do and here she is figuring out that this isn't what she wanted to do. Perhaps someone told her something else to do and she is now bucking that by getting an abortion. Perhaps she has been treated judgmentally or punitively by somebody along the way. A lot of what we have to do is to provide extra support and extra comfort in our settings. I think that's really crucial.

Gerash: I have a report addressing itself to the emotional reactions of abortion services personnel.* The most frequent reaction of these personnel was anxiety, depression, and periods of obsession, even for those who were not in conflict about abortion. There were reports of withdrawal from the procedure, which was discussed this morning as one of the ways of handling these problems. They have an automatic rotation for people in this service. There was sometimes some excessive drinking. The stress would overflow into what seemed to be resentment and hostility toward the patients, suggesting that they should have prevented this pregnancy. The authors attribute this to an acute identity

---

* F.J. Kane, M. Feldman, S. Jain, and M.A. Lipton. "Emotional Reactions in Abortion Services Personnel," *Archives of General Psychiatry*, 28:409, 1973.

crisis that the personnel experienced regarding their medical role and function. Nurses, doctors, counselors, all of us like to see ourselves in the role of promoting health, the quality of life, and the lengthening of life. The concept of perhaps putting an end to life has been a very threatening thing for medical personnel. One of the ways of coping with this is to help personnel look at the fact that they are enhancing the quality of life of these patients who might otherwise have to go to the back alley for abortions. The recommendations that they make include the following:

If at all possible, participation in these programs, in any phase, should be absolutely voluntary on the part of all office or clinic or hospital personnel. The program should have a strong leadership, medical or counseling, by someone who feels very strongly about abortion programs but who is also able to be extremely patient, open, and able to listen to a lot of ambivalent, negative feelings. Let the personnel ventilate without being threatened by it. They have also recommended utilization of group therapy sessions on a regular basis to let the personnel really ventilate and talk about their feelings and experiences. The third recommendation is to have all abortion patients in a separate section of the hospital away from Ob-Gyn. These women should demand from their doctors and the hospitals that they're not going to go on the Ob. ward, period. Another positive step would be to cut down outside referrals and deal only with patients that might normally go to that particular clinic or that hospital. The nurses and the doctors and the counselors tend to feel a little resentment that this woman is only seeing them one time for an abortion and that they're never going to see them again. The reason they feel resentment is that they feel isolated and they can't form a bond of health caring with that patient. The fifth recommendation is that physicians should be present to support the nursing personnel. This is badly needed in the termination phase for the second trimester procedures. The nurses are very resentful that they've got the worst part of the emotional trauma and the dirty medical work, while the doctor's at home, usually in bed sleeping. They have to handle all of their own feelings about the fetus. They have to deal with it and they have to deal with an intense emotional reaction from the patient all by themselves. The sixth recommendation is the need for the development of training programs in medical schools, social work schools, and nursing schools devoted to teaching people to handle abortions and to understand them better.

Vicki Ziegler, Women's Health Service Clinic, Colorado Springs, Colorado: We are promoting diaphragms in our clinic. We strongly support women's use of noninvasive birth control methods. We thought that we were very supportive but what we're finding is that, of course, those methods do fail and the woman is intrinsically in a punishing position. She has to come in for an abortion. She has to pay for it and she has to go through pain. She has to go through the grief you're talking about. We find ourselves in a real bind because we don't want to push pills and IUDs if we don't have to but we don't know what to do about that. We're starting a support group soon for all our diaphragm patients where possibly we might use menstrual extraction as a backup method. Immediately doctors and other people have come down on us with the assumption that women are irresponsible. We know you're going to fail occasionally with the birth control methods that we have available.

The other thing that seems to be assumed when we start talking about this new program is that women will automatically be irresponsible because we provide menstrual extraction as a backup or because they have easy access to abortion. I think it's important to make the connection that abortion is so unpleasant even for the most balanced woman that she would rarely choose that indiscriminately as a birth control method. She's exercising a fairly reasonable option in choosing abortion over putting hormones in her body every day. Having the combination of birth control with abortion has started to make a difference in terms of understanding that dilemma. We just haven't found a way out of it.

Gold: If you provide birth control information to women in the hope that they will use it and not have an unwanted pregnancy, you're in a bind because some of those methods fail. If we're talking about women being able to take care of themselves, don't they deserve all the information we can reasonably give them about all the methods of birth control?

Ziegler: Yes, and when I say that we promote diaphragms I really mean that relative to the fact that most physicians don't even talk about diaphragms. If they talk about them at all they mention them disparagingly and they don't give the women any information. We always explain the pill and we always explain the IUD, but in addition to that we explain very carefully the pros and cons of a noninvasive method like the diaphragm. Then we let the woman choose. Women will choose the IUD even when they read the consent form and it describes all the terrible things that might happen. Every day we provide pills and IUDs. We feel bad about that but it's a woman's choice.

Gerash: Most of the contraceptive methods that we have really leave something to be desired, but I am very concerned about a massive overreaction in women. They may feel extremely limited in the choice of contraceptives and feel that there's nothing they can do for themselves. That really isn't true. For example, you prescribe a diaphragm when it appears there may be problems with the pill or the IUD. More and more people in the private sector are beginning not to have such a negative attitude toward the diaphragm any more. It's a small breakthrough. If you have a patient who has had a diaphragm and has a pregnancy in spite of it, it's almost impossible to get her to use the diaphragm again. She doesn't trust it at all. That's also an overreaction. It has to be dealt with. Women must be informed about it in order to ask their doctors to monitor them when they are taking the pill so that they're not feeling that this pill is

144

going to do all these terrible mysterious things and they're not going to know it until they have a blood clot. They can go in for a couple of routine blood tests every six months or every year to see how their clotting mechanisms are working. They can pick up a blood pressure kit themselves and take their own blood pressure once a month.

DeDe Apple, Planned Parenthood, Kansas City, Missouri: It seems to me that there are two types of counseling needs that women have. One is informational and the other is support. The clinic where I counsel does both in groups. The object of the group session is not for me, the counselor, to be everything to everyone in the group, but for the group to be support for itself. By the time that group counseling session is finished, I could vanish into the thin air and they could sail through. I am with each patient during her procedure. It's helpful to the patient and it's helpful to me. I grieve and I cry and I laugh and I'm just as much a part of that group as everyone who's in there waiting to have an abortion, but they're wonderful for each other. They're not isolated. They have support. If they've been abandoned by the man, they have women who are willing to help them and to carry them through that moment of crisis. We have patients who get together after meeting for the first time in the group, months later, to have a good time. They share something. I share something and I think that is really important for everyone to consider as a counseling method. Group counseling is not simply for information to go from me to them but allows them to share the information that most women do have. If you get four women in a group together you'd be amazed to find out how much information they have available—not only birth control but about the abortion procedure itself. My work used to be a lot harder when I tried to do everything for everyone in the group, now that we've worked out methods of having the group facilitate itself, we've had a lot more success with patients going through a procedure and feeling good afterwards.

Brown: There was a study done recently that showed that of 61 women, all but one ovulated within five weeks after the abortion.* The average number of days was 22 and the earliest was 10 days post-abortion. There have been some studies which have shown that actual provision of contraceptive services is really the key in post-abortion contraceptive efficiency, more so than contraceptive counseling. I personally am committed to all forms of counseling surrounding the abortion, both contraceptive and personal, but where do you think the actual provision of followup birth control services fits? I know it's not always possible but I think it's mandatory.

Gold: I think providing birth control is absolutely essential as an

---

* E.F. Boyd and E.G. Homstrom. "Ovulation Following Therapeutic Abortion," *American Journal of Obstetrics and Gynecology,* 113:469, 1972.

integral part of an abortion service. The woman should leave the clinic or the hospital hopefully having made a decision of what form of birth control she's going to use immediately and having been provided with whatever she needs in order to do that. She should be seen medically for followup anyway and she can be told she can get an IUD at that time. She needs to have a packet of pills in her hand and a prescription or she needs to be told how soon she can get fitted for a diaphragm. All that needs to be done right at the time of the abortion.

Schneider: We were scandalized in our study two years ago to find that over two-thirds of the girls were not using contraception after six weeks when they had been told by their physicians to have contraception after the six week checkup.

Linda Weber, Boulder Valley Clinic, Boulder, Colorado: It may be less traumatic psychologically for most women to have an abortion rather than give a child up for adoption, but there are individual cases when it would be better for a girl to give a child up for adoption. She would just do better psychologically because of the way she feels about abortion and because of her background.

We recently did some data collection from patient responses about the use of birth control. From a sample of about 500 patients, about 72 percent of the patients coming for abortions had used some form of birth control sometime in their lives. It proves that it's not only a lack of knowledge and a lack of information about birth control. The issues are much, much deeper. We have to understand that what we are doing is sexual counseling and that is very specialized. It takes some training, and it requires a certain attitude on the part of people doing that kind of counseling. It's important that there be a certain warmth and medical understanding but also a willingness to share personal history. The counselor should be willing, under most circumstances, to share her personal history. It helps if you have some people on the staff who've had abortions themselves. It helps the understanding for the rest of the staff. Ambivalence is built into pregnancy as a whole, whether it's planned, unplanned, unwanted, or whatever. Counseling is absolutely essential to guarantee that a woman is going to come out of the experience of pregnancy feeling okay about herself, feeling that she has some understanding of what happened to her. I feel this is true not only for unwanted pregnancy but for full-term pregnancy. It would be very important to institute a much more widespread counseling service for women.

Sandra Bagley, Utah Women's Clinic, Salt Lake City, Utah: I just wanted to make one comment concerning the type of counseling that's being done. We are combining techniques. We are using both individual and group counseling and we find that works well.

146

Education and Information

Defining the Problem

Sam Downing, M.D.

The problem that we have with abortion today is twofold. One, there are too many stockholders trying to make decisions for the player who is "on the field." Second, abortion is not the problem; pregnancy is the problem. The people who are involved with abortion, when it touches their life, view it completely differently from people who are standing around on the outskirts of the problem looking in, and who are involved because they want to be, not because it really has touched their life. People who are not involved have a tendency to view abortion as the problem. The woman who is involved with the pregnancy views it completely differently.

The problem begins with conception. There are many responsible people who get pregnant because birth control fails, people who are doing the best they can to practice responsibility in terms of birth control. Other women become pregnant for a variety of reasons. It may be a 14-year-old girl, who lives in a wretched home and who goes to bed with her boyfriend because she hopes secretly that he will carry her off if she gets pregnant and get her out of that environment, or it may be a 16-year-old girl who is at the bottom rung of the family, who has never done a single thing in her life that gave her confidence and is hoping to carry through a pregnancy and maybe give herself some confidence, or she may be hoping to get admitted to a trade or professional school so that her folks will show her some respect. The woman may be a professional person, a mother who has three or four children at home and is taking her pills just as regular as a clock, or a girl who is raped, or a woman who goes in for dental X-rays or thyroid scans when she is only two weeks pregnant, too early to diagnose.

Pregnancy is great, but it is not so great if you're 15 years old and in high school. A lot of high schools, at least until recently, would ask pregnant students to drop out of school on the pretext that they might trip and fall down the steps, which would put the school in legal jeopardy. For a pregnant teenager, the problems can be enormous. What is a girl going to do for work if she is pregnant? What is she going to do for schooling and education? Who is going to pay the doctor bills for the nine months of pregnancy? The doctor bills for the labor and delivery now in Denver are somewhere between $1100 and $1500 for private patients, or $300 to $500 at Denver General or Colorado General public hospitals. Many of the girls know that their parents may stand behind them, but not financially.

They go through pregnancy knowing that nobody is going to take them to the junior prom, and maybe they have dropped out of school. Maybe their parents have decided to leave their small rural society town because of the stigma of a daughter in the family with an unwanted or an illegitimate pregnancy.

Then comes the labor and delivery, where, although there are millions of women walking by on the street who have gone through it, there is still the knowledge of putting one's life on the line. It takes a person about four minutes to bleed to death if nobody is attending her. Toxemia can end in convulsions, stroke, and kidney failure. Another possible problem is overwhelming infection within the first week of delivery. In the hospital it's called a "superinfection." Antibiotics are given in 80 to 100 times the dose normally given for an infection, and the patient still may die. The patient knows that she is putting her life on the line. She gets through the labor and delivery, possibly devoid of any moral and emotional support depending on her circumstances, depending on whether or not the hospital allows just husbands in the delivery room or allows fathers in. There's a big difference in today's society.

Then there is the problem of the unwanted child. I am sure that as you grew up your parents yelled at you and disciplined you from time to time. I know my father did. I am not talking about this kind of temporarily unwanted child, but about the child that shows up at age eight in school with gloves covering the cigarette burns on his hands because he is embarrassed the other children will see them. Eight is a very poignant age. Eight is going to the zoo and birthday parties and swings and rings and looking at the world around you. I am talking about all the battered children. Now, starting with conception, following through the pregnancy and the labor and delivery, the result may be an unwanted child. Let us draw a line down to the bottom of the blackboard with an arrow and write 18 down here. Eighteen years. The mother in the pregnancy has an 18-year, long-term debt which she may well consider an 18-year albatross hanging around her neck, especially if she is young, if she is in college, if she is a teenager, or if she is 35 or 40 years old and has raised a family. It is the fact of the 18 years, until it is possible to pat them on the fanny and pitch them out of the nest that I think is the problem for many of my patients.

The other problem is that people who are not involved in looking at the scope of this social problem only see the word "abortion." I would suggest to all of us that abortion itself is really a very small part of the problem. If we can think in terms of the larger problem, then maybe our thinking will be more clear.

I therefore do not think abortion is the problem because it is the pregnancy that is the problem. No one does nothing if they are pregnant. They are either going to carry it or abort it or attempt to abort it. How they carry it, grudgingly, begrudgingly, or happily, the circumstances differ. The question is not abortion or no abortion; the question is abortion or compulsory pregnancy.

150

Cross-Cultural Considerations

Jessica Luna

I am going to speak from an ethnic point of view and share with you some of my concerns about the abortion movement. I have been involved at different levels in my community concerning the lack of participation of Chicanos in many areas. I do not represent every Chicana, as you do not represent every Anglo woman in your community. These are my own opinions.

One of the problems concerning abortion is the lack of research examining impacts on different ethnic groups. Most of the data that have been collected are not pure; they usually mix data on various minorities and the poor. This assumes that all Chicanas or blacks are poor. Just as you have in your group different levels, we also have different levels. There are three things I want you to incorporate into your program. First, I want the inclusion of the Chicana in the abortion service. Staff are not aware of the cultural differences. Many think that Chicanas and Chicanos are not American, that they all come from Mexico. They also think that they are all on welfare, that they are not taxpayers contributing to the services that you are providing. You are leaving them out of the decisions that you are making. Therefore, I want these arrogant and ignorant attitudes concerning the Chicana changed in the abortion movement at every level. Just as with Anglo women, there are different attitudes toward abortion. We also have different beliefs, with the added cultural differences.

Chicanos also must contend with triple jeopardy. We have to deal with the Church, which plays a very strong part in family life. Most Chicanas suffer from the blessed Virgin Mary syndrome. They help perpetuate this idea so they can use it for power to control some of the things that happen within the family unit. This culture is very male-dominated, and we have to use any means we can to have equal rights. However, Chicanos do have some of the same attitudes that you have concerning women's issues. There are those who believe that abortion is an alternative.

We have had to play a very subservient role within our culture. We also have to deal with the local witch doctor, who is a very respected individual in our community. He's called the *curandero*. The midwife is usually in charge of giving abortions, sprinkled with fear. Therefore the Chicana needs different kinds of services, more followup, more research on the effects on Chicanas of abortion, more Chicanas on the staff, and staff training concerning cultural differences.

There is another part of the Chicano movement which is not so willing to come and speak before a group like you, who are disenchanted with some of the programs in the community. They are trying another approach. A lot of your programs are federally funded and state funded. Having dealt with federally funded programs, I know that some of the things that I am requesting are part of program guidelines, and some of you have not been following them. There are Chicanos who are also aware of this and who may be tapping at your door, not asking but demanding that these changes take place immediately.

I am also a Chicana feminist who has a different point of view on education concerning abortion. I have five sons between the ages of 16 and 21 and one daughter. I am very concerned with the lack of education being given to young men about abortion. One thing that gives me a feeling of terror is that some feminists say all men are monsters. On behalf of the mothers and the sons, I feel some of the new laws and ideas concerning rape, abortion, and the feminist movement, are not taking cultural differences into consideration.

I would like to leave you with the hope that you take into consideration my recommendations about including Chicanos and Chicanas at every level of your decision-making in the abortion movement. I think that we comprise a lot of the people that you work with and a lot of the statistics that you are getting. Yet many of you do not understand the changes that are taking place in our culture.

Sex Education in Public Schools

Don Shaw

My responsibility in the Jefferson County Schools, the largest system in the state, is sex education for 80,000 students. Any time one is charged with sex education for 80,000 students, it has to be exciting.

Looking at national statistics, about 47 percent of graduating seniors, 23 percent of eighth graders, and about 9 percent of sixth graders have had intercourse. In our schools the figures are 46.6 percent of our graduating seniors, about 20 to 22 percent of our eighth graders, and between six and nine percent of our sixth graders. I am glad to report that we are average in Jefferson County. The illegitimacy, pregnancy, and venereal disease rates are not average. We have low illegitimacy, pregnancy, and venereal disease rates. We have the lowest illegitimacy rate in the state of Colorado and a very low venereal disease rate. We gave a staff of teachers in another school system a test about a venereal disease and our eighth graders outscored them significantly. That does not mean that they will not get VD, but I think they have a better chance. This is a question we are going to have to try to look at and assess.

The first problem that we run into is the gap between the parent and the teacher and the child. The parent has a tendency to tell his children something two years after they already know it. That is the parent who is going to talk to the child at all. We have people saying, "Let's let religion do it." Twenty-seven percent of our children report that they have been in church once in the last year. That is not the place for education. Sixty percent of the children in an average community will not be living with their original two parents when they leave high school. The divorce rate is running around 40 percent in some communities. When people say, "Let somebody else do it," you have to look at the reality of who else is there to assume responsibility.

We are also beginning to realize that sex education starts before the child ever enters school and most of what we do is to unteach what has been taught. We teach remedial sex education almost all the way through school. We have to start the remedial sex education with the teachers. You cannot expect a teacher to teach something that they do not know. Leonardo Buscaglia says you teach what you are, and you teach what you know. So we have a long, hard process trying to educate and and work with teachers.

In 1967 when we decided that we should teach sex education, our

153

philosophy was that young children will be parents, some within four years, so we have to start some place. We start with the young children. We would like to have them coming out of our school system knowing how a family should operate, having facts and statistics instead of fear. One of the biggest problems we see in many of our young children is that they honestly saw abortion as some kind of hacking, cutting, and bleeding. They had no concept of what abortion really was.

A good education gives the child the best information available on both sides of any subject. It is hard for some teachers to give the other side. Even for premarital intercourse, we have our teachers sit down and list all the advantages of having premarital intercourse. Some of them will not even pick up a pencil because they do not want to list them or think about them. That is not the role of the educator. The role of the educator is to teach facts on both sides of any subject.

If we have 22 percent of our junior high school students having intercourse, maybe abortion and VD should be taught before senior high school. Yet when you begin to deal with these issues it gets very complicated. In most cases we do not get a chance to deal with our 13- to 14-year-old girls who do get pregnant in any kind of counseling situation. Most young girls who are 12 to 14, honestly do not accept pregnancy until the baby kicks them in the stomach. Then it is often too late. Most girls that young will not really accept the pregnancy. They have a lot of fears. Most girls from 14 to 16 will not accept that it is theirs. They say, "It's his, not mine." Our 17-, 18- and 19-year-old girls have a tendency to force somebody else to do something with their pregnancy.

There is a great difference between teaching about abortion and teaching abortion. A school system should teach the facts about abortion. The philosophy of abortion is a different thing and has to be handled in a different way. It is also important to understand the techniques of teaching. We have a lot of teachers who say, "You just tell me what to say and I'll say it." Teachers play games just like little children. The only difference is that you can walk in with little children and say, "Hey, I got a new game with new rules." They say, "What is it? Let's play." We walk in with teachers and say, "Hey, we got a new game, new rules." And they say, "Don't want to play your game. I like my game and I like my rules."

It is really amazing when you try to get 12 to 14 teachers to deal with their own sexuality. They are going to teach what they are. We take 12 to 15 teachers, two hours a week, for two years, trying to teach them how to do inservice training of teachers. We have had about 42 finish the two-year program and we only have seven who can walk in, get teachers to deal with their own sexuality for a 20-week period and not get thrown out. Our biggest problem in teaching is that we have been doing inservice training of teachers for seven years, but we still have a long way to go, while the students still tend to be ahead of the teacher. We cannot quite keep up with them.

Our students are overexposed to sex education. I laugh at any parent who says, "I don't want my child exposed." When you consider the exposure to ideas and concepts from TV, from advertising, from books, shows, and music we are facing students with enormous exposure already. Another important point is that because of this exposure and knowledge, my boy and girl in the eighth and ninth grades make more decisions in one week than my dad made in his lifetime. To learn to make decisions, you do not read about it in a book and make the decision. You have to have the responsibility and education to make decisions. And the education that you get had better include the right facts or poor decisions will result.

The Ethnic Perspective

Mary Bennet Scharf

In my experience in a special counseling program dealing with problems of integrated schools, we noticed that students come with problems unrelated to whether they were black or white. Many of these were in the area of sex education. I found myself shocked to find 12-year-old girls pregnant. I found that many had gained some information from books but there was still a lot of misinformation, especially about sex. I heard time and time again, "I thought I wouldn't get pregnant the first time. I thought I wouldn't get pregnant if it was during my period." Many thought that abortion was still a kind of cloak and dagger thing, that it was a bloody kind of procedure.

Information geared to young people about alternatives to pregnancy is almost nonexistent. The Denver public schools are not quite as advanced as those in Jefferson County. They probably are statistically matched, but Denver schools do not have a real sex education program. In some cases, the programs are started by the school nurse or a bold science or social studies teacher, but they always require parent permission. The teachers teach with whatever biases they might have.

I would also like to touch on some of the problems of abortion with ethnic groups. Abortion is viewed quite differently by many black women. Abortion is equated, in the minds of many black women, with murder and genocide. Certainly, we have reason to fear abortion and, in some cases, even contraception or family planning. Many of you have heard of the tales of forced sterilization among welfare mothers. Other women have been put in this position. A lot of black women would not consider abortion for religious reasons. We do not have the Catholic church, but we have the Baptist church, which is quite an influence on our lives. The concept that abortion is genocide is reinforced by many black brothers who feel that we must build up a black nation. This requires children, and the more children the better. We should not worry about how they are fed and clothed. This is what we need for our own self-determination. Those of you who are counseling in clinics must consider this aspect of our culture. It is also important to understand the things that happened to black women in slavery. Children were taken from them, and children are still very precious. Thirteen-year-old pregnant black women will still very seldom have abortions. They are more likely to find a mother or grandmother to take care of that child. For many young black women, having a child brings a sense of self-esteem and is viewed as evidence that she is a woman.

Discussion

Robert McCoy, Midwest Health Center for Women, Minneapolis, Minnesota: I have two questions for Mr. Shaw. The first one is: Are you able to provide the students in your school system with information as to where they can obtain family planning services? The second question is: How do you deal with our compulsory pregnancy friends who want to bring slide shows into the public schools when asked to put on presentations about abortion?

Shaw: We have problems with both of those. Our counselors and our teachers have to tell a child where to go and how to get there. They do not have to take them. We have the same responsibility with venereal disease and contraception. We have contraception kits available with all of our counselors from the sixth grade on up. If a kid walks in and says I want to see a condom, they can see a condom. It's not presented along with venereal disease information but in teaching about responsible sexual behavior. We have all that available after the sixth grade.

We have the "Right-to-Life" in our schools. It's taped and we have people there—I suppose it's a little bit more selective. We talk to our kids before they come in and they hear both sides. The senior high school students in the Marriage and the Family course are usually exposed to both sides and they have the ability to judge and think and listen. At the junior high level, we deal much more with discussions of their feelings than with information.

Downing: I'd like to comment on the slide shows. I've been involved with this at the high school and the college level. It's really kind of a psychic experience for me to go out and sit in the back of a room, because I can pick out which kids are going to faint. I don't have any medals for life saving but I've caught two kids before they hit the concrete floor with their heads during the show. If I have experienced that, I feel sure that the kids have experienced that. They know. There are some poignant questions that can be asked. To debate this topic with those showing the slides one only has to ask a series of questions that are related to the relative non-involvement of the "Right-to-Life" people. Questions like, "If this whole social problem is here what do you have to offer me during my pregnancy? What do you have to offer me during my labor and delivery, financially or emotionally? How are you going to help me solve the problem of my unwanted or abused child? What will you offer me for 18 years while the problem hangs around my neck?" That's the first question. The second question is: "Oh, well, now let's see, you're a housewife from Minneapolis, or you're a lawyer from Decatur. Do you counsel extensively on abortion? Well, of course not. Have you ever seen an abortion? Of course not. Do you go into the hospitals and do them? No. Have you discussed the sequelae, the complications, if even there really are some, with five hundred or a thousand people who've had them? Have you followed these people up for the next six months to six years to see how their life is going?" All you have to do is drop the question mark and I think the problem is solved.

Sue Ellen Alinshouse, Planned Parenthood, Fort Collins, Colorado: Could you speak to the illegality or legality of sex education in the state of Colorado?

Scharf: A principal said to me, "You don't worry about your job, do you?" And I said, "No, if I worry about my job, I'll make poor decisions." I think a lot of educators at the higher level worry about their jobs and it forces them to make poor decisions.

Even if it's illegal, I'd have to go to the courts and I would ask one question. When information is given in the classroom, I ask the parents, "Is it the truth?" If it's the truth, then I must say, "What do you want us to do, lie?" If the child asks the question, I think you have to say, "I didn't ask the question; the child did." There's one way to set up curiosity. Anytime the childs asks a question and you don't give him an answer, you cause curiosity. If you lie to him you create curiosity. We have no choice. We have to tell the truth.

I think we can interpret the law either way, but the law to me says very strongly we must teach them about drugs. It doesn't say how, when, or how much. We must provide contraception. It doesn't say at what age, how much, and we cannot tell unless that child gives us written permis- must provide venereal disease information and tell the child where to go for help. Even if the child is six years old, we can't tell unless that child gives us written permission. ⌣

That is also true of doctors. We were giving our program to the Clear Creek Medical Society in Jefferson County last month. We were horrified when we heard a doctor say, "By God, if somebody gets VD, they deserve it and I'm not treating them."

Downing: My dad told me when I graduated from medical school to just remember that the conferring of an M.D. degree does not guarantee common sense.

Mark Scott, Cherry Creek High School, Denver, Colorado: Just realizing how little we know about sex and how much there is to gain from knowledge of it, how would one go about implementing a program as you have done in the Jefferson County schools?

Shaw: I think it has to come from parents. We had parents really push ours. You have to have a parent who is very verbal. I think you have to have some people at the administrative level because you can be blocked so quickly it's scary. I think you have to have some kids who are honest.

We spent two years preparing our public field study. We had 70 meetings. We probably talked to over 18,000 people. Some of those

160

meetings went until three in the morning. Then it takes that one or two people to say, "We're going to field study it; we're going to watch it." We have to get a trust factor. More than that, it was four or five really honest students who stayed at those meetings. It takes a good parental group. It takes a group of students who will be honest with adults and say, "Hey, here's what we're doing. This is what's going on and this is what we're watching on TV, so don't kid us." It finally comes down to the administrative people who have to say, "It's good, we have to do it." It took us two years to get ready to do the field study, and then three more years in the field and pilot study. We started in 1965 and we had it into our schools in 1970, so it took us five years, and 1975 is the first year that we really had it in most of the schools. It took us almost 10 years in total. Then you have to have somebody like me who likes to fight. It's like refereeing. If you don't like it and you're scared to death, it would make you sick. I like it. I like to argue.

Downing: I'd like to just suggest some other things that can be done. A parent doesn't necessarily have to push sex education to the point where it becomes imposing on their neighbors, their friends, or the community at large. They can communicate with teachers by mail or by the phone. As a physician I was impressed in the first few years of my practice with how many problems I was poorly prepared to deal with when I got out of high school. Geometry certainly doesn't help me with deciding whether or not I should have a vasectomy at age 42. So I developed this "big six." We do our kids a disservice by not sharing these with them again before we pat them on the fanny and get them out into the world. The big six are: marriage and divorce (just the pros and cons), labor and delivery and pregnancy, birth control, sterilization, abortion, and euthanasia. There's no reason why any parent or any student cannot simply say, "I recognize these items as problems in dealing with daily living. When will you teach me about these before you turn me loose?"

Economic and Health Insurance Aspects of Abortion

Introduction

Jean Dubofsky

In this state, the problem is no longer obtaining an abortion as much as it is paying for it. The financing questions often never get raised in the legal context. As a practical matter, paying for an abortion may be a very real barrier to obtaining one. Consequently, this panel will concentrate on the economic and health insurance aspects of abortion.

The South Dakota Medicaid Experience

H. Benjamin Munson, M.D.

Welfare women everywhere, and particularly welfare women in South Dakota, have always had a hard time getting money to have an abortion. In the days before the U.S. Supreme Court decision of 1973, I can recall performing abortions for women who could not pay. Then, as now, there were some women who openly declared they could not pay. I either did their abortions free or charged them a reduced fee and asked them to pay when they could. There were those who would promise to pay soon but never did. Others wrote bouncy rubber checks. There were some who wrote checks and then had payment stopped before I could cash them. In all, most people did, in fact, pay what was charged.

In January of 1973, when the U.S. Supreme Court handed down its decision, we thought that the high court action had settled that whole question. It was soon apparent that while state interference with abortion would now be forbidden by that great decision, nevertheless the matter of whether the state must actively finance abortion for welfare women had indeed not been settled at all. We, the free choice advocates, tried to get faithful ones rallied for a confrontation at the State Capitol Building with the State Board of Social Services in February or March of 1973. That Board had announced a public meeting at which they would hear and discuss the issue of whether to pay for welfare abortions. It seemed to me that the Board of Social Services had a friendly attitude toward me. My impression in talking with their lawyers was that they would probably soon begin seeing the logic of it all and make the decision to pay for abortions as part of pregnancy care. On the day of the public meeting we were greatly outnumbered at the Capitol Building's meeting room by the angry opposition. The "Right-to-Lifers" outnumbered us two or three to one. The news media reported that those people antagonistic to free abortion for welfare patients definitely outspoke and outweighed those in favor of state funding. The Board of Social Services took the stand that "the people" had demonstrated their general opposition to having to pay taxes to support welfare abortions. The Board issued a statement that no welfare abortion would be paid for unless it could be shown that it was "medically necessary" or "therapeutic."

It took our side about a year to bring a Jane Doe case to assault the Board of Social Services' no-pay policy. The Jane Doe project first entailed sizing up each abortion applicant as a possible Jane Doe. We eventually found our courageous welfare woman, who, in spite of her precarious circumstances, declared that she was willing to be the spearhead. I hope you can appreciate the courage and the audacity that it takes for a welfare woman to bring a lawsuit against the source of the checks that are keeping her alive.

On April 14, 1974 she brought suit against the State Board of Social Services for its refusal to allow her to have equal privacy and equal protection as provided by the 14th Amendment. She also contended that the Board's policy was illegal, according to the Title XIX provisions of the Social Security Act. The case had hardly been news very long when an advertisement appeared in the paper that said: "Dear Jane Doe: We wonder, Jane, if you know that here in Rapid City, South Dakota, there is a group of volunteers on call 24 hours a day, 7 days a week, offering their oving concern for women such as you. These volunteers care about you, and the light you are carrying. They believe in you and your child. They believe that this child should have the same opportunity to live his life as you and we have. To laugh, to cry, to use the potential he was instilled with at the moment of conception." It was signed, "Lovingly, the Volunteers, Birthright of Rapid City."

The Federal District judge scheduled to hear the case declined to deal with it. He said he did not have jurisdiction, and he referred it to a three judge Circuit Court which convened that summer. The three judge federal court decided on February 24, 1974 that South Dakota's no-pay policy did indeed violate the equal protection provisions of the 14th Amendment. They directed that Jane Doe's abortion be paid for under Medicaid. The State of South Dakota appealed that decision to the U.S. Supreme Court. We waited for the answer from the U.S. Supreme Court. We waited five months until March of 1975. The U.S. Supreme Court sent the case back to the District Court, vacating or nullifying the Circuit Court's decision. It directed the District Court to reexamine the case and to determine first whether the South Dakota State Board of Social Services had specifically broken any federal or state law by establishing its no-pay policy on welfare abortions. For instance, did such a state policy violate the provisions of Title XIX Medicaid statutes? The three judge court was told, in effect, that its decision about constitutionality was vacated and nullified. The Supreme Court told the District Court it had to first find out whether or not the Board's policy broke a State or Federal law before the constitutionality of the policy could be examined.

The U.S. District Court re-examined and re-evaluated and we got a new District Court decision in September, 1975. It was a good decision for us holding that South Dakota Board's policy of disbursing money for full-term obstetrical care and the performance of so-called therapeutic abortions had established the principle that pregnancy is a condition requiring medical care. The State's Board could not, therefore, decline to finance a nontherapeutic abortion without violating the requirements of Title XIX. The District Court went on to restate that the Board's no-pay policy was unconstitutional. The District Court then enjoined the state court from continuing its no-pay policy for therapeutic abortions. Our supple and formidable adversaries again appealed to the U.S. Supreme Court.

Again we wait. We are aware of that old adage that justice too long delayed is justice denied. We do hope for the ice to thaw this coming spring.

Meanwhile, how has the state's no-pay policy affected the availability of abortions to the indigent? I have always had the policy of never turning any patient away for lack of money, but at my office, my two assistants and I have developed certain patterns of reaction, patterns of hesitancy and inquiry when a patient says she does not have money to pay. If Title XIX would underwrite all payments, we would have no hesitancy to schedule an abortion for the welfare patient. As it is, we do sometimes hesitate. Here's a sample conversation. The patient may say, "I'm on welfare and I heard that Title XIX would pay for abortion." We say, "That's not true. Title XIX has never paid for any abortion." And she says, "How much does an abortion cost?" We say, "$125 if it's early. But if it's late it could cost as much as $300. We would expect you to try to pay for it. We will, however, send in a claim to the welfare office and if they ever do pay, we will reimburse you." She may say, "I don't have that much. I can't pay it." We will say, "Well, can you manage at least a third of it as a down payment? We could then try to make arrangements with you for the balance of the payment in installments. We do ask that you make an effort but you will not be turned away." I'm not really sure how often that last phrase gets in there. It's been a policy of mine not to turn people away, but I have some misgivings about that conversation. Especially when I see that about 75 or 80 people out of 500 scheduled failed to make it in the front door during November, December and January. That is one failed appointment out of six or seven appointments scheduled. Of course, if the patient is on the schedule for that day and says during her office interview that she has no money for a down payment, she is asked to please have a talk with me first before she is taken to the examining room. In the conversation, I ask her to make some sort of promise to try to pay and then to sign that promise before resuming her place in the waiting room. We are considering why one person out of six or seven fails to materialize. I will concede that that original talk might discourage some people, but there are in fact quite a few other reasons why some patients just do not come in. These include deciding to continue the pregnancy (if you only knew the extent of some of the patients' ambivalent feelings about whether they want an abortion); fear of the unknown; forgetting the appointment; confusion about the date, the place and the hour; and transportation problems. For instance, people come to my abortion service from three or four hundred miles away, and sometimes farther. There are snowstorms that occur, stranding cars and grounding planes. In addition, the number of scheduled people who fail to come in is close to the same percentage as for my regular Ob-Gyn practice.

I have tried to make my office and my service available to everybody, but it may well be that my personnel's exasperation with certain patients' seeming lack of responsibility and our ongoing vexation with the State Board of Social Services sometimes shows. It quite possibly is felt in a negative way by certain patients who have felt embarrassed when they made their call of inquiry.

We have tried to make it clear that we personally are optimistic over the eventual outcome of our lawsuit, but we are a bit irritated over the long wait and the uncertainty of our potential payments. My lawyer friend in the local legal aid society said that this case is unique among those cases on the docket before the United States Supreme Court. It's the only case, he said, that is dealing with this particular point of law. No other cases now before the high court could dispose of this issue. "This is the one," he says.*

So in South Dakota, we are waiting. I should say one earthshaking event that occurred while I was waiting is that I turned into a sexagenarian. I do hope that we will have our case decided before the rest of you join me in that category.

---

* The constitutional and statutory issues are expected to be decided by the U.S. Supreme Court in its forthcoming rulings on *Roe* v. *Norton* from Connecticut and *Doe* v. *Beal* from Pennsylvania.

Actuarial Considerations in Insurance Payment for Abortion

John Vance

While playing a game of golf here recently, I missed a shot, as I frequently do. I remarked to a friend with whom I was playing that one of the nice things about the game of golf was that it was a difficult game to master and it was a great humbling experience. My friend challenged my understanding of the word humble. He went on to explain that he was reared a Roman Catholic in a Republican family that resided in Arkansas. He said that was an ongoing humbling experience, the likes of which I would never understand. Maybe today will give me a little insight into the trials my friend faced because I am a Catholic. I am not sure that my views relate to the Catholics for Free Choice, but that is not necessary because even Catholics are required to answer only to their own dictates of conscience. Since we are a number of individuals, we can have a number of different positions.

I am not going to discuss with you the differences in the dictates of conscience except to the extent that such differences do affect the economic and insurance aspects of abortion. Many years ago when I sold Blue Cross and Blue Shield, the family rate then, if you can believe this, was $3 a month. I related that $3 a month charge to a daily charge of ten cents; then I likened the cost to the cost of a cigarette habit. No matter how tight a man's budget was, he was willing to admit that protecting his family for health care costs was more important than smoking. Even though that was a corny pitch, it seemed to work and many enrolled in Blue Cross and Blue Shield. Of course, they kept on smoking and somehow stretched their budgets to accommodate both health coverage and the smoking habit.

Today if I were going to compare the cost of Blue Cross and Blue Shield with some family expenditure I would have to liken it to the house payment. I do not really say that apologetically. I say it more to emphasize the improved health care available today over that which was available just a few short years ago. The improvement in health care today over yesterday is really more dramatic than the improvement of the Ford car we can buy today over the first Ford that Henry ever produced You can not compare today's cost for such things as restoring hearing, eyesight, or heart function with the cost of restoring those functions yesterday. Yesterday, they were not possible. Many procedures that can be accomplished

171

today were not an expense before because they could not be accomplished. In addition to the inflationary factor that we are all familiar with, the cost of Blue Cross and Blue Shield today reflects many health-improving and life-saving procedures not medically possible yesterday. Other procedures, though medically possible, were not legally possible or not socially acceptable yesterday. I read recently that there were 1.5 million male and female sterilizations in the United States last year. I wonder what that number would have been in the days that Blue Cross and Blue Shield cost a family $3 a month. It probably would have been insignificant.

All of these new procedures and the related costs as reflected in Blue Cross and Blue Shield dues are not received with equal enthusiasm by the general public. When open heart surgery became medically possible, I am certain every Blue Cross and Blue Shield member welcomed the news, was pleased to know that this new service automatically became a benefit of his or her coverage, and accepted the fact that the rate would ultimately reflect the use of this added benefit. When a controversial procedure such as abortion is added as a prepaid health care benefit when it is legally endorsed, although not yet 100 percent socially accepted, it adversely affects to some unknown degree the insurance principle of risk spreading. Let me give you an example by reading a letter I received the day that Dr. Hern asked that I be on this stand. I quote: "Gentlemen, I am definitely against abortion. Your company participates in this terrible killing of innocent babies. My premium as well as that of Mrs. M—— can contribute to this injustice and we cannot in good conscience continue our Blue Cross and Blue Shield policy. Sincerely."

What is the actuarial message to be derived from such a letter? In the extreme, it could mean that all Blue Cross and Blue Shield subscribers who object to having a portion of their dues expended for abortions, either because they are morally against abortion or because of sex or age are not potential users of abortion services, will drop their Blue Cross and Blue Shield. This could mean only an increase in dues to the remaining members. If all remaining members were potential or even probable users of the abortion service, the insurance principle of risk spreading would be lost for that particular benefit.

As a practical matter, there are many other benefits to Blue Cross and Blue Shield membership, and the dire extreme of voluntary cancellation, as cited, will not occur on a mass basis. Cancellation will occur to some unknown degree. The degree to which this happens will be an actuarial factor in future rate determination.

Every family seems to have its skeleton in the closet. Maybe it is a drinking uncle. He is a nice guy and, generally, you are proud of him; but every once in a while he really embarrasses you. The Blue Cross and Blue Shield skeleton has developed largely in recent years and is the result of benefits relating to pregnancy and to alcoholism mandated by law. These benefits are not 100 percent acceptable to all citizens of our society. The pros and cons of mandating benefits for alcoholics is another subject, but it is related because it is a mandated issue. I would not consider highlighting these mandated benefits relating to pregnancy or alcoholism in a promotional folder designed to sell Blue Cross and Blue Shield. I would fear that through prominent display of such benefits, more prospective members might be lost than gained. Paying for abortions on single subscribers, which we do at Blue Cross and Blue Shield, is not uniformly popular among our 900,000 members. Also not uniformly accepted is the Blue Cross and Blue Shield benefit for an abortion on an underage daughter on a family contract with or without the consent of the parent.

Colorado Blue Cross and Blue Shield provides benefits for abortions in the unfortunate and unintended circumstance of unwanted pregnancy. However, the plans emphasize freedom of choice by also paying for delivery at term. One might say that Blue Cross-Blue Shield even encourages that choice by providing the newborn child with coverage from the moment of birth. Another point in the direction of encouraging the time-honored institution which we call the family is to be found in the fact that the Blue Cross and Blue Shield family rate is the same whether there be one child or a dozen.

While I do not advertise those Blue Cross and Blue Shield benefits which do not enjoy 100 percent social acceptance, I can readily defend them by reference to Colorado statutes and by reference to federal sex discrimination guidelines. These state that an unlawful employment practice is a situation in which wives of male employees receive maternity benefits while female employees receive no such benefits. Most of the small employers in Colorado are unaware of those federal guidelines. These guidelines are not yet law, but federal guidelines have a way of becoming law. By conforming and providing maternity care to single subscribers as well as to married subscribers, Blue Cross and Blue Shield in this state are not only protecting the members, they are protecting the employers who have enrolled their employees in Blue Cross and Blue Shield and may not be aware of all these guidelines. Thank you.

173

Economic Discrimination
in Abortion Services

Judy Widdicombe, R.N.

The whole health insurance situation has been an interesting one. We have very few providers covering abortion services. I can only describe what's happening in our own facility and the efforts that we have made in influencing private carriers. As with Colorado Blue Cross and Blue Shield, Blue Cross and Blue Shield in Missouri has been affirmative as far as their reimbursement policies are concerned. Usually, the larger the company, the more the obtainable benefits. With the private insurance carriers it has been different. The one carrier that we are still having a major difficulty with is Metropolitan Life. It's the only one that has consistently refused to reimburse, and they write group policies for some of the unions. People covered by these contracts are utilizing our service and they should receive benefits. We get letters from the main office of Metropolitan Life saying that this situation has not arisen out of injury or illness to the patient and hence is not coverable. I am not sure that all of us would agree, and I must say that my bias comes in when I see that it is signed by someone named O'Shaughnessy. The policy of the company not to offer abortion benefits or sterilization benefits has been clearly stated. We also had problems with Aetna. Those have been resolved and they are now paying.

In the beginning, we required that the woman pay whatever she could afford to pay when she came in and then we would help her file for any benefits that might be coming to her. We are now amending that policy. We are beginning with selective companies that we know will pay. We are not requiring money at the time of the procedure and we are just taking insurance policies. We are going to do that for a limited amount of time and see whether or not we can stay solvent as the companies continue to pay.

Economic access is a continuing problem for women. We have talked about whether facilities provided reduced fees. It is always a quandary for us if a woman has insurance that we know pays but cannot come up with the actual cash at the time of the procedure. How do we deal with that when there are so many other women who have neither public nor private third party reimbursement and also no cash? The unfortunate thing for me is that I have to make sure that that bottom line comes out somewhat with a smile on its face. We cannot consistently run in the red and we have a fairly large staff. Employees do not like my saying, "I can't pay now; I'll pay you in two weeks."

I would like to present some strategy for those of you who have to go back home and work with private carriers. In most metropolitan areas there is an organization called the Claims Managers Organization. They often meet on a monthly basis. They have people come in who speak to them about problems. I have been going to speak to them for the last three years on an annual basis. I educate and inform them about what's happening with abortion. We help them work through some of the problems that they are finding.

I am firmly convinced that confrontation is important and confrontations do not always need to be negative or hostile. In fact, it can be very positive. Confrontation in a give-and-take atmosphere can be very productive in creating some social change.

The other thing to do is to write to the companies and keep harrassing them, if you will, because that is actually what it becomes. Do not let them say, "I'm sorry, the policy of our company is that this is not a therapeutic abortion, hence we cannot pay for it." I refuse to accept this and I write back and give them excerpts of the Supreme Court decision in 1973. After a few months of controversy and firing letters back and forth, they have yielded. I am sure through their own legal counsel they have decided that they can no longer refuse to reimburse.

As we look at the Medicaid sector, we find that these monies are federally distributed but they are actually state controlled. Each state varies. I can respond specifically for the State of Missouri. We have had a Medicaid hassle there as we have with everything else. They refused to pay us, and they did so on a number of bases. One was that they could not give clinics numbers. We were a whole new breed of cat, and they really did not have any way to reimburse. This lasted about ten seconds with me. We pushed the issue and they finally refused to pay on moral grounds. We made the decision to file suit and did it in a little different way. We had suit brought against the State of Missouri and Mr. Singleton, who is the Director of the Social Services Department, by two physicians rather than a pregnant plaintiff or a group of pregnant plaintiffs. What the Supreme Court is going to be addressing is whether or not physicians have the right to bring a suit against the Division of Social Services in the name of women.* If they do in fact rule against us, we're going to have to go back to the drawing board unless the Pennsylvania case will be broad enough to decide whether or not the states will have to reimburse.

---

* The U.S. Supreme Court in July 1976 in *Wulff* v. *Singleton,* held that the physicians did have standing to sue and remanded the case to the federal District Court for re-hearing on the substantive issues.

Just to give you a little economic insight, the Medicaid suit will have cost us about $22,000 by the time we are finished. That is really very inexpensive as many court cases go because it has been through all the lower courts. My concern is that we are constantly fighting battles that take up monies that could be put into services. That money could be providing better services and a broader range of services for women. I resent having to do this on a consistent basis when we are no better off now than we were three years ago as far as court cases are concerned.

One of the things that we did not talk about that I would like to mention is the cost differential across the country for the service. We find some insurance carriers who will pay $100, some will pay $150, and some will pay $125. In our state Medicaid will pay only $75 for the physician.

There is an increase in cost for abortion services at the outpatient level. It is not going to be the antiabortion people who do us in, it is going to be the insurance companies in the area of malpractice. I think those of us who have free-standing clinics have found ourselves neither fish nor fowl.

We are faced with a tremendous malpractice crunch in covering not only the bricks and mortar, the corporate structure and the staff. The private physician who comes in on a sessional basis to provide services is not covered by his other malpractice insurance. Our insurance costs from 1973 to 1975 have gone up two and a half times and we have lost the primary coverage for our physicians. I think there is no way in which clinics who are providing nonprofit services can continue to absorb this. There is going to have to be an increase in cost. Our cost is going up to $170 as of April 1st.

This is distressing because my goal in setting up services was to gradually get the cost down to about $100. In early 1974, we decreased the fee from $175 to $160. Unfortunately, because of malpractice and the 40 percent increase in the cost of services and supplies, we are having to raise it back to $170. There are those who do it for $125 and I applaud these people. Unfortunately, we are not able to do it and still meet the needs of the lower socioeconomic group women. A third of the women seeking services at our facility are in the lower socioeconomic group.

Part of this reflects the fact that there are three other providers in St. Louis, none of whom take reduced fee patients. We are getting a large number of these women, and there has been no way that we can pressure any of the other providers to cooperate. One of those facilities is a department of Ob-Gyn in a teaching institution. We do need many institutional changes.

Discussion

Dubofsky: My experience in dealing with insurance, and particularly private coverage, has shown that the definition of maternity coverage will often control whether or not an abortion is paid for. It used to be that most insurance companies said that they simply would not pay for abortion. That has changed. Now one of the requirements often is that the person be carrying maternity coverage. Depending upon the insurance company and the way they write their policy, you may find some real problems here. Some of them will say that maternity coverage is only available for a family, and this will exclude the first child of a couple. It will not pay when both carry single policies through their employer, or it will exclude a single person who has heretofore not had a reason to carry family coverage. A second problem is that for maternity coverage, some companies will have a requirement that you have to have been insured for ten months prior to the birth of the child before they will cover the costs of delivery. You run into some difficulties here with attempting to cover an abortion.

Under disability insurance, which is usually written separately from health insurance coverage, many companies will say that they do not cover complications of pregnancy. If there's a complication because of some aspect of a problem with abortion, you may again find that disability coverage is excluded. I think disability insurance coverage tends to be further behind than health insurance coverage in this area. Finally, some of the programs are offering insurance coverage for optional maternity care; in other words, you can pay for it if you want it. You may find the rates are so high that it is less expensive just to pay for the costs of the delivery or the cost of an abortion, depending upon whether or not there are complications. Of course, the possibility of complications is probably why one would buy the insurance.

I think you'll still find that even though companies make insurance coverage available for single persons who want abortions, there are a lot of other fine print clauses that have to be taken into account. Also, we still hear a lot about whether childbirth is a medical problem or a problem of choice. Dr. Hern, I believe, has written several articles in regard to this, and if anyone has questions on that he might be able to respond to them.

Hern: As a matter of fact, I wanted to raise a question about that. I have raised some questions in some things that I've written about whether or not pregancy really is "normal" in the traditional and accepted Ob-Gyn sense or whether in fact it qualifies as an illness. I'm perfectly serious about this. I have expressed this in a couple of papers, the most recent of which is called "The Illness Parameters of Pregnancy."* Basically, what I've done is to challenge the idea that pregnancy is normal. I have pointed out the fact that there are certain mortality risks which women experience with pregnancy. The physiologic changes that go along with pregnancy produce these mortality risks. In fact, the important factor to be concerned with is the woman's perception of the pregnancy in terms of whether or not she sees this as something which is desired or not desired. This tends to dictate the appropriate treatment for the pregnancy. Under this premise, the question becomes not how do you justify an abortion, but what is the appropriate treatment for the pregnancy? This has several other implications, some of which are legal, medical and economic.

Judy Widdicombe has sent me copies of the letter from an insurance company which says that since pregnancy is not the result of injury or illness, abortion will not be reimbursed. But what if you call pregnancy an illness? What if you are able to demonstrate the fact that it fits into our cognitive framework of illness and that women have certain definable risks of serious complications which can be fatal. This does pose serious problems for the insurance carriers. As Mr. Vance pointed out, it disrupts the concept of risk-spreading because there is a certain class of people who have specialized susceptibility to this illness and that is women. It is not uniform. We can look at the epidemiologic aspects of this and point out that, if we are going to cover this actuarially, we have to define what those risks are. My question to the panel is, if this concept is accepted as valid someday by everyone else besides myself, will it have any bearing at all on the behavior of the health insurance system, public or private?

Vance: Quite aside from anything other than the actuarial side of it, there have been people over the years who have questioned Blue Shield's policy of charging one rate for the single individual and another rate for the family individual. They ask why we don't have rates for the family of one child, rates for a family with three and four and five and so on. Aside from any moral considerations, we just don't think it makes that much difference. We think that a family of two which is beyond the childbearing age is into a period of life where they are going to require other services that the younger family will not require. One really offsets the other. The only way you can get around the actuarial problems of this is to mandate by law that all carriers provide certain benefits. If there is one plan trying to provide benefits, whether it be for abortions or alcoholism, and there is some other program that is not providing those things, then the people who don't anticipate using those services will join the other plan. Then the cost of that

* W. M. Hern. "The Illness Parameters of Pregnancy," *Social Science and Medicine* 9:365, 1975.

particular benefit for the people who think they might want to use it is prohibitive. You would be better off putting your money in a sugar bowl to pay for it when the time comes.

There are people who honestly believe that alcoholism is an illness. There are others who honestly believe that it's something you bring on yourself, and if you're going to bring it on yourself, put your money in your own sugar bowl and pay for drying out when the time comes. There is a law in this state requiring that benefits be provided for alcoholic treatment centers. You can go to one of these treatment centers without even going to see a doctor. You just go and turn yourself in. Whether or not some of these things can be actuarially rated and successfully included in health programs will depend on whether or not it is mandated that all carriers provide it. Then I think it would be actuarially successful.

Widdicombe: One of the things that just dawned on me is that we try to find all sorts of other labels for abortion so it may be more acceptable in one place than another. When we say termination of pregnancy, abortion automatically floats into our head. I'm not sure that we ought not to start thinking that termination of a pregnancy can occur in a number of different time frames and in different situations. It may be spontaneous abortion. It may be induced abortion. Termination of a pregnancy may occur with a live birth. We need to attack it from that standpoint. We've learned this weekend that there are tremendous risks in all of these. There's a risk in spontaneous abortion. There's a risk in induced abortion. The risk that has been discounted is the risk to termination of pregnancy with or without a live birth.

Maybe what we need to start doing is to see the pregnancy as one event with termination of that pregnancy possible by a number of different routes. That's really the issue.

Munson: I was grateful for having had Dr. Hern's article, "Is Pregnancy Really Normal?" in our confrontation with the state's lawyers in South Dakota.* They were trying to raise questions about whether or not it really was the state's business to have to pay for an abortion. After all, they were saying, pregnancy is a normal thing. It would just take care of itself if you would wait long enough, wouldn't it? Fortunately, I had access to this article which set down so nicely and systematically the abnormalcy of pregnancy and the fact that here is a woman with a tumor growing inside her. If it was any other condition in which you had this syndrome of problems, you'd say, "Hey, that person is sick; that person needs to have a doctor." Here's a "normal" condition, but it's so abnormal that the

---

* W. M. Hern. "Is Pregnancy Really Normal?" *Family Planning Perspectives* 3:5, 1971.

treatment for it is for everybody to go to the hospital. Five percent of the people have a life-threatening major operation as a termination for it. There are tremendous strains occurring on the heart and lungs and kidneys, and sweeping changes take place in the bloodstream. I will certainly agree that the State Board of Social Services ought to be facing up to the fact that here is an abnormalcy that they have an obligation to pay for.

There are two other ways that Dr. Hern's question about whether pregnancy is an illness might be asked. One of them is really what Mr. Vance was talking about when he says that there is some degree of choice in whether you're pregnant or not. Sometimes abortion has not been covered, or pregnancy in general has not been covered, because there is a question of whether one chooses to be pregnant. Along the same line of thinking, you can say somebody chooses to ride a motorcycle and they choose to smoke. The possible outcome of that choice is normally covered by health insurance.

Another way of looking at the problem is the question as it comes up in the Medicaid program. Some states have excluded nontherapeutic abortions on the basis that they're not medically necessary. That comes back around to the illness question. One way the question comes up is whether or not abortion is medically necessary. I think that's what's being litigated in some of the Medicaid cases.

Shelly Norman, Rock Mountain Planned Parenthood, Longmont, Colorado: I hope to be able to provide just a little bit of optimism for those working with Medicaid. We have an excellent rapport with our welfare department in Boulder County. We are reimbursed for our Medicaid patients. Our understanding with our Medicaid technicians is that once a person has been approved for Medicaid, whether their papers have come through or not, they are eligible for the services. I would suggest that all of you go back to your county welfare department, talk to the Medicaid technicians and their supervisor, and find out what is really going on. We don't have those kinds of problems and I don't think it's inherent in the system.

Unidentified: Would you give us a broader overview of the cost of abortion around the United States and the ancillary services with it?

Widdicombe: If we're talking about first trimester abortion, we're talking anywhere from a low of $75 to probably $250. There's a physician in our area who charges $225 for an office-type, quasi-clinic procedure. Of course, the costs are very different. His cost is inclusive of everything, although he doesn't give anything. He doesn't give Rhogam unless the patient is 12 weeks or over. He doesn't give her any counseling. The services that that patient is receiving for $225 are really not acceptable medical practice even though it's a physician who is providing the service.

There is another clinic in our city that charges the same as we do. Although they seem to follow us, everything is extra. Rhogam is $35, pre-procedural visit is $10 and a post-procedural checkup is $10. Patients get a prescription for medications. You can't look at total costs or the top price. You have to ask a few more questions about what the patient is getting for the amount that she's being charged.

In the in-hospital situation, with general anesthesia, the cost is increased and the physician's cost is increased. It may cost up to four or five hundred dollars for a first trimester abortion. There's no question that the ambulatory delivery system is the most efficient and is the most cost-effective. Unfortunately, because each facility is set up differently, it has a different corporate structure. Some are profit-making, some nonprofit, and some are not-for-profit and tax exempt. The way the clinic is structured often determines how the service is being provided. My clinic has a Board of Directors. We are a not-for-profit, tax exempt corporation. Nobody owns the clinic. Nothing is getting creamed off the top. Everybody gets a salary commensurate with the position they hold. Our nursing salaries are compatible with the standards of the community. We had to set our own counseling salaries because there was nothing in the community comparable to what we were doing. The starting salary for a counselor at Reproductive Health Services is $8,400 a year and that was just raised. The salaries are not outlandish for the Midwest. The problem is, unless we can band together and begin to demand of providers that the services be of a quality nature, women are going to continue to be exploited whether abortion is legal or not. That's why we're here now: to find out what is acceptable, what is good quality service, and how could we bring some pressure on the providers.

Most second-trimester abortions are being done within a hospital. They're running anywhere from $250 to $700, depending on whether it's an evacuation from below the local anesthesia, up to and including the saline and/or prostaglandin in the hospital, which requires at least a tow-day stay in the hospital.

Hern: The cost of second trimester abortions in Colorado is generally about $500 to $600. It is unusual to see a patient who has this done anywhere for less than about $600.

Legal Aspects of Abortion

Introduction

Sarah Weddington

To introduce and begin discussion on the topic, "Legal Aspects of Abortion," I would like to review briefly the *Roe* v. *Wade* decision and mention some of the current areas of legal debate.[1]

The *Roe* v. *Wade* decision was the first United States Supreme Court decision to establish the right of a woman to make a choice about whether or not to continue or terminate an unwanted pregnancy. There has been a good deal of confusion about what the Court said.

The Court first said that there is a constitutional right involved. Where is that right? Obviously, the word "abortion" doesn't appear anywhere in the U.S. Constitution. Yet the Court went back to a line of cases that emphasized the right of an individual to make decisions about things that are vital to one's self-interest. For example, one former decision held that an individual had the right to marry whomever he or she chose and that states could not pass laws against miscegenation. In *Griswold* v. *Connecticut,* the Court held that individuals had a right to use contraceptive methods and that the state could not constitutionally pass a bill prohibiting their use.[2] The Court also considered all the social aspects of pregnancy in terms of the effect of pregnancy on the woman, including its medical and psychological impact and its impact on her family.

The Court then turned to the second test. Once the Court determined that there was under the Constitution a fundamental right of the individual to make a choice about pregnancy, it then queried, "Can the state overcome the constitutional right by showing a compelling reason why it must regulate in this area?" The State of Texas was arguing that it had a right to protect the life of the unborn. The Court indicated a series of ways in which we, as a government and as a people of law, have never treated the rights of a person after birth as being the same rights as those existing prior to birth. For example, the Constitution of the United States speaks of "all persons born or naturalized" as citizens. In fact, there was a case about the time of World War II in which a couple from Germany were visiting in this country. A child was conceived; the couple went back to Germany where the child was born. The child later sued to become a U.S. citizen. The Court denied citizenship saying citizenship is a right of birth in this country and not a right of conception. The child was not a U.S. citizen.

Income tax deductions or exemptions are available only after the birth of a child, not during the period of pregnancy. When a woman who is pregnant travels outside the country she gets one passport, not two. We celebrate birthdays, not conception days. Property rights begin at birth under most state laws. In limited instances they are retroactive if the fetus is born alive. If the father were killed during the pregnancy and the fetus were later born alive, the child would have the right to inherit. The fetus does not inherit if it is stillborn or miscarried. We showed that in Texas, for example, self-abortion was not a crime. Abortion was a crime only for somebody else who helped the woman. The penalty for abortion in Texas depended on whether or not you had the woman's consent. If you had her consent, it was one thing; if you didn't have her consent, it was twice as much. Abortion was not murder in Texas, murder being specifically defined as the killing of one who has been born.

We showed that the state had never taken a legal position. The Court held that the state, in equating life before birth to life after birth, had failed to prove a compelling reason to regulate. Therefore, the woman's right was supreme.

The Court went on to make some other pronouncements. You will sometimes hear charges that the Court "legislated." In some ways it did. When the cases were heard, there were many cases pending before the Court on the issue of abortion. You have all seen a situation where a state law is declared unconstitutional, and immediately, the state passes the same law with just one or two minor provisions changed. I am sure that what the Court wanted to do was to give some guidelines to the state legislatures about what the court felt they could and could not do constitutionally in hopes of eliminating the need for future cases.

The Court approved the following type of regulations: during the first trimester of pregnancy, a state can regulate to prohibit anyone other than a licensed physician from performing an abortion. Most states have a medical practice statute which says that no one but a licensed physician can practice medicine; the "practice of medicine" would include abortion. The Court said because of the increased medical dangers to the woman involved during the second trimester of pregnancy, the state could, if it wished, regulate the kinds of health facilities in which abortion services could be available. Then the Court said that in the third trimester of pregnancy, because of the increased potential for life and because of the still increased medical danger to the woman, the state could also, if it wished, say that abortion would then be available only in instances where the life or health of the woman was endangered.

Even though the Court approved state regulation and laws in those instances, the Court did not say "that is now the law." What the Court did say, in effect, was: "We declare the current laws to be unconstitutional. If a state wants to pass a new statute, that is the kind of statute we think would be constitutional."

There are a number of other areas that are now being presented for legal discussion. One is the rights of minors. No minors were involved in our case; the question of minor's consent was not presented to the Court.

Another issue is spousal consent. The Court decided that Mary and John Doe, who were original plaintiffs and were married, did not have standing to sue because Mary was not pregnant at the time of the suit. The Court decided *Roe* only on the basis of Jane Roe, who was not married. Therefore, the issue of whether or not a woman needed her husband's consent was not presented to the Court in our case. Some of the other issues that we will discuss will be the Medicaid cases, the responsibility of public hospitals, and those other kinds of issues which we are now in the process of debating and presenting for Court decision.

With that as an introductory remark, I would like for you to hear Cyril Means, who was the attorney who did much of the background information on how abortion laws came to be. Cyril's writings were on the Supreme Court bench as the judges heard our case, and I know the Court found Cyril's work very helpful in its deliberations.

REFERENCES

1. 410 U.S. 113 (1973).
2. 381 U.S. 479 (1965).

Recent Trends in the Legal Status of Abortion

Cyril C. Means, Jr.

The first case I am going to mention has been decided. It is a little-noticed case and was decided on November 11, 1975. It is very significant because, although very short, it contains in the opinion a paragraph in which the Court looks back at *Roe* v. *Wade* and attempts to put it in a nutshell.[1] There have been an infinite number of academic writers and judges of lower courts who have tried to do that. However, when the Supreme Court itself looks back at one of its great decisions, such as *Roe* v. *Wade,* and says "Now what we meant by that is this," it is time to listen.

The case I am referring to is *Connecticut* v. *Menillo.*[2] It was a pre-*Roe* v. *Wade* abortion performed by a nonphysician in Connecticut. His case went up to the Supreme Court of Connecticut after *Roe* v. *Wade.* The Supreme Court of Connecticut said that the language of the Supreme Court in *Roe* v. *Wade* was pretty strong. They have something in there about the Texas statutes having to fall "as a unit." Although they did say that a state could require that only a physician perform an abortion, our old Connecticut statutes did not differentiate between physicians and non-physicians. Therefore, they, too, must fall as a unit and therefore, Mr. Menillo, a lay abortionist, cannot be convicted. It is true the Connecticut legislature can enact a new statute in which it will say that only physicians may perform abortions, but until it does that, nobody can be convicted.

The State of Connecticut appealed that decision to the Supreme Court of the United States. The Supreme Court reversed the decision. They said the Supreme Court of Connecticut had gone too far. Yes, the Supreme Court did say that the Texas statutes had to fall as a unit, but what the Court meant by that was the whole intermeshing network of Texas statutes on abortion. Because one of them was unconstitutional, the other ones went down too. The Court made it perfectly plain in *Roe* v. *Wade* that a state could require that the performance of an abortion be by a physician. Therefore, even one of these old statutes, like Connecticut's 1860 statute, can be enforced against a nonphysician. That is all the case is about, but it does contain this one very important paragraph which says: "The rationale of our decision in *Roe* v. *Wade* is that, during the first trimester, the patient mortality in abortion is at least as safe as the patient mortality rate in childbirth."

That is the understatement of the century because, as of now, the comparison is something like eight-fold. In other words, abortion performed in the first trimester is about eight times as safe as childbirth. They were being cautious and not getting into any statistical squabbles. They went on to say: "However, the premise of that conclusion is that the person who is performing the abortion is a physician." Since that was not satisfied in this case, the reasoning does not apply and this lay abortionist cannot take advantage of the decision.

That is a very important point because they have really telescoped into a single paragraph the rationality of their decision in *Roe* v. *Wade* in the comparative safety test. Because abortion performed by a surgeon or physician is safer than childbirth at the present time, the state has to show a compelling state interest in order to compel a woman to take the greater risk to her life of childbirth.

Of course, we have familiar examples of instances where states have been permitted constitutionally to assert such a right. The United States can send men to war, but there, the compelling state interest is national defense. The state, for example, can force persons to undergo compulsory inoculation although it is known that there is a small death rate in connection with that. There, of course, the compelling state interest is the public health. Here, the Court found, there is no such compelling state interest, at least in the first trimester of pregnancy. There are two state interests which may become compelling at later stages which do not become compelling that early. As Ms. Weddington has pointed out, the first state interest they found becomes compelling only at the end of the first trimester and that is in the interest of maternal health—not fetal health, but maternal health. The second one is an interest which the state may, if it wishes, assert in the potential life of the fetus. That becomes compelling only when the point of viability is reached.

The first case that I want to talk to you about is a case from Missouri. It involves a statute passed by the legislature of Missouri in 1974, subsequent to *Roe* v. *Wade,* in which a very deliberate and obvious attempt was made to whittle down as much of the liberty guaranteed by *Roe* v. *Wade* as the legislature thought it could get away with. The name of the case is *Planned Parenthood Federation of Central Missouri* v. *Danforth,*[3] Danforth being the name of the Attorney General of Missouri. One of the sections of the law defines viability. The legislature of Missouri has literally lifted the language out of the *Roe* v. *Wade* opinion. It says: "Viability is that stage of fetal development when the life of the unborn child may be continued indefinitely outside of the womb by natural or artificial life supportive systems." It is a trifle more specific than the *Roe* v. *Wade* language, but not by very much.

The attack being made on that is on the ground of vagueness. You may say, "How can that be vague which the Supreme Court of the United States itself has said?" The answer is, vagueness is judged according to its context. When the Supreme Court is pronouncing a decision on the meaning of a constitutional clause, it does not speak with the kind of precision which is required of a legislature when it is enacting a criminal statute. The vagueness rule is that a criminal statute has to give the individual, who is defined as a person of ordinary intelligence, notice of the conduct which is being prohibited so he or she can know what is being prohibited and what is not.

When the Constitution itself is vague, as it is in the 14th amendment, the Supreme Court, naturally, is going to try to be a little bit less vague when it interprets it. But the Supreme Court is not a legislative body. It is not enacting criminal statutes. It is merely giving guidelines to the state legislatures to indicate what kinds of criminal statutes they may enact and what kinds they may not. It is up to the legislature to define with greater particularity in such a way that it does not intrude upon or impinge upon an area of constitutional liberty defined by the Court. In this way, it does give fair notice to persons of ordinary intelligence exactly what kinds of acts are or are not prohibited.

Viability is a concept which has been a very fertile source of dispute among doctors. Textbooks of classical medicine talk about 28 weeks. There have been rare instances where it has been alleged that fetuses early in the 20th week have survived, although there is only one such case that was thought to have been authenticated. The doctor who was supposed to have delivered that fetus admitted that he was not really sure. The Court itself said that 28 weeks was the norm, but sometimes it could occur as early as 24 weeks.

In a criminal statute, the legislature is obliged to observe several caveats. One of these is not only that it define the conduct with particularity so that a person of ordinary intelligence knows what is being prohibited, but also so that it enables the prosecution to prove its case beyond a reasonable doubt. Viability is a medical fact which exists out there in the world of reality with respect to every given fetus at some moment in time. However, to ascertain that moment in time with respect to any given fetus is an extraordinarily difficult task. What doctors have to do is to make an informed guess. The only way that one really could know with respect to any given fetus at any stage of gestation would be to induce a premature birth at that point and then wait and see if the fetus did survive and did not die within the neonatal period normally reckoned at 31 days. That is obviously not a form of experimentation which one can resort to in advance in order to try a criminal case. Therefore, in all cases in which the doctors are going to be testifying as witnesses, what they are going to be doing is engaging in retroactive guessing. These guesses are more or less well informed, but they certainly do not arise from that degree of certainty which enables the prosecution to prove its case. In criminal cases it must prove it beyond a reasonable doubt. There is another intriguing section that has been put into this Missouri statute. This is section 6-1. It reads as follows: "No person who performs or induces an abortion shall fail to exercise that degree of professional skill, care and diligence to preserve the life and health of the fetus which such person

193

would be required to exercise in order to preserve the life and health of any fetus intended to be born and not aborted. Any physician or person assisting in the abortion who shall fail to take such measures to encourage or to sustain the life of a child, and the death of a child results, shall be deemed guilty of manslaughter." The District Court held that provision to be unconstitutional. It upheld all the other provisions of this statute, including the one on viability. That one, of course, goes directly against the whole tendency of *Roe* v. *Wade*. *Roe* v. *Wade* held that a fetus is not a person until it is born and that consequently, until the birth of a fetus, or until its emergence as a result of abortion, if it does emerge alive, there is only one person present: namely, the mother to whom the physician is to attend. She is his patient. What this statute is attempting to do is to compel, under the sanctions of criminal law, a physician to treat that fetus as if it were a person and therefore a second patient prior to its birth or its abortion alive. I do not think there is much doubt that that portion of the statute is clearly going to be held unconstitutional under *Roe* v. *Wade*. That is the one section which the lower court held unconstitutional.

The other two sections which are of principle interest here are the spousal and parental consent provisions. Although the Court left those questions open in *Roe* v. *Wade,* the rationality of the decision does seem to militate against those requirements. It is not to say that the begettor of the child has no interest in the fetus. It is to say, however, that that interest cannot be protected by the state through the vehicle of the criminal law. It is quite conceivable that a state might, for example, make it a cause for a divorce if a woman, against her husband's consent, insists on aborting any child that he had begotten. This provision goes much farther than that. It says that any married woman must obtain his consent, whether the spouse or the husband is or is not the begettor of the fetus. The patently unreasonable character of a requirement of that kind is clear because consent is required even where the husband has not begotten the fetus.

Parental consent is obviously a somewhat more questionable area. In dealing with adults as two parties to a marriage, one is dealing with persons who are *sui juris:* that is, the law regards them as people protecting their own rights, normally exercising personal autonomy. However, there is a large area of law where children are not given this right of autonomy. The state is attempting to defend this statute on the ground that many children are not capable of making decisions in other areas and that the law does not allow them to until they reach at least 18, or in some cases, 21. Therefore, is it not reasonable to the legislature to put in a similar provision here?

The argument being made by the challengers is that the situation in which a pregnant teenager finds herself is already an adult situation. The very fact that she is pregnant means with respect to the pregnancy decision that she has already behaved as if she were an adult. What we are running into here is a kind of curious situation where, biologically, the person is already an adult, whereas socio-culturally, we do not regard her

194

as yet an adult for all purposes. In any case, the law as it stands does not put the burden of rearing an unwanted child born to such a teenager upon the grandparents whose consent was withheld. It leaves that saddled upon the teenager who is going to bear the child. Consequently, the argument is made that it is extremely unreasonable to impose, under penalty of criminal law, a consent requirement on the part of a parent with respect to such a pregnancy.

The Attorney General of Missouri attempted to defend the law by interpreting these in various ways which would make it less obviously in conflict with *Roe* v. *Wade*. For example, he tried to interpret the famous section 6 as only applying if the fetus is delivered alive. Of course, the very language of "fetus" shows that a standard of prenatal diligence is being imposed upon the physician. The very reading of the language makes this plain. Curiously enough, that statutory language of section 6 is the very same thing which the Commonwealth of Massachusetts is asserting as a standard of common law care in the case of the *Commonwealth* v. *Edelin*.[4]

In Massachusetts, the argument had to be made on the basis of common law rather than statute because at the time Edelin performed that operation, which was a hysterotomy, there was no statute in Massachusetts on abortion. The old statute, the one from 1845, was declared unconstitutional along with *Roe* v. *Wade*, and the legislature had not yet enacted any new statute. It is very interesting that section 6 in the Missouri statute and similar sections in others of these new state laws merely codifies the argument being made in the Edelin case as a matter of common law.

There is one other provision of this Missouri statute which is particularly infamous and completely inconsistent with *Roe* v. *Wade*. That is the one which proscribes saline procedures. It is an actual section which says that salines may not be performed and other forms of procedures must be used instead. From the point of view of the patient, saline procedures are more safe than childbirth. Therefore, under the comparative safety test laid down in *Roe* v. *Wade*, the proscription of them is clearly unconstitutional.

However, the argument that the state makes here is much more subtle than that. It says that may be so, but there are other procedures which are even safer. They say: how about prostaglandins? We simply do not have enough experience yet to know whether prostaglandins are safe. Today, patient mortalities are measured in units per 100,000. You have to have 100,000 procedures before you have a statistically respectable universe in which to compute a rate. There just have not been a hundred thousand prostaglandin procedures so far. I do not think the state is going to be able to make out that case but it raises an extremely interesting point. Suppose that there are a series of procedures of varying degrees of safety to the patient, all of which are safer than childbirth. May a state pick and choose amongst them and say you must use one and not the other? That is a point which was certainly not addressed by the Court in *Roe* v. *Wade*, and it is

195

a curious one. If later on the demonstration could be made on it, it might prove a perplexing one. It would appear to me that that is getting into the intimacies of the medical decision in a way in which a legislature has never done with respect to any other kind of medical decision. There are a lot of other types of physical conditions for which people get treated where the doctor does have to use a comparative safety test. He may have a whole battery of remedies, and he may think about one being more safe in one respect than another; but normally that is the kind of decision that is always left to the doctor. Why the legislature should be allowed to get into this is a little odd, but I could not say with confidence what the courts might say on that if it got a proper case

The next case comes up from Pennsylvania and it is called the *Doe* v. *Beale* case.[5] It involves the question of Medicaid reimbursability for abortions. Back when *Roe* v. *Wade* was pending, there was a whole passel of other cases pending, and all but one of them were disposed of in one-line opinions as a result of the decision in *Roe* v. *Wade*. The one that was not decided was a case called *Klein* v. *Nassau County Medical Center*.[6] It involved, as its name implies, a suit against a public hospital on Long Island. What had happened there?

The New York Social Services Commissioner had promulgated a regulation saying that Medicaid reimbursability should apply only for "medically indicated" abortions. He had not said that when New York's law was originally liberalized back in 1970. He said it along about 1972. When the Court got this case, it decided that it would ask the Solicitor General of the United States, who was then Irwin Griswold, for an opinion, not on the constitutional question, but on the statutory question. There is a statutory question with regard to the HEW legislation as to what a state may do in addition to what the federal Congress has already done.

Under Title XIX of the HEW legislation, a wide range of options is left open to the state in deciding to fund or not to fund various types of medical treatments. What Solicitor General Griswold did was to say that this is practically an accordion. If the state wants to stretch it out like this it may; if it wants to contract it like this it may; but whatever the state does, the federal government has got to match with matching funds. The state is under no obligation to finance any particular kind of medical treatment. He went on to say something about cosmetic surgery being an obvious sort of thing which the state might very well say it did not want to cover and which most states do not cover. On that basis, the Court then reversed, remanded the decision, and sent it back to the District Court in Brooklyn, saying, "Please reconsider in the light of *Roe* v. *Wade*." They had shunted aside the statutory question. I think that the Court expected that that case would come back fairly promptly. Then they would be able to decide all the questions, the constitutional questions and the statutory questions, in one big decision. Unfortunately, that case, *Klein* v. *Nassau County Medical Center*, has never come back up to the Supreme Court. It is still pending in the court to which it was remanded. I went over there about a year ago and talked to the law clerk and discovered that they are now patiently trying to discover what is going on under this order in every one of the 218 counties of New York State. It will probably take them years to complete this survey and they are not going to decide until then. I assume that the Supreme Court must have lost patience by now, and it has decided that that case is never coming back up.

Doe v. *Beale,* which has come up from Pennsylvania, presents the same issues in a very interesting way. Pennsylvania promulgated a regulation which says that the only abortions which can be reimbursed under Medicaid are those which would qualify according to certain guidelines laid down. Those guidelines are virtually a replay of the A.L.I.-type model penal code law, such as Georgia had, and which was declared unconstitutional in *Doe* v. *Bolton.*[7] In other words, it covers endangerment to life or health of the mother, rape or incest. Those abortions that can qualify under those guidelines are reimbursed. All others are called elective and they are not reimbursed. These regulations were attacked in the federal district court in Philadelphia. It went up to the Third Circuit, and at first, a panel of three judges decided it. The whole court considered it so important they ordered a reargument before the Third Circuit *en banc.* About 15 judges participated in the final decision in that court. They decided that the regulations were invalid. They did not hold them to be unconstitutional because they said they were only going to decide the statutory question. The Supreme Court has said in recent HEW cases that they want the statutory questions decided first. In a very fine opinion by Judge Van Busen, he said this regulation of the Pennsylvania authorities conflicts with Title XIX of the HEW law and that went up to the Supreme Court on a petition for *certiorari* by the State.

The Supreme Court has invited the present Solicitor General to submit a brief as *amicus curiae* on behalf of the United States which says what the government thinks the statutory position is. Griswold submitted a brief on exactly that same question back in 1973 in the Klein case. I guess they wanted to know what the current Solicitor General thought about it. Solicitor General Bork filed a brief in which he said exactly the same thing that Griswold said. In other words, it is completely up to the state. It can fund or not fund, and it is up to the federal government to match what the state does fund.

I think Judge Van Heusen's opinion is the better view on this, although there is one Second Circuit decision from New York that conflicts with it in a case coming from Vermont. Judge Van Heusen's reasoning is that the Supreme Court has said that a woman who is pregnant has two procedures before her, calling for a choice. She can either have a childbirth or she can have an abortion. When a state, or any other governmental body, attempts to impose upon a woman any kind of regulation which influences her choice in one direction or the other or coerces her choice, it is violating this fundamental right which was originally affirmed in *Roe* v. *Wade.* That is inconsistent not merely with the Constitution, but also with a provision in the HEW legislation itself which says that, in preparing plans of coverage of various types of medical activities, a state must be "reasonable." In other words, there is a built-in due process clause right in the statute itself.

It seems to me that Judge Van Heusen's reasoning is the better reasoning. I look forward with great anticipation to what the Supreme Court decides on that case because it will be very important.

At the end of his brief, Solicitor General Bork has said that he does agree that this is a question of great public importance, and he encourages the Court to grant *certiorari*. With that sort of a statement from the Solicitor General, I think the Supreme Court will grant *certiorari* and will decide this case.* If it decides it the way that we would like to see it decided, that will probably be the end of the matter. Of course, Congress could amend the statute to say that the states shall have the power to exclude abortions. At that point, there would have to be a decision on the constitutional question of whether that act of Congress or such a regulation like that of the states would indeed violate the constitutional provisions of the 14th Amendment as they were laid down in *Roe* v. *Wade.* We have two bites to the apple, and the bite we are working on now is the statutory construction problem. If we win on that we may never have to get to the constitutional issue.

There has been a whole series of cases on public hospitals, and we have won them all in the lower courts. The distinction made by the lower courts had been uniform. Public hospitals, if they perform childbirth services, must also be open for the performance of abortion services. This is the choice between these two procedures with which the woman is medically confronted when she becomes pregnant. All it is is state action, except that here it is the whole state trying to forbid every hospital, public and private, from doing abortions under certain circumstances. It is not just a public hospital whose local board of trustees has decided it does not want to do any.

In private hospitals, the rulings have been fairly uniform with only one exception. That is the one in the Fourth Circuit in Virginia.[8] Whether they are religious or nonreligious, if they are private, they are private. Even the fact that they have obtained Hill-Burton funds is not enough to invest them with sufficient state action to bring them under the 14th Amendment and compel them to perform abortions.

There was a Beaumont, Texas case called the Greco case which involved a hospital which was private.[9] It had been given tremendous amounts of state aid in its building and foundation. It was built with tax money, then it was leased on a $1-a-year lease to a private association.

---

* Certiorari granted July 1976. U.S. Supreme Court No. 75-554.

The contract between the county and the hospital provided that the hospital would take a certain number of public patients. There was a great deal that could be alleged to be the necessary amount of state action to make that hospital, even though in name private, in fact public for 14th Amendment purposes. That went up to the Supreme Court and the Supreme Court denied *certiorari*. There was a shrieking dissent from Chief Justice Burger and Justice White, who said they thought this was definitely outrageous. The Court should not have denied *certiorari*. They should have faced up to deciding this issue. There are nervous Nellies among our ranks who think that this may presage a weakening of the Court on the issue of abortion. I do not agree with that at all. I think it could be explained by a completely different fact. The Court is in a great quandary on this whole question of private vs. public action for 14th Amendment purposes. They often do not like to decide ticklish issues until they get just the right case to decide them. They did not figure, I think, that this was the right case.

On the Edelin case, the position was, as I say, that there was not any statutory law on the subject at the time that Dr. Edelin performed that abortion. He started off trying to do a saline. He ran into a contraindication because he obtained what are known as bloody taps. If you get blood instead of fluid when you try to extract the amniotic fluid, you know that something is wrong. You are either into the blood system of the mother, or perhaps the blood system of the fetus, maybe even the placenta; but you are not where you want to be, which is getting amniotic fluid out which you are going to replace with a saline solution. He got another doctor in at that point and said, "You do it; see if you can succeed," and he could not either. He got a bloody tap. That was the head of the department. The only thing they could do at that point was to go to the hysterotomy, which is a miniature Caesarean section.

The very curious thing about this case is that the Commonwealth tried it on one theory throughout. The judge never ever disabused the jury of that theory until he issued his final instructions. In a hysterotomy, the fetus is not as developed as it would be at term, but it is big enough so that the physician's hand can go in and detach the placenta from the uterine wall and take out the fetus. The theory on which the Commonwealth tried this case was one completely innovative in the field of medicine and law. It was that, once a placenta had been detached by Dr. Edelin from the uterine wall, that that fetus was born, even though it was still inside the mother. Therefore, it then became a 14th Amendment person. Therefore, he then became obliged to exercise toward it the standard of diligence that he would have to toward the person already born. In other words, it became a second patient. When the one doctor who was willing to testify that, in his view, a birth had occurred intrauterinely, was asked if he could quote any other doctor who had ever said such a thing, he said "yes." He mentioned the name of a doctor who had written an article in a medical journal. Fortunately, Bill Homans, who was the lawyer for Edelin, happened to have a copy of that medical journal. He handed it up to this doctor and said, "Can you find it in the article?" He could not. It was a completely ridiculous, outrageous, unprecedented theory. That was the theory on which that jury was allowed to try that case. There were numerous objections by the attorney for the defense, but Judge Maguire did not do anything to disabuse the jury that that was the proper theory upon which to try the case until the very last moment when he had to give his charge to the jury. When he did, he gave it in perfectly correct terms. He said that for a person to be a proper subject of manslaughter, he must be born outside the womb of his mother and he must be alive.

Of course, the Commonwealth can argue that they cured any previous error, but you cannot try a case that has lasted over 30 days with the jury hearing evidence on one theory, and then suddenly in the last minute say, "Well, now, that isn't the right theory." Obviously, they are going to be influenced. Obviously, they were. The religious proportions of the jury were, I think, something like ten or eleven Roman Catholics. That is not surprising in view of the fact that Suffolk County in Massachusetts is a very heavily Roman Catholic community. An attempt was made to exclude from that jury anyone who would admit to a prejudice on the subject that he could not overcome when instructed as to the contrary on the law by the judge.

A poll was taken of eligible persons to be drawn for the jury of *Commonwealth* v. *Edelin* by a polling outfit. They were asked various questions. A very large sample, about a thousand people, was asked as to whether or not they had been influenced by the teaching of their religion on abortion, and if they were serving on a jury, could they put these aside. Would they, if the judge instructed them otherwise, be willing to decide in accordance with what the judge said the law was? Over 13 percent of the respondents to that questionnaire said that they could not. Once Judge Maguire saw that, in fairness to him I have to say that he said, "I will conduct a very careful *voir dire* here," and he did. He excluded anybody who would answer the question that way. Of course, that does not exclude some latent bias. There is no way of making it surface in the course of a *voir dire* examination. It does appear from certain statements made by some jurors after the hearing and even by the tone of voice in which the foreman delivered the verdict that there was prejudice here. It is a most unfortunate case which I hope the Supreme Judicial Court will reverse without it having to go to Washington.*

The Morgenthaler case is a Canadian case. Dr. Morgenthaler was literally Mr. Abortion in Eastern Canada for around 20 years. For many years, he was left completely untouched by legal authorities. They

* The Massachusetts Supreme Judicial Court unanimously reversed the manslaughter conviction of Dr. Edelin in a decision handed down on December 17, 1976. In part, the decision to reverse was based on the grounds that the instructions to the jury were inadequate in separating the prosecution's views on "viability" from the established legal meanings. (*Commonwealth* v. *Edelin,* Order No. S-393, Massachusetts Supreme Judicial Court.)

all thought he was just great when he was operating clandestinely and not making any waves. Then he fell into the terrible catastrophe of having been approached by a women called Eleanor Ripel-Rhein. She is the author of a book on abortion in Canada, is quite a crusader, and happened to have a connection with Canadian National Televison. She said, "Dr. Morgenthaler, you must perform an abortion on national television in Canada. That is the way to promote the cause." That was his undoing. He did it, and the very next day the Royal Canadian Mounted Police were coming out of the woodwork in his office. They arrested all the patients there, seized his records, and his troubles have not ceased ever since.

In any case, he was tried and he asked for a French language jury. In Quebec, you can ask for either an English language jury or a French language jury. It was a solid Roman Catholic jury, but that jury acquitted him. He was tried in the Court of Queen's Bench in Montreal, and then a very unusual thing happened. The Crown appealed the acquittal on a point of law. That is not possible in common law. It is certainly not possible in this country, and it did not become possible, even in England, until very recently. There has been a statute on the books in Canada for many years that has permitted the Crown to appeal on a point of law. Never before had it been thought that, on such an appeal, the appellate court could do anything but agree. The Crown got a bad instruction or something and the law is different. Never before had an appellate court done what the Court of Appeals for the province of Quebec did in this case, which was not only to reverse the judgment and order a new trial, which they normally do under their statute, but to substitute a judgment of conviction for the judgment of acquittal that the judge had given below. Chief Justice Hugusen of the Court of Queen's Bench refused to enter such a judgment of a conviction for the judgment when it came down on remand. It was not until the Crown got a Writ of Mandamus against him that he would do it. He finally then did, and sentenced Henry Morgenthaler to 18 months in prison.

Eventually the appeal on that was taken up to the Supreme Court of Canada which reluctantly concluded that this is possible under the statute. It is completely unprecedented in the history of English, American and Canadian law, but the statute says it can be done. That has resulted in the introduction of a bill in Parliament which will forbid this situation in the future. After it had won in the Supreme Court of Canada on that, the Crown said that it was going to bring a prosecution for 12 other cases in which evidence was seized on the day they raided his office. They brought a second case to trial involving a second abortee. This time, again, a French language jury acquitted Morgenthaler. The Crown again appealed to the Court of Appeals for the province of Quebec, hoping to succeed as it had before. This time the Court of Appeals refused and affirmed the acquittal. Why? The answer was: this time, as opposed to the first trial, there had been evidence submitted of a defensive necessity. There was a passage

201

in the Supreme Court of Canada's opinion in which they had said a defensive necessity would be a good defense to an abortion prosecution in Canada. The defensive necessity is that of throwing the excess passengers out of overloaded lifeboats to save the remainder. It is a similar defense, but it is not quite as dramatic as that. The way it was made in this case was as follows: Under the Trudeau statute which was a cruder form of the old ALI bill here, a hospital is completely free to do abortions or not do abortions, whether the hospital is public or private. In Quebec, no French language hospital was doing any abortions at all. The English language hospitals that were doing them were so few and their facilities were so overloaded that they could not possibly handle the demand. Competent witnesses testified that this girl who had been aborted by Morgenthaler would probably have had to wait so many months to get an abortion she would meanwhile have given birth to a child. Therefore, the jury accepted this defense of necessity.

Of course, that would apply to any other prosecution that the Crown would bring under these circumstances, even as they exist today in Quebec. As a result of the affirmation of the acquittal by Court of Appeal in the case of this second abortion, the Federal Minister of Justice in Canada, acting under a provision for which there is no analog in American law, vacated the conviction in the first case, and ordered a new trial. Now Morgenthaler is going to go through a new trial on that first case. He will be able to make the same defense of necessity and he will undoubtedly be acquitted again. If that happens, I am sure the Crown will cease and desist. He was confined until after this new Court of Appeals decision, but he is now out. The Crown is trying to go to the Supreme Court of Canada on the second Court of Appeals decision but it is not likely that the Court will grant permission.* It is one of the most extraordinary cases in the history of Anglo-American law and it has caused a tremendous amount of publicity in Canada and a focusing upon the issues that interest all of us. It points up the difference between a country which does not have a binding Bill of Rights, such as we do in our Constitution, and a Constitution like ours which can be judicially enforced.

* Dr. Morgenthaler was acquitted a third time by a jury on September 18, 1976. On December 11, 1976, Quebec's Justice Minister halted all further prosecution on Dr. Morgenthaler, termed the abortion law "unenforceable" and called for a new law. (See H. Giniger, "Quebec Halts Trial of Abortion Doctor," *The New York Times*, December 12, 1976, 21:1.

REFERENCES

1. 410 U.S. 113 (1973).
2. 423 U.S. 9 (1975).
3. 420 U.S. 918 (1975).
4. Order No. S-393, Massachusetts Supreme Judicial Court, (1976), 359 N.E. 2nd 4.
5. 523 F. 2nd 611 (Third Circuit, 1975).
6. 412 U.S. 924 (1973).
7. 410 U.S. 179 (1973).
8. *Doe* v. *Charleston Area Medical Center,* 44 U.S.L.W. 2233 (1975).
9. *Greco* v. *Orange Memorial Hospital Corporation,* 513 F. 2nd 873 (1975).

U. S. Commission on Civil Rights Report

Carol Bonosaro

I was the Director of The U.S. Civil Rights Commission report study group, and the author is a brilliant black attorney, scholar and university administrator named Dr. Mary Berry, who, interestingly enough, is personally opposed to abortion. She approached the topic out of a context of legal scholarship and could reach no other conclusion. The title of the report is *Constitutional Aspects of the Right to Limit Childbearing.* In true federal government fashion, it is a bit misleading. In that report we discuss only the issue of abortion and not other methods of limiting childbearing. It is not much more misleading than the phrase "abortion on demand." I have always wondered whether the alternative is "abortion at random."

The Commission began to think about this topic and approached it from the point of view of a legal report. It became increasingly clear that debates, when they occurred at all in the Congress before passing pieces of legislation designed to limit the right to abortion, were very often not well informed. It is rather difficult to secure the Congress's attention with some thoughtful legal, social, or economic discussion of the topic.

For example, during the hearings of the Subcommittee on Constitutional Amendments of the Senate Judiciary Committee, one of the Senators was hearing the testimony of a doctor on various relevant medical issues. He was compelled to ask that doctor during his testimony just how many ova the average woman produced during the normal act of intercourse. When I tell that story, sometimes men do not quite get it but know that it ought to be funny. That really illustrates the quality of some of the discussion.

The Commission's report, of course, is one which favors the right to choose abortion, which is not the same thing as being pro-abortion. The Commission also makes it quite clear that the American people have, indeed, the right to amend the Constitution. What the Commission is arguing in that report, however, is that any such amendment would have some rather devastating effect on the Bill of Rights, particularly on the first and ninth amendments as well as the 14th amendment.

First, the Commission considered the effect on the First Amendment. Our argument was that any constitutional amendment prohibiting abortion or restricting the right to abortion would represent a constraint on the First Amendment. Such an amendment would stem from wholly or partially religious motives. There is no wholly secular reason that can be cited at this point for limiting the right to abortion such as occurred a hundred years ago or more when the anti-abortion laws were developed. At that time, one could cite the lack of antiseptic procedures and, therefore, the risk to maternal health. This was a secular reason.

No secular reasons have been advanced during the course of the present arguments. The Commission felt that what was really at issue was wholly or partially religious motives. Such a constraint on the First Amendment would represent an assault on the freedom of conscience, which is protected by the First Amendment. In simple terms, we would be compelling every woman to accept a view that a person exists from the moment of conception, even when that view would conflict whith her own religious view. Under current circumstances, the right to abort does permit each woman to exercise her own religious views for herself.

Organized religious involvement in this issue does not conflict with the First Amendment. That is not what we were arguing. We do recognize that there are several religious denominations that are indeed opposed to the right to abortion. The Commission made a novel argument under the First Amendment section. We use the excessive entanglement of government and religion approach, which has traditionally been used only when material resources are involved. This occurs when the government is talking about giving money or supplies of some sort. The Commission moved beyond this argument because we felt that this issue represented and excessive entanglement of government and religion because of the lack of a purely secular reason to support any anti-abortion constitutional amendment or any anti-abortion legislation at the federal level. There was no valid state objective being served. Also, since there is no consensus on when life begins, a primary effect of such legislation was the advancement of a particular religious view.

We went through some history with regard to the adoption of the Ninth Amendment, which was designed to meet the objections of some people at that time that the absence of mention of any right could be construed as a lack of that right. Even after the adoption of the Ninth Amendment, some still felt that there were not sufficient restrictions on state actions. Many states adopted declarations of rights and many of them include freedom of conscience and personal liberty clauses. This is one of the reasons why some people feel that even a states' rights amendment to the Constitution would not accomplish very much. It has been suggested that a state with such a Bill of Rights, incorporating a freedom of conscience and personal liberty clause, might find itself in violation of its own Bill of Rights if it then adopted anti-abortion legislation.

The Commission went on to discuss the freedom of women to abort and reviewed the common law, based on the work of Cyril Means, which is the definitive work. It then approached the question of erosion of the right to personal privacy which the Supreme Court has recognized as a Ninth Amendment right. Again, there has been demonstrated no compelling state interest which would permit the state to infringe on that right. We felt, therefore, that such a constitutional amendment would erode the Ninth Amendment.

The Commission also devoted a fair amount of attention to the 14th Amendment. We talked about the implications of amending the Constitution to change the meaning of "person." Let me deal with the states' rights amendment first. The Commission report argued that a state statute making a fetus a person would be of no federal constitutional significance since the word "person" in the Constitution has a particular meaning. Secondly, when a woman's right to privacy would be in conflict with the state's "fetal" right as established pursuant to a states' rights amendment, the federal claim would have primacy. It is based on the 14th Amendment, which prohibits state interference with 14th Amendment rights.

A states' rights amendment would not protect a state statute from the compelling state interest argument: that is, having to demonstrate a compelling state interest which required the state to prohibit or limit abortion.

Under the 14th Amendment argument, we also presented the notion that a woman who was required by virtue of such statutes to submit her body to cary a child to term without her consent arguably has submitted her personal liberty to another. The fact that she must submit to the higher mortality rates for pregnancy and childbirth, to pain and to possible loss of income and career, given societal treatment of pregnancy and motherhood today, certainly permitted us to make that argument. At possible loss was her own personal liberty. There is no compelling state interest in requiring this. We arrived at the same conclusion which the Supreme Court did; that is, that the only state interest is in setting medical standards for the performance of abortion in order to protect maternal health.

The Commission did devote a fair amount of time to the concept of equal protection. What has really been at issue in the past is still at issue given noncompliance with *Roe* and *Doe:* discrimination against poor women, among whom minority women are disproportionately represented. If one had access to sufficient funds, one could always hop on a plane and go somewhere or be able to secure an abortion where one lived. Poor women have traditionally suffered through the necessity of proceeding with the pregnancy or enduring a self-induced or back-alley abortion with its higher mortality rate and incidence of septic and incomplete abortion. We made an argument that what one would be doing by amending the Constitution would be to chip away at equal protection and at the 14th Amendment.

We considered some of the interesting things that would happen under various types of law with regard to fetal rights. For example, under current tort law, one can recover for an injury at or after viability if a child is born alive. What would happen in the face of a constitutional amendment that confers personhood on the fetus? Could you sue a mother, for example, for smoking and therefore injuring the fetus in some way? The whole question of how to determine the date of conception is another issue

207

which Cyril Means has addressed. Under tax law, would we begin taking deductions for fetuses? How would the IRS determine that indeed a fetus had existed from a particular date? How would the moment of conception be determined? In criminal law, there could be manslaughter-murder charges for a woman and a doctor if a menstrual extraction were performed. Would it have been demonstrated that a fetus did exist? It would create chaos in law.

The Commission moved on to another issue. Apart from the question of the effect on our Constitution, what sort of eroding effect would an anti-abortion amendment have on civil rights enforcement generally? The argument the Commission made was that success in the strategy of withdrawing by means of a constitutional amendment a right which the Supreme Court has found to be part of the Bill of Rights, a constitutional right, would very possibly be a forerunner to other efforts with regard to unpopular or difficult-to-enforce rights. We have had long experience with states' rights as a guise for violating the Bill of Rights and 14th Amendment. We think that there is a valid federalist principle of states' sovereignty but not as a rationale for denial of constitutional rights.

The Commission made two major recommendations. The first was to reject all constitutional amendments, whether they would prohibit abortion per se, whether they would guarantee a right to life, whether they would confer personhood on a fetus, or whether they would simply leave this matter up to the states. The Commission uniformly rejects any and all proposed constitutional amendments. The Commission also recommended that the Congress reject any legislation which nullifies or limits *Roe* and *Doe*. I am sometimes asked what sort of legislation is pending. It is almost never pending because it is seldom introduced on the floor with sufficient notice for anyone to give any thought to it. The legislation passed during the past two years has never been subjected to hearings. That creates a real problem if you are interested in responding to such legislation.

We also recommended that all of the anti-abortion legislation passed by the Congress to date be repealed. Specifically, there is an amendment to the Legal Services Corporation Act which prohibits the use of any of those funds, and consequently, attorneys' time, for abortion cases. There is no other legal action which is similarly prohibited. Likewise, there is a prohibition on the use of monies under the Foreign Assistance Act for abortion. There were the fetal research bans which accompanied the creation of the special commission to study protection of human subjects and fetal research at the National Institute of Health. There is the conscience clause of the Health Programs Extension Act which says that federal funds cannot be withheld or withdrawn from a hospital which refuses to perform abortions on the grounds of conscience, morality, or religion.

There is a rather interesting argument which can be made for the notion that an institution does not have a conscience. The Commission did not argue that *individuals* cannot exercise such conscience; rather, an institution could not be exempt on some theory of institutional conscience. Therefore, one ought not remove the federal handle in that way.

Our current and future concerns at the Commission include federal noncompliance. It was not until September 1975 that the Defense Department finally decided that it was time to comply with the Supreme Court decisions and told all of its military bases that they could not follow state statutes which are not compliant with *Roe* and *Doe*. Some of the military bases around the country were doing just that. If there were unconstitutional abortion statutes in those states, the military bases followed that lead. They have been told as of September 1975 that the federal government should be in compliance with the Supreme Court decision. Likewise HEW has told the Public Health Service that compliance with *Roe* and *Doe* is a good idea and outlined implications for PHS facilities. There are some other places in the federal government where policy is unclear, including the Peace Corps, which goes through some rather convoluted efforts to permit their employees to secure abortions when they desire them.

The Commission is very concerned about state Medicaid statutes which are designed to prohibit abortion or at least payment for abortion under Medicaid provisions, as well as limiting access to public hospitals. We are particularly concerned about these issues because of the effect of such statutes. They represent denials of a constitutional right. There is some good evidence now with the Guttmacher report that the effect of such statutes really falls most heavily on poor women who do not have options.[1] If you are poor, living in a rural area of a state which has some repressive abortion legislation, and there is no public hospital in your area which performs abortion, you really have no option. You proceed with childbirth irrespective of your choice.

The Commission has a study planned for the next fiscal year to address four issues: first, the question of sterilization, stemming from a concern for the kind of coerced and uninformed sterilizations which received major publicity a few years ago. The controversy has died down, but we strongly suspect that the same issues remain. Second, we want to deal with the question of abortion further. Namely, we want to look more precisely at compliance with *Roe* and *Doe* around the country. We want to get a better fix on precisely the extent of noncompliance, whether it is by unconstitutional state statutes or by public hospitals which refuse to provide abortion services. We want to look at the effect of federal restrictive statutes and regulations. We think there are still nooks and crannies in the executive branch of the federal government that are not in step with the judicial branch. Third, we want to look at some of the litigation issues that we suspect may not be resolved within the next year because litigation is time-consuming and costly. Fourth, we want to assess all of these things from the point of view of precisely what effect they are having on real women in this country. It is a crucial study that needs to be done rather quickly. It would be very helpful for us to get feedback from the people who are working in this area everyday, whether in litigation or clinics, with regard to the utility of that study.

Two years ago, I was convinced that what really had the best chance of passage in the U.S. Congress was a states' rights amendment. In the Bayh subcommittee, a states' rights amendment reportedly lost by only one vote. It has a superb chance of moving somewhere simply because there are a lot of people in Washington who do not really want to get involved in this issue. They try to straddle the fence, but it cannot be done, even, as many think, with a position in favor of the states' rights amendment.

I hope I am wrong, but I think that there is not yet a significant movement in this country to retain the right to abortion. The fact that there is a conference here is very encouraging to me. We are not yet really seeing on a national level the kind of movement that there needs to be. The major problem is that we have not awakened enough people out there who really do believe in the right to abortion, and that it is possible to lose this right. There is a majority of public support for this as a personal, private decision. That message has not been translated into something that decision-makers can understand. I would urge you to think of some innovative ways in which we can begin to work to protect that right.

REFERENCES

1. C. Tietze, F. S. Jaffe, E. Weinstock and J. G. Dryfoos. *Provisional Estimates of Abortion Need and Services in the Year Following the 1973 Supreme Court Decisions, United States, Each State and Metropolitan Area,* New York: The Alan Guttmacher Institute, 1975.

Legal Status of Abortion in Colorado and Other Rocky Mountain States

Jean Dubofsky

Many of the problems facing states depend upon the kind of statute that was on the books when the *Roe* decision came down. Some states has Texas-type statutes. Other states had Georgia-type statutes. Some states have acted to develop new legislation. Other states have not done anything. You can have a combination: no statute, some new sections and new statutes, or some remaining old sections of statutes that were in existence in 1973. Colorado had, and still does have on its books, the Georgia-type statute. It was adopted here in 1967. Shortly after the U.S. Supreme Court ruled, the Colorado Supreme Court ruled on three pending criminal cases. Attached to its opinion was a copy of the Colorado statute, underlining those sections of the statute which failed because of the U.S. Supreme Court ruling. It left the consent provisions that a minor must have a parent or guardian's consent, that a spouse must consent if the wife is living with the husband, and that an abortion must be performed with the supervision of a physician.

The consent provision relating to minors has since been overruled in a Federal Court decision in the U.S. District Court of Colorado. That particular lawsuit was filed by a Legal Services attorney. Several of the cases that have been filed in this region have been filed by Legal Services attorneys, particularly Utah and South Dakota cases. Under the new legal services legislation, cases can no longer be brought by those kinds of attorneys. They tend to be the people who see the cases when they involve minorities or poor women.

To go back to the Colorado case, it involved a woman under the age of 18 who was living with a foster family. She had not been able to obtain her mother's consent for an abortion. The court went to great lengths to interview this woman and to have her interviewed by social workers, psychiatrists, and attorneys. It finally determined that the woman had been well counseled and therefore was able to give her consent to this procedure. In the process of reaching that decision, the court had a lot of language about what kind of consultation someone should have and what a woman's circumstance should be in order to be a minor and still give her consent to abortion. However, after all that language, the court simply threw out the provision of the Colorado statutes which said that a minor could not consent to an abortion. The court could not write the legislation

211

for the State of Colorado. It simply gave some guidelines and left it at that.

That case is on appeal to the Tenth Circuit. To my knowledge, it has not been argued yet. It was appealed by the attorney for the mother. The case was called *Foe* v. *Vanderhoof*.[1]. The Governor and the Attorney General who were defendants in that case changed in January of 1975, and the new Attorney General and the Governor decided not to appeal the court's decision, so it is only being appealed by the mother, whose attorney is the attorney for the "Right-to-Life" group in Colorado.

Spousal consent, to my knowledge, has not been litigated here. There were several cases in Colorado prior to the 1973 decision. Hospitals in Denver and Boulder were requiring a woman to prove that if she was not living with her husband, she had to have filed divorce papers. In both instances, the State District Court in Denver and the State District Court in Boulder ruled that that was not the case. I have not heard of a hospital making that a requirement since those decisions. Neither case was appealed.

In other states in this region, there have been new statutes. For example, in Montana a statute has been adopted since 1973 which would require written notice to parents and spouses of the person seeking the abortion; which would prohibit advertising and fetal research; and which would require a very elaborate warning before a woman's informed consent could be said to be obtained. That particular litigation is still pending. I presume that those portions prohibiting advertising would fall as a result of the Supreme Court decision in the Virginia case in 1975.[2] That is a very interesting decision from other than simply the abortion standpoint. It signalled the Court's decisions in the whole area of right to know as a portion of free speech. From a practical standpoint, hospitals, doctors, and state governments normally should heed their attorneys' advice that various actions that they might contemplate following the *Roe* decision would be illegal.

In many areas of the law, two or three circuit courts will rule on a particular issue, such as whether or not Medicaid requires payment for abortions, and that ends the question. It never necessarily gets to the Supreme Court. Everyone thinks, "The courts are going this way; this is what we'll do." That has not been the case in this area.

There is no Medicaid case pending in Colorado. Medicaid has been routinely covering the cost of abortion. Utah, North Dakota, and South Dakota have had cases in this area. In Utah, the court ruled that Medicaid should be covering abortions.[3] In South Dakota, the ruling was the same.[4]

Even if Medicaid payments do not cover the cost of abortions, you still have before you the issue of whether a public hospital is required to provide services free or to pay for abortion services. In Colorado, that would be Denver General and Colorado General. It involves the question of use of hospital facilities, which has been mentioned before. If the hospital is private, it seems that they are not required to perform abortions. In Colorado, that means that abortions are not available in large areas of the state. In Grand Junction, for example, the hospital is a Catholic hospital. I think the statistics showed a year or so ago that in the San Luis Valley, for example, in the southern portion of the state, there had only been one abortion performed in the last year. Most of the abortions are performed in Denver or Boulder. It really has to do with the willingness of a hospital to allow the procedure to be performed there, or to the existence of clinics.

Much of the litigation in this region now concerns whether or not a hospital must allow sterilization to be performed. Some of this litigation will have effects on litigation involving abortions.

REFERENCES

1. 389 F. Supp. 947 (U.S. District Court for Colorado, 1975).
2. *Bigelow* v. *Virginia,* 421 U.S. 809 (U.S. Supreme Court 1975).
3. *Doe* v. *Rampton,* 366 F. Supp. 189 (U.S. District Court for Utah, 1973) and *Doe* v. *Rose,* 499 F. Supp. 1112 (U.S. Court of Appeals, 10th Circuit, 1974).
4. *Doe et al.* v. *Westby and Woodward,* U.S. District Court for South Dakota, Western Division, Civ. 74-5017.

Discussion

Weddington: One of the interesting things on the issue of minors' consent to abortion is that, in most states, the law says that you cannot force a minor to get an abortion. There was one case out of Chicago where the parents wanted very much for the girl to have an abortion. She was 16. At one point, she was even put in jail overnight for her refusal to abide by her parents' decision. That order was then reversed, as I think it should have been. I think the law throughout the country will develop that a minor cannot be forced to have an abortion against her will. Second, the law in most states is that it is the minor's decision, if she does carry the pregnancy to term, whether she would give the child up or keep it. A parent cannot force a particular decision upon the minor. Third, in many states, it is the law that a minor has the right to decide about contraceptives. Certainly a married minor, an emancipated minor, or a minor living apart from parents can make that kind of decision. Minors in most states can consent to treatment for venereal disease. A whole line of cases and statutes recognize the right of a minor to make decisions about sexuality. However, a minor still needs parental consent for abortion in most states unless she is married. I think that is a good argument that such a result is wrong and does not make snese. A minor ought to be able to make a decision if she is old enough to understand the implications of it. While consultation with parents or others may be helpful in some situations, the final vote should not be the parents'.*

Unidentified: It looks to me from the court ruling thus far that the minors will have a constitutional right to abortion. If the state cannot intervene, it cannot intervene to give parents a right to intervene. But it does not look as though a minor has a right to contraceptives. We have a constitutional right to abortion, but no right to contraceptives.

Means: There was a Supreme Court decision, *Baird* v. *Eisenstadt,* which said that a state could not make it an offense to provide contraceptives to a minor.** It's a very complicated case because there was not a majority of the justices behind any one theory of the decision. There is a second case that is coming up on *certiorari* before the Supreme Court

---

* In July 1976, the U.S. Supreme Court in *Planned Parenthood of Central Missouri et al.* v. *Danforth, Attorney General of Missouri et al.,* invalidated portions of a Missouri statute requiring the written consent of a parent or guardian to the abortion of an unmarried woman under age 18. See the Appendix for the text of this decision.
** 402 U.S. 432 (1972)

along with the Medicaid reimbursability case from Pennsylvania. This case comes from Utah and it involved contraception and minors and parental consent. It does not involve abortion. Utah has adopted a provision in its regulations that contraceptive services and advice may not be given to minors without the minors' parental consent. The lower court there has held that invalid and that is the companion case to the Pennsylvania case on abortion. On that one, Solicitor General Bork has taken the view that that is inconsistent with the federal statute, but there, the Congressional intent was much clearer. There were some reports in the Senate and the House which said that the public policy of the United States was in favor of making these contraceptive services available to minors "on a confidential basis." They couldn't have been talking about just the general medical confidence because every patient has that, vis-a-vis his doctor and the public. What must have been meant was confidentiality from the parents. Bork apparently has bought that argument. At least we're going to have his support in the argument of that case.

Weddington: A case on minors' contraception is now before the Supreme Court. However, if the Court does decide that minors do have a right to make a decision for themselves regarding abortion, I would feel comfortable advising people at that point that they could go ahead and give contraceptives to minors who have the mental capacity to make an informed decision.

Dubofsky: The Colorado statute provides that anyone over the age of 14 may receive information and contraceptives without consent from the parents.

Ann Eichorn, Religious Coalition for Abortion Rights in Northern California: It has been our experience that the confusion about the Supreme Court decision usually is in the language concerning the third trimester. Is it a correct interpretation to read that the state may prohibit an induced premature delivery in the cases where the health and life of mother is endangered? To use the language of abortion for that prohibiting clause in the third trimester is confusing when in fact you're talking about a premature delivery.

Weddington: I don't think you'd ever have a bill passed that would say that. You are correct in saying that a state cannot restrict medical practice where a mother's life or health are involved.

Means: I would just like to address myself to one point that was implicit in the last question. There is a very interesting semantic difference between the use of the word abortion by the medical profession and its use by the court and the legislatures and the legal profession. It turns on this point of viability. In medical textbooks, a doctor will not call a termination of pregnancy which he brings about after the point of viability by the word abortion. He will call it either a termination of pregnancy or an induced delivery or some other expression. That is not the way the Court is talking. That's not the way the legislatures are talking. They're using the word abortion to cover any termination of pregnancy during any time during the whole period of gestation. There is that confusion between the two professions and there's just no way of reconciling it. So you simply have to figure out who is using the word at the given moment to know what was meant.

Bonnie Purcell, Women's Health Service Clinic, Colorado Springs, Colorado: Say the Supreme Court decision goes through and minors can have abortions without parental consent. What would be the position of school nurses and counselors refusing this information or informing the parents without the teenagers' consent?

Unidentified: There would be no criminal liability in either kind of conduct. What would happen on civil liability is not clear. If the minor brought suit saying the doctor or medical personnel violated her right of privacy by informing her parents without her consent, it would be hard to get a decision favorable to the minor. All of the people who would hear the case are most likely parents and would feel that parents ought to be involved in that kind of decision.

Unidentified: There's no way to prevent the damage that a minor might incur on her person or her state of mind?

Unidentified: I don't see any kind of lawsuit they could bring right now.

Dorothea Howe, Abortion Referral and Counseling Service of Colorado: I am replying to Ms. Dubofsky's statement that she thinks Medicaid is paying for abortions. I want to share with you how it actually works. A woman came to me at 20 weeks. She was too late to get into Denver General. Neither she nor her husband were employed. Denver General has a cutoff date of 20 weeks, but you have to get in at 16 weeks because it takes them four weeks to get going. I sent her to welfare with a statement from the doctor that she was pregnant and needed an abortion. A caseworker called on her and told her that she was qualified but that it would take a month to get the paperwork done. I said, "That's OK, the doctor will bill later." She said, "Then you will no longer qualify because you would get it under Aid for Dependent Children and you'd no longer be pregnant." This woman is having to go through an unwanted pregnancy and, of course, we have another case of welfare. These are the kinds of things we run into in practice.

Dubofsky: That would be a decision by an individual caseworker. I don't think it necessarily reflects the state's policy on Medicaid. There are some very great difficulties in Colorado, however, because Colorado's Medicaid is tied to welfare eligibility. Colorado is one of a minority of states that does not have welfare available for people who are called categorically needy. This means that you fall under the same category but your income is slightly above welfare levels.

Legislative and Political Aspects of Abortion

Legislative Experience and Tactics

John Bermingham

I feel a little as though I were a World War I soldier talking with some people just fresh off the Vietnam battlefield. My experience all goes back to 1967 and much has happened since then. Perhaps some of my comments and some of the history that I can relate to you will contribute to the background.

My own attitude was formed from an interest in world population problems. In 1960, I became a member of the board of Planned Parenthood here in Colorado. I ran for the legislature in 1964, and at that time there really was no interest in abortion or birth control and population matters. I don't think I was ever asked my opinion on those things at that time. But I did have it at the back of my mind that I would like to do something about birth control.

Actually, an effort had been made to pass a birth control bill in Colorado in 1963. It was introduced very hurriedly and failed. After my election, I ended up as Chairman of the House Welfare Committee, which was an ideal vantage point. With the help of some others, particularly Ruth Steel, we put a bill together, introduced it, and got it passed. That birth control bill really did not do anything. All it said was that people who worked in county health offices, county welfare offices, and county nurse offices might talk to their clients a bit about birth control. That is all it did. Yet we had a fantastic commotion over that, certainly as much as we had two years later on the abortion bill. But that paved the way.

In 1967, the abortion bill was introduced to the House. Either Dick Lamm who introduced the bill or George Brown asked whether I would be willing to carry an abortion bill in the Senate. I sort of shrugged my shoulders, because I did not really know much about abortion at that point. To me it was less emotional than birth control. I have learned differently since. Eventually I said yes and introduced it in the House.

I should tell you a little bit of history and a little about the legislative process. I do not know whether it works this way in Congress or in other state legislatures but I am sure there are analogues. When a bill passes the House and is headed for the Senate, physically it's taken from one body to the other. It is introduced in the second body and at the time it is introduced, the presiding officer in the body assigns it to a committee. The presiding officer in the Senate at that time was Mark Hogan, a Catholic, and it was well known that he was going to send that bill to the State Affairs

Committee where Will Nicholson was chairman. He was a Catholic, and that was going to be the end of that abortion bill.

The bill then has to go down to the basement just for technical numbers and that kind of thing. We persuaded the clerk in the basement to hang onto that bill until we whistled. We did not whistle for two or three days, but we suddenly discovered that Mark Hogan was out of the building and Fey DeBerard, the president pro tem, was available. He gavelled the Senate to order and then assigned the bill to me instead of Senator Nicholson, and we were on our way. You have to do things like that. When you get into the thick of the legislative process, you had better know these things. If you are not pulling them on them, they are pulling them on you.

When that bill got up to the health committee, we had hearings and I remember being startled by one witness who put a fetus on the table in front of me. I think I stood up and said, "Get that thing out of here." You do not really know how you are going to react in those situations and apparently I reacted right on the spur of the moment and he took it away. We eventually did get the bill passed. The day it passed in the Senate, I walked out of there and someone was carrying a placard behind me saying, "Herod was a piker!" These things happen. It's all part of the commotion.

When I ran again in 1968, abortion had become an issue and the churches in the area all denounced me from the pulpit. The fact that I had been willing to stick my neck out generated so many people who wanted to work for me, and would work hard for me, that it far outweighed the statements that were made from the pulpits. That had not been in my mind when I got into the fracas but it worked to my advantage, I believe.

In 1970, I was at the Congress on Population and Environment in Chicago. Harriet Pilpel gave a speech on how voluntary birth control has never been tried in this country because there were so many barriers and so many obstacles. There was just that one statement and two or three examples that she gave that prompted me to go back to the drawing board. In 1971 I introduced a very comprehensive birth control bill that struck down a lot of barriers and said that hospitals may not refuse to give out information and so forth. That served as a pattern for other parts of the country.

When that 1971 birth control bill was introduced, we introduced an abortion bill at the same time. Colorado's 1967 abortion law had been the first to be passed in the United States. All it did was say that abortions could be granted for serious reasons, such as to save the life of the mother, or if the fetus was deformed. It was a quite limited bill. So in 1971, at the same time we introduced this birth control bill, we introduced an updated abortion bill which was to do virtually what the Supreme Court eventually did do. We played the abortion and birth control bills together in the legislative process. The abortion bill failed by one vote and two days later we came to the floor with the birth control bill.

There was a legislative reaction on the part of the Senators, a sense of relief. They had been very upset over the abortion issue and they said, "This is the way to go." It passed with only one or two noes. This bill affected hospitals, nurses, educational institutions, and public schools, and strengthened the rights of minors to obtain information. Thus with two bills, one may be moved at the expense of the other.

In 1972 we tried again. A bill was introduced in the House to make the state abortion law similar to what the Supreme Court eventually required. There was a tremendous furor. because it was slipped in as an amendment to the criminal laws rather than as a direct abortion bill. There was such an outcry that the bill was withdrawn. In 1972 when I ran for re-election, I was again confronted by a Republican candidate who tried to defeat me in a primary. He found that he was not qualified as a Republican, so he ran as a third party candidate. He was an out-and-out "Right-to-Lifer," trying to prevent my re-election to the Senate. He failed and in 1973 we tried again. We were working on the bill when the court decision came down.

With the Supreme Court decision behind us, it is a new ball game, but there is lots going on. Otherwise you would not all be here. I will just stress one or two things. There is nothing more important in the whole process of legislation than adequate preparation. Anything you can do to be better prepared is worthwhile. Your bill should be properly prepared. You should have your arguments pro and con. Your lobbyists should be well-informed, non-abrasive people. They should be people who can go up to anyone and know all the angles, all the arguments, the statistics, the lingo and so forth. You may never know where your friends are. You may decide, well, there's a fellow that I'm not going to have much luck talking to. But I happen to know a county commissioner that is a good friend of his. So you go get that county commissioner to talk to the fellow in the legislature. You go around the left end and you can stir up votes that way.

The type of people that you have as witnesses at the hearings is important. You do not want many of the intellectual types who know from theory what it is all about. The legislators are average citizens, and they react in a very average way. A little drama is going to help. They come in with a fetus on the table. We brought in a doctor who told of one of his patients who had been turned down on a request at Denver General several times for an abortion because she could not qualify in any way. Finally she arrived. She had driven herself to the hospital after having taken a pistol and shot the fetus through her stomach. That's a shocker of course. But it is the kind of thing that you may want to bring in.

Congressional Activities

Karen Mulhauser

I work with the National Abortion Rights Action League in Washington. Abortion rights organizations include a wide spectrum of medical, religious, social and legal groups that are working to preserve legal abortion. NARAL is representative of all these interests. The situation that we are dealing with in Washington is different from the situation that we just heard described, involving the passage of good legislation. At the national level, we are fighting for the status quo in working to preserve the Supreme Court decisions of 1973. The struggle to preserve the right of every woman to choose legal abortion is somewhat different. I think many of us relaxed right after the Supreme Court rulings. A lot of the groups that had formed across the country at the state level to work to repeal abortion laws folded. People felt the Supreme Court had taken care of it for us. It took passage of three national laws restricting the availability of abortion in one year before we began to realize that we have to re-form these state groups. We have to work very hard to protect this right.

In 1973, Congress passed three restrictive laws. There is a restriction on the Legal Services Corporation Act (P.L. 93-355) that limits legal service lawyers from assisting women who seek abortion. There was a rider to the Public Health Services Act of 1973 (P.L. 93-45) known as the "conscience clause," which has two important parts. First, individuals need not participate in abortions. We all agree that if a person is opposed to abortion, it is not constructive for that person to participate in the delivery of abortion services. The other part of the conscience clause, the institutional or entity conscience clause, says that a hospital or a facility need not allow abortions to be performed. Since an institution itself can not have religious or moral principles, it is difficult to understand how it can have conscientious objections to abortion.

The other amendment that Congress passed in the year after the Supreme Court decision was to the Foreign Assistance Act of 1973 (P.L. 189). It said that U.S. funds that go to other countries for foreign aid cannot be used for abortions. Even if abortion is legal in those countries, and the U.S. is assisting their family planning programs, abortion cannot be used as a method of family planning. All three of these amendments are still law.

The subsequent attempts by the anti-abortion groups after that first year have been less successful. I think it is partly because we began to realize that we had to work to preserve the Supreme Court decision. When I first moved to Washington and started lobbying for NARAL, we would go into offices and hear that the letters from the constituents were 1,000 to one against abortion, or 500 to one against abortion. In the early months of lobbying for abortion laws, I do not remember any office saying that they had more letters from people supporting abortion than those opposed to it. Congress responded by passing restrictive legislation. However, once we began to send letters to members of Congress some began to feel more comfortable voting against restrictive legislation.

Some members of the 93rd Congress polled their own Congressional districts. Of the 93 Congressional polls that we are aware of, only five polls found a majority opposed to abortion or supporting a constitutional amendment. Seventy-three of these polls showed a clear majority supporting the Supreme Court's decision. There were 15 polls where there was no clear majority. The message to Congress is clear. They are not polling their constituents as much in the 94th Congress, but there is no question from the results of polls in the 93rd Congress that they had to look beyond the mail that came into the office to get the views of the voters. Also, there have been a number of national opinion polls showing an increasing trend toward support for abortion rights. I think this has helped Congress in defeating anti-abortion legislation.

Among other legislation introduced in the House and the Senate in recent years is language that would prevent Medicaid money from being used for abortions. You may be familiar with the Bartlett amendment to the Labor-HEW appropriations bill in 1974. This failed in conference. Senator Bartlett later introduced similar language in the 94th Congress as an amendment to Nurse Training and Health Revenue Sharing Act of 1975. There was a tabling motion which succeeded. Again he failed. These kinds of failures have frustrated the anti-abortion movement.*

We are beginning to feel confident again, perhaps, too confident. The anti-abortion people are getting geared up again. They are frustrated with the 94th Congress. They are frustrated because their bills are not passing. They are frustrated because their attempts to pass a constitutional amendment were defeated in the Senate Judiciary Subcommittee on Constitutional Amendments in 1975. I like to note that this happened on September 17th, the anniversary of the signing of the Constitution, because it is a nice reaffirmation of the Constitution. They are frustrated because they recognize that there is not much chance of a constitutional amendment passing the House of Representatives this Congress. This frustration is being directed back to the States and to upcoming elections in the congressional districts. They would like the next Congress to be more sympathetic to a constitutional amendment.

* In the fall of 1976, anti-abortion forces succeeded in attaching an amendment to the DHEW-Labor appropriations bill banning the use of federal monies for abortion unless the woman's life was in danger. This restriction has been enjoined, pending Supreme Court review of its consitutionality.

NARAL and other pro-choice groups are occasionally accused of being on the defensive and asked why we are not more aggressive. We have a good law now and if the anti-abortion people are introducing legislation that is opposed to abortion, we have to defend what we have. If the anti-abortion people are going out in the congressional districts and are supporting candidates who are opposed to abortion, we have to go out in those districts and defend the individuals who are supporting abortion rights. If we are going to continue to have good legislation, we have to have good members in both state legislatures and in Congress. People have asked me why NARAL didn't put up a presidential candidate. How come you are not running for President? First of all, I am too young. But also the major candidates, at least in the Democratic party, are all opposed to a constitutional amendment that would outlaw abortion. Wallace is the only Democrat who would support a constitutional amendment. Because of the anti-abortion positions of both Reagan and Ford, it is hard for a pro-choice voter to choose a Republican candidate for President. The major Democrats who are running for President are against a constitutional amendment so we do not really need to have an abortion rights activist running for President. We do have to respond to the campaign of the Pro-life Action Committee.

Ellen McCormack, a Catholic Long Island housewife, filed in July 1975 with the Federal Elections Commission to run as a Democrat for President. Most of us would not give to a fringe, single-issue candidate that we know is going to lose. But we might give to a movement that we believe in strongly. It was a very clever idea to get an anti-abortion, so-called "Right-to-Life" candidate for President, because she has now qualified under the federal campaign law for federal matching funds. The new Federal Elections Commission enumerates various requirements for a presidential candidate to qualify for federal matching funds. He or she must receive $5,000 in contributions of $250 or less from 20 states. She has met these qualifications. A couple of weeks ago, NARAL filed a formal complaint with the Federal Elections Commission, enumerating those parts of the federal campaign law of which she or her political committees had been in violation. Violation of these statutes cause criminal penalties including imprisonment and fines. Unfortunately, we failed. She is receiving her matching dollars from tax payers. By now she has received a check for $100,000 and is going to ask for more. We disagree with the Commission's decision. These funds are going to be used almost entirely to promote the Pro-Life Action Committee, or the "Right-to-Life" committee's anti-abortion message through TV commercials and radio spots. It is a single issue media campaign, not a presidential campaign.

This is something that we as individuals can fight. We can form local coalitions. You can get five or six people representing such groups as Planned Parenthood, ACLU, religious coalitions for abortion rights, and AAUW and go to your local TV station and request public service time to match the time that the anti-abortion movement is receiving through Ellen

McCormack's commercials.

A presidential candidate can say almost anything, because the message is part of a political campaign. If a TV station decides to sell time to any presidential candidate, the station must also sell time to other presidential candidates. What we may find in many communities is program managers who would just as soon not sell time to McCormick but are compelled to do so. Some may be receptive to giving public service time for pro-choice TV spots. Planned Parenthood and NARAL have produced spots which are available through either organization. If the anti-abortion spots appear in your community, we urge you to use our ads. If you do not yet know your TV and radio program managers, approach them before the spots come so that you will know them before you actually ask for time.

The State Legislatures

Jeannie Rosoff

I was asked to comment on what happened in the states following the Supreme Court decisions. If you listened to Senator Bermingham, I am sure you understand that the main reaction of the state legislatures to the Supreme Court decisions was one of relief. The ball was in somebody else's court and they did not have to worry about this issue any more. However, after just a few months, the anti-abortion organization came to realize that they had lost a big battle but the war was not over. There was a resurgence of activity at the state level. The degree of activity was probably less than before because the anti-abortion movement is really not very large. It is very vocal and very active, but it does not have that many bodies. A lot of people are now camping in Washington and harassing Congress so there are fewer people left in the state legislatures to harass state legislators.

Most states did nothing in reaction to the Supreme Court decisions. They heard the decisions and acted as if it was the law of the land, as it is. A few decided that whatever law they had on the books was still going to be their law until it was thrown out. In fact, it took a lot of litigation to do just that. Of the states that acted, some acted positively. They moved toward getting their laws in line with the Supreme Court decisions. In some cases, it was clear that the law was patterned in good faith after the Supreme Court decisions. In some other cases, it was not clear whether the Supreme Court decisions were fully understood or whether somebody was trying to be clever and write a law which appeared to follow the Supreme Court decisions but incorporated more restrictions. There were some extreme examples of obstructionism as with the state of Utah. It adopted a new law which had the most inventive provisions to restrict access to abortion. One of them was that a minor had to have consent of both the parents and also one of the grandparents. There was a great deal of creativity in the writing of these laws. Most of them, of course, ended up in court very quickly. There were a number of approaches to restricting access to abortion, but a prime one was clearly the question of consent: the husband's consent, the putative father's consent or parental consent. The most extreme example of this approach, of course, was the Utah statute, but many states passed laws which required the consent of somebody besides the woman herself. Some states also passed legislation that said that a woman would not be deemed to have given her consent to an abortion until she had had explained to her in exquisite detail the stage of gestation of the fetus, what would happen to the fetus during the course of abortion, and how the fetus would get dismembered. This obviously was not intended to encourage abortion.

Some bills were passed which imposed several conditions in the first trimester which were clearly out of line with the Supreme Court decisions. The Supreme Court said that in the first trimester, the abortion decision is up to the woman and her physician but it did not say where abortions had to take place. A number of laws were adopted which required that they be performed only in hospitals or only in clinics specifically licensed by the states. A couple of state legislatures, Missouri being particularly ingenious in this regard, added special restrictions on how abortions could be performed in the second trimester, specifically outlawing saline abortions (which is the prime method of doing abortions in the second trimester). There were some attempts to write into law various descriptions of what constituted a viable fetus and what the responsibilities of the physician might be in relation to a viable fetus. There were some reporting requirements which, in perhaps half or more of the cases, were innocent enough. There are some advantages to reporting various health events for monitoring purposes. In a few instances, however, the legislatures went much further than this and clearly intended these reporting requirements to act as restrictive provisions. Last, but not least, there were also a number of attempts to restrict the use of public funds for abortion, mainly the use of Medicaid funds. Most of these inappropriate or improper measures have since been thrown out by the courts.

There has been a difference in the level of anti-abortion activity at the state level in the three years since the Supreme Court decisions. For the first two years after the decisions, there was a great deal of activity by state legislatures trying to impose restrictions of one kind or another. This past year there has been a real lessening of activity, not only in terms of the number of bills passed but even in terms of the number of bills introduced. Whether that means that in years to come these efforts will diminish further is hard to tell, but I think they probably will.

One last type of initiative by state legislatures which should be mentioned is that many state legislatures went on record memorializing the Congress as to the need to pass a constitutional amendment. This is not a binding procedure. In legislative terms, it is like sending a message to your Congressman. It is like saying, "I'm very unhappy about something and I wish you would do something about it. Good-by." Some state legislatures, which probably did not want to pass restrictive abortion laws, tried to satisfy the portion of the electorate which was unhappy about legalized abortion by passing such resolutions.

The Church and Politics

Jan Gleason

I am the president of Catholics for a Free Choice and I am also on the national board of NOW. I never did share the optimism of some women that *Roe* v. *Wade* was going to be the permanent law of the land. Historically, abortion has always been around and it has been illegal. As far as its legality goes, it is like a badminton game. It goes back and forth. In 1973, I wrote a resolution which I took to Houston, at our national convention of the National Organization for Women, where we reaffirmed our support of *Roe* v. *Wade*. We also raised objections to the various constitutional amendments. When we talk about politics, it is more than just running an Ellen McCormack for President of the United States. These roots go very deep. What we in NOW are learning is that there is a tremendous amount of behind-the-scene politicking going on with the Roman Catholic hierarchy. As women, we do not like it. Catholics for a Free Choice feels the same way. We have a part-time lobbyist who works in Washington and we try to make people aware that the Roman Catholic bishops do not represent Catholic people. The bishops do represent a great deal of power in general and they have tremendous psychological power with the press. Bishop Maher, as you know, excommunicated the San Diego County NOW members last April 1975. He did this because we were visible and vocal on the abortion issue. As a result of that, the news went across the nation and we had many demonstrations in San Diego. We had 400 women in front of St. Bridget's Church and he still really has not learned that women do not like what he is saying. The latest incident is that he confirmed to Joan Casale, the local president of NOW, that women who use an IUD would be considered murderers. This was announced yesterday on TV. You have to realize that when you are dealing with this type of mentality, as long as you keep it in the Catholic press, nobody knows. When it starts getting out, women start thinking, "What does this mean to me, one of six million IUD users? Can they really pass those constitutional amendments? And if they do, is the IUD going to be a lethal weapon? Are they really going to have fetal police? Are you going to have to send your Kotex in to the IRS for your $650 deduction?"

These are topics that traditionally have belonged to women's culture and men are not comfortable dealing with them. Bishops are not any better at dealing with them than anybody else. About a month ago I asked the Internal Revenue Service for an audit of the Roman Catholic diocese of San Diego. I had sent them a memo signed by Bishop Leo T. Maher, the wording of which was very similar to the announcement in November at the National Catholic Conference of Bishops convention, of a pastoral plan for pro-life activities that would involve every identifiable national, regional and local Catholic agency, and would be organized on the basis of Congressional districts. They are to be called citizen's lobbies, and the bishops refer to the parishioners as "constituents." Bishop Gumbleton said, "Nobody will believe the Catholics aren't involved. I don't think Catholics will believe it either."

In spite of this, the Roman Catholic hierarchy continues to lobby with impunity. They have a certain mystique with the press. Being a bishop or cardinal carries more weight than being a housewife. Since I had never felt that way I got thrown out. I would go on TV and say, "I believe in the law of the land and women have the right to control their own bodies." Furthermore, women have this right in light of Vatican II documents of religious freedom. It is a Catholic document. Women have the right to use their conscience. These bishops do not want to hear this because for 200 years they have been teaching Catholic women that they are subordinate to men, that they have no head and sex is evil.

I am concerned about their lobby because they are attempting to be the most decisive political force in the third century of this country's history and the Catholic press states so publicly. They go on to outline their political potency. Catholics are concentrated in ten states with the greatest number of electoral votes.

Yet the Constitution does not say that you have a "right to life." The Constitution says you have a right to not have your life taken away without due process. Thus the fetus will be given rights that no citizen enjoys. Do not forget the "enabling" part of the amendment. When you have this biological right to support, what is that going to do to the economy and to taxpayers? Do you know what is involved? Do you know that if they pass a constitutional amendment, you are going to have a totally different economic and social structure when they pass the legislation that will go with it?

We are sick and tired of having 300 bishops tell 100 million women how they are supposed to think and what they are supposed to do with their bodies.

The View from Congress

Cynthia Kahn

Congresswoman Pat Schroeder is fairly relaxed about the status of the abortion legislation before Congress, considering that there are some 60-odd bills that are currently being considered. The Senate Judiciary Subcommittee that is dealing with these bills has voted to take no action on any of the constitutional amendments affecting access to abortion. In the House of Representatives, the subcommittee on Constitutional Rights, which is chaired by Congressman Don Edwards, Democrat from California, has held two hearings on abortion resolutions and will be holding five more days of hearings. It appears that the measures currently before Congress will be voted down in subcommitte. I should hasten to add, though, that it is terribly important to keep up the pressure. Part of the reason that we are winning again is the action of NOW and NARAL and all the groups putting on the pressure. A second explanation is that three or four of the key congressmen who were responsible for putting in all of the anti-abortion legislation in the 93rd Congress were defeated when the 94th Congress came around. There is no real knowledge of whether they were defeated by women who were angry at their anti-abortion stands, but certainly their defeat has struck the fear of God in the hearts of other Congressmen, or at least the fear of the electorate. A third explanation is the economic downturn, which may explain the lack of current activity at the State level as well. People really are more concerned about jobs, about unemployment, and about economic issues that face them than they are with the abortion issue.

The vocal anti-abortion people are really only a very small minority of the total population. Partly as a result of their lack of success on the congressional legislative level, the "Right-to-Lifers" have begun to focus on electing more amenable candidates to Congress. I think that's probably an issue that we really ought to be very much aware of. They are now turning from the legislative arena to the actual election process and trying to get more of their people elected, people who will support their views and will put more legislation into the hopper.

There was a CBS news report that outlined all the presidential candidates' stands on abortion. As I watched that news report, I became very angry. Jimmy Carter had just won in the Iowa primaries and was looking pretty good as a national presidential candidate. He was asked for his statement on abortion and I want to read it to you. Jimmy Carter says: "I think that abortion is wrong. I think that the government ought to do everything it can to minimize abortion. I think the Supreme Court has ruled that women have complete control over the process in the first 13 weeks. I do not favor the Supreme Court ruling nor do I favor a constitutional amendment to change that. I have never favored a constitutional amendment to give unrestricted abortions nor to give States local options." I had great difficulty understanding what exactly he was saying and Birch Bayh's response was: "I'd rather not judge Jimmy Carter on what he's said or hasn't said." He really has taken both sides of the issue on abortion. The other presidential candidates, Bayh, Udall, and Harris, are for the Supreme Court decision and obviously against a constitutional amendment. Jackson and Shriver are against the Supreme Court decision but are also against a constitutional amendment. Wallace and Reagan are against the Supreme Court decision and for a constitutional amendment.

It is important to understand that we absolutely should not choose our presidential candidate on the single issue of abortion. There are many other issues that arouse strong emotions in people. Gun control is one of them. Israel is another one and abortion is probably the third. Yet you should not make your decision on a presidential candidate on the basis of any one single issue.

In terms of what pro-choice people can do or ought to be doing in anticipation of the campaign and elections, we cannot attack the anti-abortionists on the narrow issue of abortion. You cannot let the "Right-to-Lifers" frame the issue as being one of abortion. It is necessary to look at it at a much broader level in terms of the quality of life. Nobody believes abortion is marvelous. Women do not want to go out and have an abortion just because it is really fun and everybody ought to have the experience. Abortion is the ultimate back-up for birth control, and ideally, that is what it should be. We should focus on the quality of life, on family planning services, and on research in contraceptive technology and social services that ought to be provided to a family. If you ask "Right-to-Lifers," they tell you that they are not concerned about quality of life. They are not in favor of job programs for people. They are not in favor of food stamps. They are not in favor of family planning services being available on a broad level. That wider range of issues is where we ought to be focusing our political attack, not simply on abortion itself.

Secondly, in terms of a general strategy, we should keep the federal government out of abortion decisions. Theologians have been arguing about when life begins for thousands of years. Do you want the federal government to step in and make that decision? It is absolutely crazy. It should not go back to the state legislatures and it should not be an issue for the federal government. This is a private decision between women and their doctors. Please comment on strategies that you think would be beneficial in the November election.

Discussion

Gleason: I can tell you what we're doing in San Diego. Next month we're working with a religious coalition for abortion rights. This is a group of 22 religious and ethnic groups that are opposed to any type of fetal amendment or restriction on a woman's right to choose. We agree that it's a decision of conscience. In the state of California, the Religious Coalition for Abortion Rights is putting on a one-and-a-half day seminar covering the legal, medical, and theological aspects of abortion.

Rosoff: I agree with Jan that the recent entry of the bishops into the fray was very important but perhaps for slightly different reasons. For the last three years, the visible groups in the anti-abortion fight have been the "Right-to-Life" groups. We have been fortunate in our opposition because they are so way out and so unreasonable and so crazy that eventually they turn people off. When a witness comes to Congress and says that abortion is absolutely terrible and the Senator or Congressman says, "Well, do you think that more research in contraception would be a good thing in this case?" and the witness says "No, that would be terrible too," it gives the Senator or Congressman some pause. Then if the Senator or Congressman says, "Well, do you think the answer is in more family planning?" and the witness says, "No, family planning is also murder, and we're not going to have it either," at that point everybody turns off. The danger in the entry of the Catholic church into the debate, in a more organized and more persistent way than formerly, is that the bishops are usually pretty good politicians and they understand what's possible and what's not possible. The real danger in the years ahead will not be the adoption of a constitutional amendment of the type which has been introduced up to now, but the search for an "acceptable" compromise. Politicians get very tired of having an issue which they don't seem to be able to get rid of and, after all, compromise is mother's milk to politics. There are many people in the church who are able to try to engineer this kind of compromise and that is why I feel the bishops' more active involvement increases the danger.

As far as the political campaigns are concerned, I would like to make a point on the position of the candidates. I, too, find it personally annoying to see a candidate genuflecting and saying, "I oppose abortion and all abortions are terrible, but I'm not going to do anything about the Supreme Court decisions." What is more salient is that they are all saying they will oppose a constitutional amendment. The first clause is, "I oppose, I'm upset, I'm disturbed." That's the candidate's privilege. The clause which is important is, "I will not change the law of the land, I will be against a constitutional amendment." If you look at it this way, the candidates fall into three categories. All of the Democrats except George Wallace say that they will keep the law as is, whether they're unhappy with it or not. George Wallace and Ronald Reagan would seek a human life constitutional amendment. Our President Ford, who somehow has not yet been mentioned in the course of this discussion, apparently wants something which nobody else wants. He would like a states' rights amendment which he said he would not seek but would support. Since none of the various sides in this controversy have any interest in the states' rights amendment, it is the best equivalent to a non-position.

We should not get tangled in the rhetoric of what candidates say, their facial expressions, their personal feelings and so on. The only important thing is whether they will seek or they will not seek a constitutional amendment. That is where the dividing line really is.

Mulhauser: We polled all the candidates a couple of months ago with a very detailed questionnaire, asking for more than just their stand in support of the Supreme Court decision or in support of a constitutional amendment. We asked for instance, if the candidate supports Medicaid payments for abortion. Even though there's more of a variation in the middle group that would support some restrictions on the availability of abortion, it is still very clear that most of the mainstream presidential candidates, at least among the Democrats, are not going to support a constitutional amendment. It's important for us to remember that Presidents are not in a position to affect change, anyway. Presidents are supposed to uphold the law of the land. That's the very least we can expect from our President.

In terms of strategies for campaigns, I think the strategy has to respond in part to the strategy that's being used by the opposition. It's partly going to have to be a public relations campaign. It also has to include support for the good candidates. While I would agree with Cindy Kahn that we shouldn't focus just on abortion, I think we do have to know what the candidates' positions on abortion are. We have to know if they will or will not support a constitutional amendment if they get to Congress. It would be helpful for us to ask the candidates for their positions and when we learn their positions we should let them know how we feel. If we're getting requests for financial support from candidates, we should let them know why we are or why we are not giving money. One possibility is to return those postage paid envelopes to tell them why we're not giving. It would be negligent for us to not pick up on this issue when the opposition is making it a very prominent issue in campaigns. The TV commercials that Ellen McCormack is using are not going to affect the presidential campaigns that much, but they're going to be used in congressional districts. Those opposed to abortion will probably target the congressional districts where they might be able to replace someone who is presently opposed to constitutional amendments. They are going to have an effect at the local level that they might not have at the presidential level.

We need to be there to respond.

NARAL is planning five regional meetings during the month of April. They are planned for activists from NARAL and other pro-choice groups who already have a fairly good informational level about the issue but need to come together for strategy planning and to solve local problems.

Bermingham: I would agree that you should not pick your presidential candidate on the basis of what candidates think about abortion. The amendment has to go through the Congress by a two-thirds vote in each house and then be passed by the states. The candidate is going to have his eye cocked to the electorate when deciding on what kind of statement he makes, for better or worse. Once the election is over, he has nothing to do about it. The real action is in the Congress and in the feelings that are articulated by the people of America. The danger that you've been mentioning is that the "Right-to-Lifers" will somehow create an impression that they're in the majority and that they're much stronger than they really are.

I go back to the time when the birth control and abortion bills were in the Colorado legislature. The mail against these bills would stack high, but the mail for them was very low. We then began to notice that the mail and the telegrams against the bills all would come in on Mondays and Tuesdays, obviously written after church on Sunday. After the bills had been passed, the letters and mail came from those in support. For those of us with our necks out, we really wished that those who supported the bills had written ahead of time. It's always the "anti's" that write the letters ahead of time and then those in favor thank you after you've done it. So when you see an issue developing, speak up early, get your letters or your telegrams in early. Don't wait until after the action to thank the legislators who are working for you. Get your support in ahead of time.

Also, I stacked up the "anti" letters to see where they came from. I separated those from my district from those that came from elsewhere in the state, and then arranged the ones from my district by street address to see where they came from. I had 61 precincts in my district and probably 75 percent of the letters came from three precincts. There was a Catholic church in each precinct. The moment I saw that, I realized what a tiny proportion had been so terribly vocal. But the legislative candidates and the congressional candidates don't have the time or inclination to do this kind of analysis, and they really think that these people have a much broader base of support than they really have. It's up to you to counter that impression.

Karen Schecker, Right to Choose, Tempe, Arizona: The Catholic bishops took some polls and found out that most Catholics supported a woman's right to choose abortion under certain circumstances.* Also, most people do not vote for or against a candidate based on any single

* S. Saldahna, W. McCready, K. McCourt and A. Greeley. "American Catholics," *The Critic* 33:14, 1975.

237

issue.* I thought the bishops said they were willing to take the lead in organizing all of the various anti-choice groups behind one constitutional amendment. They would not suggest the wording of the amendment. I thought that meant they were ready for a compromise, realizing that because the various anti-choice groups were spread out over about eight constitutional amendments, the only way to win was for all of them to back one. They would only accept one that would be a compromise to the traditional Catholic position. From what I'm hearing from you tonight, that is erroneous. They're still going to push for a constitutional amendment that would do away with abortion for any reason whatsoever.

Rosoff: I think in terms of political tactics. I can't imagine the Church ever saying anything publicly except that we want what we think is right. What is right in our mind is a constitutional amendment. That's too simple a level of politics. That's your opening statement at the bargaining table. If someone came up with a compromise and the compromise was not too untolerable to people, for example, legal abortion in the first trimester but no legal abortions in the second trimester, except for absolutely dire circumstances, then it would not be inconceivable that the bishops would have a statement which said, in effect, well, we still reaffirm our stand against abortion and we think a constitutional amendment would be better, but in the interest of cutting down on the number of murders that go on we will support this particular measure. You can throw your political power behind a compromise just as a sort of lesser-evil type of position. I think this is what I was trying to say was the real danger.

Gleason: The Supreme Court decision spelled out very clearly what the state has a right to do and what the woman has the right to do. The only way that that can be overruled is by a constitutional amendment. That is not counting all the restrictive riders like parental consent or interested parties' consent. The only way to make a compromise is to go with a states' rights amendment.

Schecker: But I had thought that since there was a tie vote on the states' right amendment that that would be what they'd be pushing for?**

Rosoff: We're afraid that there might be a search on for a compromise. The nature of the compromise is a little hard to tell. I don't think that a straight states' rights amendment would be the compromise. I think it's unacceptable to all sides. The advantage from the bishops' point of view of the "Noonan Amendment" is that, besides being a states' rights amendment, which the bishops are against, and have said they are very

---

* Yankelovich, Skelly and White, Inc. National Poll conducted October 1976. Only 13 percent of all respondents and 15 percent of Catholic respondents reported that they would vote for a candidate solely on the basis of his or her position on abortion.
** In 1975, the Senate Judiciary Subcommittee on Constitutional Amendments failed to report out on a tie vote a constitutional amendment proposing to return to the states the power to regulate abortions.

strongly against, is that it had some words in there about recognition of the value of human life. That's what the bishops like about that particular amendment. I don't think at this point we can say what would be the nature of a compromise. What we can say is that we are entering a dangerous phase where more reasonable people are entering the debate and where some people are, in fact, going to want to settle the issue once and for all.

Lynne Ellison, Rep. Pat Schroeder's office, Denver, Colorado: I'd like to hear from the panelists on how they would look at state restrictions or laws making counseling mandatory for women seeking abortion.

Gleason: I think it's terrible. I think it paves the way for brainwashing.

Bermingham: When we were dealing with the abortion bill in 1972 and 1973, before the Court decisions came down, one of the things that we were putting into the bill in order to sell it was counseling. We were told at that time that counseling was important. The big discussions are always on the possibility of a constitutional amendment, but I think the real action is in these restrictive riders and state statutes. That's the place to be most watchful.

Rosoff: It would be unconstitutional. Let me just explain the reasoning. The Supreme Court has said that in the first trimester, the state cannot intervene. The decision is between the woman and the doctor, and the only thing the state can require is that the doctor be licensed. There have been a number of Court decisions since then reaffirming this principle. For example, the city of Chicago adopted a series of guidelines and regulations for standards in abortion clinics which were perfectly reasonable. The courts threw them out, saying you cannot treat abortion differently from any other kind of medical procedure. If you do not have counseling for all sorts of medical procedures, you cannot have anything special for the termination of pregnancy in the first trimester. In the second trimester, it can only be in such a way as to protect maternal health.

Terri Willis, Sacramento, California: I was at the California State Capitol talking to some consultants last week and they're concerned about what their candidates are going to say when they're on the campaign trail. They are faced with some difficult questions about abortion and I would like to ask our panelists if they have any suggestions for how our candidates who support the Supreme Court decision can handle the questions.

Kahn: Let me just answer for Pat Schroeder. It's been a little easier for her as a woman candidate because it's not a difficult decision. She regularly gets pamphlets that say vote for anybody but Pat Schroeder because she's supported abortion reform. She just tends to ignore that kind of statement. It's probably the easiest thing to do.

Bermingham: If the candidate is in favor of the Supreme Court decision, the candidate should just say so and that will probably put an end to it. Tell candidates not to argue and don't be weak about it. Don't waffle, just say I'm for it. Take the consequences.

Mulhauser: There are a few examples of politicians who have tried to find a middle road. There is no middle road. You can't be for both sides or against both sides, and it's much better to make it very clear to voters where you stand. There will be a minority of the hard-core anti-abortion minority who is going to vote against a candidate who supports abortion. There's no way you're going to win that vote, even if you mildly support the Supreme Court decision, so that you should come right out and firmly say that you support it. Congressmen are beginning to adopt a new posture of, "I have my own personal problems with abortion but I support the Supreme Court decision." That doesn't bother me so much because that means there are more members now who are saying they support the Supreme Court's decision or that they would not impose their own views on others. I don't think we should be hard on a candidate who may or may not have personal problems with abortion but is saying that he does. If that makes it easier for him to say he's against a constitutional amendment or supports abortion rights, or will not impose his own views, then let's let him say it.

Gleason: All you have to do is have the candidate say, "I support *Roe* v. *Wade* as the law of the land. I believe in separation of church and state." You can go into history and it gets you off the hook right away because it's right and it's true. Most people in the country do know what the first amendment is: freedom of religion, freedom of conscience. *Roe* v. *Wade* called it privacy. We call it conscience. The Supreme Court is protecting your right to your conscience. We asked Senator Tunney and here's how we worded it. "Would you vote to take away the constitutional right to make a decision of conscience regarding abortion from 100 million women?" He said, "No, I wouldn't vote to do that." So, you know, be artistic.

Hern: One of the more vulnerable sections of the Supreme Court decision is the part regarding the second trimester. The Court decision said that the state may make reasonable regulations to protect maternal health, even though it may not restrict the right to abortion. This can result in the state passing a law saying that the abortion has to be done in the hospital. That could be discriminatory in effect. Even though we in the medical community may define medical practice as having the abortion performed in the hospital, the very rapid changes in technology may make that idea obsolete. Then we are stuck with a similar situation in which there is economic discrimination against women who cannot afford to have this done in the hospital. They may not find a hospital where it will be allowed because of the Church amendment which says that hospitals don't have to provide the abortion. What do you think is the likelihood of any state trying to enact such a law and what would be the best way to counteract such an effort?

Rosoff: Some states have passed such laws, and at this stage of the technology, they may not have been intended to be restrictive laws. The key words are "reasonably related to maternal health." If the technology changes and second trimester abortion could be performed with all safety in different types of facilities, I think the Courts would certainly be willing to review these types of provisions again. What is reasonable under certain conditions may not be reasonable under others. There may need to be some litigation in this regard as things develop, but I don't see that as any terrible threat.

Bermingham: I don't see it as a great threat either. The main argument against the one you raised is that the technology does change. You can convince a fair number of legislators about that. You can also ask them why is it different from appendicitis. Why the special treatment of this operation compared to others?

Mulhauser: The Supreme Court is going to hear the Missouri case that does have the restriction on the performance of saline abortions. They may be getting into the area of the limits of states' rights to define "reasonably related to maternal health."*

Unidentified: Approximately how many states have passed restrictive legislation since 1973?

Rosoff: Half of the states did nothing at all. There are about 13 states that have passed one or more clauses which were intended to be restrictive. The remainder of the states have passed some legislation which could have a restrictive effect or could not, such as reporting requirements, or requirements as to what constitutes the woman's consent. A minority of states have gone the restrictive route. The majority of states have done nothing at all, and some states have enacted laws of unknown impact.

Renee Ward, Midwest Women's Health Center, Minneapolis, Minnesota: I'd like to ask if you see any new attacks on the horizon at the state legislative level. For example, in our state the family planning bill was up and one provision said that no monies would go to an agency in which abortion referrals were made. Last year in another family planning bill, it was proposed that at least 50 percent of the money should go to natural family planning methods and to those who teach them.

Rosoff: I see more mischief. I think you have to remember that the main effect of all this agitation is not so much that laws really get passed and stay on the books but the effect it has on a communal belief that abortion is still a very hot issue. Therefore, hospitals tend not to provide abortions. There were a number of states with no restrictive abortion laws in which not one abortion was reported in 1974. It had nothing to do with the law. It had to do with the level of agitation which makes everybody in the community believe that if the hospital is going to provide abortions, the world is going to cave in. That's where I think the real damage takes place.

Steele: I have one observation and one question. I would see it as a tremendous detriment, as former Senator Bermingham suggests, to try to write in any kind of provisions relative to counseling. We look too much to

---

* In the *Danforth* decision of August 1976, the Supreme Court ruled that these provisions of the Missouri law were unconstitutional.

changes in laws to bring about things that we, as citizens, certainly could bring about in other ways. There are a lot of doctors in institutions who are not able to serve women as well as they might like because of real problems in the management of the hospital. It isn't just management being resistant, it's simply that there are so many kinds of problems in a given hospital that abortion is only one of many. Aside from changing laws, there are a great many things we can do to change the climate and the practice relevant to abortion. Secondly, I'm curious to know if any of you feel that the kinds of television spots which will accompany the Ellen McCormack campaign could have the same kinds of effects which were witnessed in Michigan?*

Mulhauser: I personally am encouraged by the lack of response in New Hampshire because I understand that she put several thousand dollars into buying spots and promotional pieces in New Hampshire and, in spite of that, only got a thousand or so votes. The CBS and New York Times poll of voters as they left the polling booth showed that abortion was a very minor issue. It's hard to know what kind of effect the TV spots will have in the Congressional races. I think the presidential primaries are different from the Congressional races. It's hard to balance the effect of the backlash that she's generating. We're getting a number of calls and a little bit of money coming in, because NARAL is doing something about her filing with the Federal Election Commission. I think she's doing a lot of our work for us with her TV promotional spots. It's hard at this point to balance the support she will gain and the counter support that we will all reap from this.

Joyce Wilkie, Denver, Colorado: I've heard that there's a good chance that family planning funds are going to be cut in the coming year. I wondered if you had any more information on that, and if you could perhaps give us some ideas on how to counteract it.

Rosoff: Last year President Ford called for a 21 percent reduction in funds for family planning services and other health services. The Congress rejected this, but this year, the President is making the same proposal. It will not occur if we all do the right thing, which is go to our Congressmen and tell them that they better restore the funds, and what's more, they should add some more money to this program. As a matter of fact, that's the best alternative to abortion there is. If Congress is so concerned about abortion, they will have to justify their stand on what they do in behalf of family planning.

Kahn: I might just add that I think that that's the feeling that Pat Schroeder has. That's the feeling in Congress. Those family planning funds will be restored. There is a great deal of feeling for cutting back on

---

* In 1972, a referendum was held in Michigan on a bill which would have liberalized that state's abortion law. The bill had widespread support and was expected to win, but was defeated in the wake of a television-oriented, anti-abortion media campaign. (See, P. Hendrickson. "The Admen Who Beat Abortion" *Detroit Free Press,* March 4, 1973, p. 10)

government services across the board. The difficulty is that some of us believe that some areas ought to be cut more and other areas ought to be expanded.

Bermingham: Some feeling does exist at the state level. The key in the Colorado legislature is our Joint Budget Committee, which consists of six people. It is a matter of lobbying those people so that they don't cut back across the board, five percent on everything, whatever it may be. Fortunately we have in the legislature, on that committee, Sentor Ruth Stockton, who was one of the early supporters of the birth control and abortion bills.

Kahn: I have a question to ask the rest of the panel. I'd like to know what connections the rest of you feel there are between the "Right-to-Life" movement and the anti-ERA (Equal Rights Amendment) movement?

Gleason: It's very strong. When I was in Philadelphia, I managed to watch TV and on it they had a group of anti-ERA people charging down the street, marching with banners. It was the Thomas More Society, which is Catholic. They are traditionally opposed to allowing women to be fully developed persons. When the Bishop sent somebody out to talk with me, I said, "I don't understand all this flap about the fetal amendment and an egg as a person. What have you done to help make women persons legally?" He replied, "What's the ERA?" He had never heard of it, but some of them have heard of it and a lot of them are working hard against it. It's the old mind-control propaganda. You're educated and you think. You forget that a lot of people who watch TV don't think. Part of our national moblization for NOW is to research and encourage research on the misogynism of the Catholic hierarchy. It's a very real thing.

Workshops

Workshop

Religious and Ethical Aspects
of Abortion

Marty Drew: I begin with the belief that opponents of abortion are not misguided, fanatic, religious zealots. Nor do I believe that proponents of abortion are murderers or death peddlers. It is my belief that experts in the fields of medicine, social science, law, bioethics, philosophy and religion have looked at the same factual data. The disagreement and the differences of opinion emanate from differing values and philosophies. There are differing biases and points of view on the value of life at varying stages.

It is my belief that if dialogue is to become possible, we must begin the difficult process of dissecting our own positions on the value of life: what is it, when does it begin and the role of conscience. We must attempt anew to listen to persons whose views are different from our own. It is much more difficult to admit that our views contain the possibility of error. I am here today as a Catholic priest. I am here as a Christian, a person who believes in the gospel, a person who believes that the scriptures have and do contain much that is important on the whole question of life and conscience. I am here in these roles and with some knowledge of the question of abortion and conscience.

The question of when life begins and the role of conscience are issues which have been around for a long time. They have been discussed, argued, and debated for over a thousand years. The same differences of opinion which exist in the field of bioethics exist today in the field of ethics or moral theology. The debate is not between Protestants or Catholics, nor is it between modern and traditional theologians. I would like to share some of the opinions and beliefs that have emerged through debate within the Church during the past thousand or so years. I hope that a small overview might enable each of us to move toward the goal of becoming more knowledgeable on the question of humanity.

First of all, I do not believe there is any doubt that, for many of the great teachers in early Christianity, abortion was explicitly prohibited. Christianity brought with it a new sense of human dignity and worth. Man, as contrasted with the world around him, was viewed as a participant in God's creation. The prohibition of abortion in the early Church, however, rested primarily on the contention that, from the moment of conception,

247

the embryo is a human person. That theory was never a universal one. Great teachers of the early church, like Gregory, Basil, Tortoli and others, supported it. But even in the early church there were many individuals who did not hold to this belief.

It would be erroneous to say that these other individuals favored abortion. While they did not give approval to it, condemnation of abortion was lacking. Some of these individuals were Jenadeus, Jerome, and pernaps even St. Augustine. These individuals preferred a theory of a "delayed infusion of humanity." This opinion, which I refer to as "delayed infusion," held until the 12th or 13th century. It was even embraced by a person who was considered the greatest theologian within the Catholic tradition, St. Thomas Aquinas. Thomas Aquinas made a distinction between conception, which is caused by parents, and animation or hominization, which is the infusion of humanity into a fetus. This comes about through the creative intervention of God. For Thomas and many of the moralist theologians like Alphonse Liguori and Cardinal Mercier, conception and hominization did not coincide. Animation or hominization occurred when the fetus was ready for it. From this period, through the 19th century, there was a definite movement within both Catholic and Protestant traditions to view abortion as wrong under any circumstances. John Calvin, one of the few reformers to speak about abortion, stated that, if the woman expels the fetus from her uterus, it is considered an inexorable crime. Here in the U.S. in the 18th and 19th centuries, the Protestant tradition repeatedly expressed its condemnation of abortion. It was thought that the destruction by parents of their offspring before birth was an abhorrence, a crime against God and a crime against nature.

The 20th century, with its new knowledge of life and death, its renewal of exegesis, its emphasis on individual freedom, individual decision, and the role of conscience, has brought about an explosion of many new moral issues. Consequently, we see statements from major Protestant traditions expanding their perspectives and beliefs on the question of abortion, life, the quality of life, and therapeutic abortions. We find many great Protestant thinkers like Carl Barth and Paul Ramsey defending positions which today we would commonly identify with the "Right-to-Life" movement. On the other hand, we see individuals within the Catholic tradition, like Father Richard McCormick and Joseph Donzeel, both of whom are very respected Catholic theologians, who have recently attempted to reopen the question of the beginning of human life. It is important to note, and I stand here as a Roman Catholic, that the Catholic church has never definitively spoken on this matter, despite all that we read in the press. It is questionable whether this would even be within its competence. Correspondingly, the traditional views of Judaism and the Orthodox tradition are becoming more diverse, especially in attempts to define the limits of therapeutic abortion.

In any discussion of the ethical dimensions of abortion, it is imperative to recognize diversity. There is a tendency to look at those authorities and principles which support one's particular view and to view them with an open mind. There is a tendency to choose to look at those individuals and authorities and principles which are opposed to one's view with a closed mind. If we are ever going to reconcile differences, it will come because today or tomorrow we have begun to admit there are important values in the arguments presented on every side of the question. To accelerate the polarization is not only a disturbance to dialogue, not only a disturbance to bioethical research, but a disservice to millions of Americans who continue to struggle with these questions.

Does a woman have absolute rights over her own body, up to and including the ninth month of pregnancy? Am I as an individual man, or as a member of a society rendered impotent on this question? Does the fetus at every stage of its development possess human life in the same and full sense as you or I? These are important questions; questions which have been debated, and they are debatable in law, bioethics, medicine, philosophy, and theology. If our knowledge and reason cannot lead us to resolve those issues today, neither should our biases or emotions. To admit that one might be in error is difficult but perhaps it is the only sane and ethical premise with which we can and should begin. If there is anything clear about the issue of abortion, it is that it is complicated, delicate and difficult.

What makes it so difficult is that those who affirm the rights of the woman and those who deny these rights, those who affirm the rights of a fetus and those who deny these rights, accept basically the same data of the sciences and use the same data to justify their affirmation or denial. Yet we must make decisions, especially the difficult ones. To the extent that debates and discussions through which we make our decisions are intolerant, inflammatory or ill-formed, we do not do a very good job of creating a decision-making climate or milieu for ourselves and for others.

In conclusion, it is my hope that as decisions are made, there will be responsible discussion and debate based on facts and issues as we understand them, and regard for the values of compassion, freedom, conscience, and reverence for life. The decisions are never going to be easy. I think we must start with the premise that individuals, wherever they are have a right to their beliefs; that they are acting in good faith and care, and that they are concerned about society and about the greater questions which face our society. To start from any other premise is not only wrong, it prevents us from moving ahead on this important question.

Jan Gleason: I would like to read the position of Catholics for a Free Choice: "It is an individual woman's right to make decisions regarding abortion and contraception in accordance with her own conscience without fear of criminal prosecution. We oppose any efforts to deny this right of conscience through constitutional amendment and/or federal and state legislation. Any interference by the state is a gross and unconscionable invasion of personal privacy and a direct violation of a female person's human, civil right to responsibly control her own reproduction."

We do not have a pro-abortion stand. It is a religious stand. It is a woman answering the call of her own culture and her own conscience. For those of you who are not Catholics and who are not aware of the document on religious freedom that came out in 1965, I want to read one paragraph from that. It reads: "This Vatican Synod declares that the human person has a right to religious freedom. This freedom means that all men and women are to be immune from coercion on the part of individuals or social groups and of any human power in such ways that in matters religious, no one is to be forced to act in a manner contrary to his own beliefs. Nor is anyone to be restrained from acting in accordance with his own beliefs, whether privately or publicly, whether alone or in association with others." Knowing that, I felt quite comfortable with supporting the Supreme Court abortion decision. What we are saying is that women are acting in accordance with the Church's latest documents. Catholic theologians have written to me and they have written in publications like *America* that they also support it. The fact that a male bishop would ex-communicate NOW members but not members of the AMA or ABA, just the women's groups, reflects the bishop's misogynism. There was no due process or notice of an opportunity to be heard. It's very reflective of a basic misogynistic attitude of the Church. If the bishops' own theology states that you have a conscience and the bishops attempt to deny women the right to use it, what does this do to a woman's mind?

As far as debating whether abortion is right or wrong or whether women should have the power to make this decision, remember that these bishops are speaking first of all from a woman-hatred standpoint but also from a male cultural standpoint. A woman reading the Bible is going to come up with a totally different interpretation. Women are not in the positions of power in the Church. They are not ordained, and are told they are not fit to be ordained. They don't publish. They don't own the Catholic press.

If we read the Bible, we can see very clearly that Jesus was a product of a planned pregnancy. He was to be a prophet like Moses, a priest like Melchisadec, a king like David, through the race of Shem, the nation of Israel, the tribe of Judah, and the house of David. Now if that isn't planning, I don't know what is. Leave out the opinions by the church fathers and take the words of Jesus or paraphrases thereof. He said, "That which you see the Father do, go and do likewise." That is all the mandate I need from the scriptures to advocate family planning. Common sense tells you that you have the ability to reason at age seven and your reproductive organs evolve at 14. We should not still be having a debate. We should be pushing to promote our women's culture and our women's ways of looking at things. A lot of the men, present company excepted, have lost the ability to perceive that there is another culture that wishes to speak out. I can feel it even here. There are many feminists here and they want to speak from their own point of view. Getting back to the misogynism, the mind-body dichotomy, a woman by Church definition becomes a body and body is

250

sexual and sinful. Therefore women take the role of sinner; further, they are not supposed to have a mind. Saint Augustine and Jerome, among the early church fathers, said that women are supposed to be subservient. The male is supposed to be the leader. This is a very destructive concept. It is not surprising that the two big issues that women have responded to in this country and in other countries, are self-image and self-help. For example, we in the National Organization for Women received many calls when we said that a woman can use her birth name or maiden name without having to go to court.

This misogynistic bias of the bishops and of other churches is very destructive. There is a double standard that only one part of the culture has power, the male part. The clerics take a vow of poverty, but they own all the church property. We do not own any of it. They take a vow of celibacy, but they are very interested in our sex lives. They take a vow of obedience, but they want us to obey. I believe that we must "obey little and resist much" because we must ultimately account to ourselves. We must use our own consciences and our own minds to talk with people, to find out what has occurred in their lives that was helpful to them. Oftentimes, simply making a decision helps a person to grow and women must do this. They have been taught that they cannot, but their whole growth depends on learning to do this.

It is very current to have theories of personality which strip away, eventually getting down to the real personality. Feminists do not accept this. We think more in terms of a dynamic in which women must develop the initiating as well as the receiving factors existing within themselves.

Until women are ordained and are in the churches, we will be discussing this same problem a hundred years from now. Men have been discussing it for 2,000 years. It can go on forever. Unless women are accepted as priests in the Church, women will start their own churches. The secret of the women's movement and its success is that NOW and Catholics for a Free Choice operate as quasi-churches. People come in to feminist groups because we give them respect. Sometimes we respect their knowledge and sometimes we respect their ignorance. We try to teach them. We are not getting this respect from the organized churches with their misogynist bias.

Reverend Alex Lukens, Jr.: I have been involved with the Clergy Consultation Service and with counseling at Presbyterian Hospital. Whether the abortion issue is seen as a symptom or a problem in itself, it is extremely important that we gather together to talk and to share our expertise as people struggling with very real problems in an age of tremendous change

First let me suggest something that may or may not be helpful when you are dealing with the church. Probably the most disastrous event in Western history was the baptism of Constantine. At that point, the community of religious integrity joined itself with the state. The state's primary purpose was protection, either of itself or of its poorer citizens, depending on where you lived. What unfortunately came out of this was that the Church, whose primary function in society was morality and integrity through demonstration and suasion, became identified with power and control. The state, tending to be protective, had to shift to become a moral arbiter. We have lived with that confusion at one level or another until the recent age.

I suggest to you that from the Church's point of view, and it may also be true from the state's point of view, we are now probably in the greatest moral crisis since Constantine. I think we have things backwards in this country. I think we tend to take life too seriously and persons not seriously enough. I think we get confused about what rights are. I think we are afraid of moral issues because they are deep and painful. I suggest to you that from my perspective, the possibility that the battle over the extremes in the morality of the "termination of life" may well be a defense against dealing with the very real, painful, terrifying, exciting feelings that are involved in the relationship between men and women and parents and children. We have trouble dealing with feelings and relationships, especially in families. I see this as the area of more important moral, integral work for us as people. Unfortunately, we have been saddled with a concept of family which I think we are beginning to discover has not been as supportive and helpful as it might have been: the "nuclear family" in which there are two parents and two and a half children. Unless the adults can feel wanted, surely we cannot expect our children to feel wanted. If we do perceive the extent to which any of us has any rights, certainly one of them ought to be being wanted. We are not wanted in a vacuum and we do not deal with issues in a vacuum. We are wanted in a real, concrete, physical situation of parents or parent substitutes. *Constitutional Aspects of the Right to Limit Childbearing,* published in April, 1975, by the United States Commission on Civil Rights, makes it very clear that the issue is not rights per se: that is, the right to choose as opposed to no right to choose. The issue is alternatives. What are the realities of alternatives that are available? A woman may want a child but for reasons of social condition, poverty, or lack of available support of any type, may well have no choice but to abort, even though the law guarantees that she should have the right to continue the pregnancy. Another issue that presents itself here is that, from an emotional and physical point of view, statistics show that termination of pregnancy early in the pregnancy is far less traumatic than carrying an unwanted pregnancy to full term.

I think we need to learn better how to talk with each other. I have a fantasy that part of what will come out of this conference is an increased awareness that the problems in living that bring someone to a clinic for an abortion are themselves real issues and real needs. Someone mentioned that the number of people paying less than full fee in the clinic where she is working has increased from 11 to 33 percent. This says to those of us who are professionals that an increasing number of these problems are coming to the attention of the health care system. The extent to which actors in the health care system are going to deal with their own feelings and their own moral problems bespeaks a hopeful sign that we can begin to focus on health: personal, emotional and theological.

Eleanore Boyd: Within every ethical system is a value system. Without referring to religion or revelation, where does value come from? It comes from man. Man bestows value on beauty, on health, on happiness, on prestige, on intelligence, or wealth. All these good things receive their value from man. Man is the source of values. So what if we say that man has relative value? Relative to what? To things? What if we begin calculating the value of man in terms of the things to which he gives value? But things have no value unless man gives it to them. If the source has only relative value, things have even less. If man is qualified by things of less value than he (or of no value), then he has increasingly less value, as do the things he qualifies. We come to the bottom of the spiral and to the swamp of relative value and we find nihilism: there is no real value.

I do not think we are ready for nihilism. Where do we look for an ethical system? We look for something common to all of us, something all of us can give allegiance to. We have such a system, and in this bicentennial year, I believe that this document is doubly important.

"We hold these truths to be self-evident, that all men are created equal." Here we have an ethical system beginning with a universal statement. All men are created equal. Not just the people in this country, not just the men in those times, but all men are created equal. And they are "created," not "born."

"They are endowed by their creator [whether you understand creator to be God, or nature] with certain inalienable rights." He is endowed with these rights by the very fact of his being. They are not imposed from without or granted to him by a government. They are his. He carries them by the very virtue of his being a member of the family of man. The particular inalienable rights of which Jefferson speaks are those which it is the purpose of government to secure for man: "life, liberty, and pursuit of happiness." Why does man have to worry about a government securing them for him? Rights are concerned with what *ought* to be, not what is. "Ought" does not always correspond to "is." It is the purpose of government to see that "ought" corresponds to "is" as mucn as possible.

Three rights are mentioned: life, liberty, and the pursuit of happiness. Is there any ranking in these rights? Is one more important than the other? One is certainly more necessary than the other. It is the sine qua non of all other rights. Liberty can't exist without life. We can't pursue happiness without life. There is no free-floating liberty or free-floating pursuit of happiness. They must be attached to a life to be experienced. So the rights here implied are life, life-liberty and life-pursuit of happiness. When we take away life, we take away the possibility of a person's ever having any of a human being's other rights. It is not life against liberty. So the right to life, since it includes all other rights, must outweigh any other right.

It is often assumed that the whole abortion controversy could be solved if we could only convince the other side that life really begins at the moment the sperm fertilizes the egg. An increasing number of abortion proponents are admitting the biological fact that, indeed, human life begins at fertilization. In fact, I feel I may assume that most of you agree that a human being is present from the moment of fertilization. Obviously, the controversy is not over. What is the controversy?

The controversy is over the value of human life. The author of a recent California medical journal article recognized the problem. He wrote that the semantic gymnastics of those who refuse to admit the fact that we are destroying a human being would be ridiculous if they did not point to the fact that we are not ready for the new ethics necessary to accommodate abortion. Medicine is now not merely in the arena of curing. It is in the arena of killing. Since we are not ready for the new ethics, we must justify our actions in terms of the old ethics, by saying there is no life or it is doubtful if there is life. This was a number of years ago. We have progressed or regressed to the point where we say, "Yes, life is there, but life itself is of relative value."

In order to decide whose rights are of more value than another's life, we must discriminate, and abortion is discrimination in the worst sense of the word. The unborn child is discriminated against because, like all victims of discrimination, he is helpless and powerless. We can safely discriminate without ever fearing we will be discriminated against in this particular manner. We are safe; we are born; we will never go through the prenatal period again. Perhaps we overestimate our safety and we have not analyzed it thoroughly. Perhaps we have stopped with the particular, and we have not recognized the general principle. Logic gives no mercy and logic gives no dispensation.

I also contend that the abortion ethic discriminates against women. It is considered an infirmity to have a womb. A child aborted because of sex is most likely to be a girl. Women are expected to control their reproductive capacity as if it were a disease. The wombless, unproductive male body is the epitome of perfection. The means of controlling her reproductive capacity do not have to meet the test of safety anymore. The drug or device must be proven to be dangerous before it is taken off the market. Women are presented with figures which seem to indicate that abortion is safe than childbirth. The significant long-term complications of abortion are dismissed.

I am not one that thinks that the statistics lie. A thorough use of statistics will give you an accurate picture if you understand the statistics. Many women consider abortion not because it is expedient to them, but because it is the virtuous thing to do. There are many reasons a woman may think abortion is required of her for the good of others or of society. The modern woman has new freedom. She has new rights and she should have more rights than she has. She has freedom to exercise the rights that were always hers, but often the new freedom is being used as a means of further exploiting her. Unless a woman uses her new freedom with integrity toward herself, toward those for whom she has responsibility, toward those who are oppressed as she herself once was and is, then we are all, men and women, in a worse situation than before. We must demand our rights without having to sacrifice our natures and deny the bodies that are part of us.

We must say, "Here I stand before you, a woman as my creator made me. Not only do I deny no part of myself, but I am proud I am the way I am made. Biologically I am fulfilled by giving birth to a child. This does not mean I can be fulfilled in no other way. If I am pregnant in an unfortunate circumstance, it is only the circumstance that is unfortunate. Rich or poor, married, single, or raped, this thing between this child and me is a marvelous, unrepeateable thing. I have never been so important to myself or to anyone else. If society thinks that it can make me distort my nature and make a human sacrifice of my child on the altar of its utilitarian religion in order to solve its real or imagined problem, it can go to hell." Quite possibly it is already on the way.

There is less reason for abortion now than at any other time in history, and we should not tolerate it. There is less reason economically. Socially, we have eliminated the illogical stigma placed on the illegitimate child. There is less reason medically since there is no reason that any woman cannot bring her child to term safely, given the proper medical care. Surely we have enough resources and ingenuity to solve our problems in such a way to enable us to protect and accept and love this new, most helpless member of the human family and his or her mother.

Discussion

Meyers: At the University of California at San Diego, we have an excellent genetics clinic and they use one of the few methods of determining sex before birth. They don't do it if people just want to know the sex. They do it if people want to know about a problem that's going to occur. One of the few times that people make the decision to abort the fetus because of its sex is in a sex-related genetic disease like hemophilia. They're much more likely to abort a male fetus than a female because that's the one most likely to be affected. There are a lot of other things they can tell in the genetics examination and amniocentesis. I'd like to know how you'd feel knowing that you were going to have a child that would die before it was three years old and you knew that it would die with great suffering. Maybe you had already had a child that had died under the same circumstances and with great suffering. How would you feel about abortion, or how would you feel about someone else having an abortion in these circumstances?

Boyd: I appreciate this kind of concern more than I do a lot of other concerns. I would like to refer to a quote by Sir William Lyley who is the world's leading fetologist. He said, "The harm in the world comes not from the physically and mentally retarded. It comes from the spiritually retarded." It is very difficult to say that you are going to eliminate the suffering that this baby may go through. It seems illogical to me. I understand that we feel bad about these deformed and mongoloid children and it tears us up, but it seems illogical to kill them to prevent them from suffering. It doesn't to you?

Hansen: Some 20 inborn errors of metabolism can be detected by amniocentesis. Anatomical defects which are inconsistent with continued life can also be detected, such as meningomyelocoele where the spine is exposed and nerve elements are exposed. Mongolism can be determined by amniocentesis. All of these things can be detected by amniotic fluid studies prior to the 20th week of pregnancy and abortion can be performed. I would like the panel to address itself to the lack of quality of life in these pregnancies if the child were left to go to term delivery.

Lukens: I'm in a bind on that one. I have worked long and hard the last two years with a guy who is 54 years old and was born with spina bifida and meningomyelocoele. It sure raised a lot of ambivalent feelings in me, coming down very strongly in terms of terminating life. It involves issues of informed consent and so on. On the other hand, I'm not sure I agree that if you know the child. is going to die, you are simply postponing the sentence. Is that fair?

Boyd: For those who don't know what spina bifida is, it's an incompletely formed spine. Sufferers often die from infections when they get older. I have had to take care of deformed children and those with the basketball heads, the hydrocephalic. It was very disturbing to me to have to listen to them cry, and to have to think that maybe my time could be spent better with children who are healthy. I worked in these places. If a woman is pregnant and could see these children, she could go home and make her own decision. She's the one who's going to have to do all the work at home if she doesn't care to institutionalize the child. Even with the mentally retarded, one of the most beautiful experiences I ever had in my life was when, before I decided to go to law school, I went to apply for a job with the mentally retarded institute. I walked into the room and the children all stopped what they were doing. They ran over and put their arms around me. There was never a word spoken. It was just like a magnet. The administrator said, "Well, I never saw anything like that before." I said, "They know that I love them." There's a way we have of communicating at a different level. I think it would be up to the individual woman to decide how much of a commitment she would want to make to a child that would be handicapped. We can't make that decision. The woman has to decide. Just making the decision is spiritual growth. What will happen to that person if something happens to me? We don't know. My children are all healthy. I don't know what I would do.

Unidentified: Just a very quick comment. The situation that is described is one of the first that faced me as a counselor with a 17-year old girl who was pregnant. As a social worker, I've worked quite a bit with low income persons. I have lived in ghettoes and worked in housing projects. For the individual who was facing this decision, when my own opinions were perhaps more confused than they are today, the question came down to the quality of life. Perhaps it was stated best by the question of whether there was going to be life after birth for this individual, rather than before birth, and whether she was really going to be capable of providing anything. I felt it was my responsibility at that time and still do, to help her sort out her own beliefs and values and not impose mine. My beliefs and values might direct toward one particular choice. The most important thing was for her to be able to examine very clearly, without pressure, her values, her beliefs, her philosophies, her strengths, her capabilities; look at all the alternatives; and then make the decision that was best for her. My role was to support that. That was difficult for me. That was part of my learning process.

Grimes: I'd like to respond, not as a physician, but rather as a biologist, which was my training before I entered medicine. This question of when life begins is really a specious argument and it involves some very questionable biology. I do not think it's a given fact that life begins at fertilization. It's difficult to define the beginnings of life. It really began sometime in antiquity. Human life, as we know it, does not begin, it can only end. Let me explain what I mean. First of all, I am human because I contain the genetic stuff of human beings. I am alive biochemically because I metabolize food and I generate excretion products and so forth. This defines human life for biologists. When I was six months old, I was human and I was alive although my form was different and you might not have recognized me. Nonetheless I was human and I was alive. When I was a two-week old blastocyst in my mother's womb, I was very different in form, but nonetheless I was very human and I was alive. When I was a sperm and ovum in my parents I was human and I was alive. My form was different and you would not have recognized me. I think this shows you that the genetic stuff of which we're all composed does not create de novo, but rather is a continuum since way back in time. Furthermore, the definition that new life starts when fertilization begins has serious faults. I'd like to give you a couple of examples. First of all, let's say that spontaneous mutation occurs in a small blastocyst early in pregnancy. Does this mean that this is new life? In lower species for example, sometimes frog eggs or sea anemone eggs do not need fertilizaiton to grow into full adults. You can agitate them or prick them with a pin and they parthenogenetically grow on to become a full frog. Is this frog not a frog because it was not fertilized? The question resolves itself to what do you define as human life?

Kirton: Do you want me to define human life? Like you said, it begins with antiquity.

Boyd: I notice you said you didn't go back to antiquity, though. You began with the sperm and the ovum. Yes you did.

Grimes: No, I didn't.

Boyd: And it was a different form and we would not have recognized you.

Grimes: That's right.

Boyd: Then you say you have gone back to antiquity.

Lukens: I think there is something inherently different in an evolutionary sense in what we identify as the personality of human beings as compared with the "personality" or behavior of other species. Konrad Lorenz has commented that there is probably much less qualitative difference between human beings and other species than we've tended to assume, but there is probably much more quantitative difference between them than we've tended to assume. My prejudice as a theologian is that there is a difference in the area of self consciousness, and that this is an area we're just beginning to examine.

Boyd: What we are talking about is not just life; we're talking about an individual human life. Genetically, you're different from your mother and your father so you are a little bit different life than they were. A transplant from the unborn child would be rejected by the mother; that's how genetically different we are. The beginning of an individual organized life is what we're talking about.

Workshop

Teenagers and Abortion

Sidney Werkman, M.D.: Florence Uyeda is a pediatrician. She will discuss experiences from the standpoint of a public school education system. Nettie Fisher will speak about counseling, especially abortion counseling and counseling people who are pregnant and concerned about their situation. Peggy Hess is with the Jefferson County School system and is involved in educational services for people who are pregnant. I thought we might start with Dr. Uyeda, whose experiences are very immediate and who can tell us what it is like for a young woman to be involved with pregnancy.

Florence Uyeda, M.D.: I have two jobs. One of my jobs is with the school health services here in Denver. I examine pupils in elementary, junior high and high schools. This past semester, a high school student told me that she had missed her period for a few months and wondered if drinking from a stream in which there was a dead antelope could have caused her menses to stop. We talked about that for a while. When I got her on the table and saw her belly out to here, I did not think it was the dead antelope that was responsible. Luckily, she came from a good, supportive family. She was upset for a while and then, with help, was able to go home to her family with her problem. I do not know how it was resolved since I am not her physician.

At West High School, another girl had a desire to see what a baby would look like if it came from both her and her boyfriend since they were madly in love and were both such attractive young people. He was not planning on dropping out of his first year of college nor was she planning on not finishing high school. They did not believe in contraception and they certainly didn't believe in abortion as a choice, but she really did want to get pregnant.

My other job is in the clinic at one of the local hospitals. In taking a history when patients come in for annual checkups, I always find out what they know about sex education because that is part of my job. One 16-year-old girl had menstrual cramps. I put her on birth control pills, but her mother was against her using birth control pills even if it was for controlling cramps. Her mother took her off the birth control pills. Three months later, her mother said, "I don't think that Kotex box has been going down at all and I'd like you to give my daughter another checkup." The pregnancy test was positive. The mother said, "Well I'm against abortion, so she's going to have to suffer the consequences of whatever she's done to get pregnant." Then she added, "Oh, by the way, I don't think her 12-year-old sister has had periods for a while, but, of course, 12-year-olds are not regular." Then I asked the mother, "When did the 12-year-old start her periods?" "She started at age 9." I said, "By 12 she should be regular unless something else has come up such as an emotional or physical problem." This was a sad happening in this family; on Friday I diagnosed the 16-year-old as pregnant. On Monday, when I examined the 12-year-old and put my hand on her tummy, there was another baby on the way. This time though, the mother, who was against abortions, said, "There's no way that this 12-year-old kid is going to go through a pregnancy." It took a month but both of these girls are not pregnant right now. I gave the girls a choice and it was a difficult one, especially for the 16-year-old who was really frightened of the abortion. She wondered what it really means. The 12-year-old was a sixth grader without any previous sexual experience. She was frightened of the ninth grade boys who said they would beat her up if she did not do it and they would beat her up if she ever told her mother. They both finally agreed that an abortion was what they wanted. I told the 16-year-old, "Next time, if you want to get pregnant, you have to plan ahead. Make sure you are in good shape physically and emotionally so you can have a good healthy baby."

I do not want any more battered kids to be brought into the world. With these kind of kids, the chances are great that they are not going to be great parents, but with education, they might be good parents. I said, "I don't care whether you're married or not. I just want you to have a happy experience being a parent."

In my sex education discussions with teenagers, we talk about contraception and sexuality. I always include the fact that I think sex is a great thing. It feels good, but if the students are not ready for the responsibility, they have to forego those pleasures for awhile until they are ready to accept it. We talk about what happens if they get pregnant while in school. What about their folks, what would they think? We talk about abortion. I would say that most of the teenagers rule out abortion: "It's wrong, period." This area of sex education needs attention and needs it now.

It is true that the teenager is somebody who is at a most sensitive, delicate age. One of the issues that we brought up was how to handle the very young teenager who is pregnant and who comes for abortion counseling or service. There is the question of forcible involvement in intercourse and almost-rape situations which some of them get into.

Nettie Fisher. M.S.W.: An adolescent generally finds herself in the whole dilemma of dependence versus independence: "Help me" versus "Mom, I'd rather do it myself." One of the most critical and difficult patients, not just in terms of physical but also emotional aspects, is the teenage patient. The patient is not really completely in control of her own destiny. She can come into a clinic and say, "I want an abortion," or, "I'm having problems with this pregnancy; I want to keep it."

They are always basically under some type of coercion or pressure, whether it be from the male partner, parents, older siblings or peers. They do not come in as independent agents able to control their lives at that point. For example, one teenager came in and said, "I don't want an abortion but I'm going to have to have one because my mom said I couldn't live at home otherwise."

You need very particular skills in working with problem pregnancy teenagers. A lot of these girls have no intention of going through an abortion. Many of them are very opposed to abortion. An even higher percentage are opposed to adoption. If you are counseling in this area, you need to feel that it is not just problem pregnancy counseling. You can give the alternatives, but you need to have skills in working with families, bringing in external support systems, and intervening in some external systems such as the schools. For example, in this state it is illegal to remove a pregnant girl from school. Yet, through certain kinds of subtle coercion techniques, girls are pushed out if they want to continue their pregnancies. If they are not pushed out of the actual academic program, they get pushed out of social functions. That is very important to teenagers.

The other thing we must do is examine how people are able to resolve problems for themselves. Unfortunately in our society we have a tendency to think that at 18 you are grown. All of a sudden, you can make your own decisions, even though you have not had an opportunity to make a decision up to that point. People need information to make responsible decisions. An amazing number of teenagers are not very well educated in terms of sex and sexuality. There are a lot of myths, rumors, and old wives' tales floating around as far as the teenage population is concerned.

Some myths that you hear about quite often concern contraception, about what contraception is and what it is not. When I was working at Colorado General Hospital, a young girl came in and said, "Every time I have intercourse, I make sure I have it with two different boys." "Why?" "Well, that's contraception. I can't be pregnant because if I have sperm from him and sperm from him, they fight it out and they die." The other myths center around the idea of being mothers. The whole fantasy is having this cute little Gerber baby that never cries, never soils its pants, meets all of your needs, and is just a neat little person, all in one little bundle. I call that the myth of motherhood. The next ones concern the ideas that they have from their own families about abortion. This is from a wide religious, cultural, and economic spectrum. Abortion has not been a topic that has been easily talked about, not only today but for many years. It just happened. Parents are major educational influences on sexuality for kids, but they do not talk to kids about abortion. They say, "Well, the church says . . . ,"or "I don't believe it's right." Many of us have our opinions, but we have obtained information that sometimes balances out those opinions. These kids have not had the time nor developmental maturity to process different opinions.

I think a person working with a teenager who has a problem pregnancy needs the skill to assess and to help her explore her situation. The second needed skill is the ability to understand a family as a unit and to understand family dynamics. More often than not, you are not just going to have to work with the teenager, you are going to have to work with her total family. The third skill involves working with the family to enhance the well-being of your identified patient, the adolescent.

For example, a little girl came in for an abortion; I think she was 13. She was in for her third in about 11 months. The mother had decided that the solution to this problem was to move across town because it was the fault of the 14-year-old boy next door. In the same period of time we ended up treating another 12-year-old sister who was pregnant. We started working with the whole family, including a couple of sisters; discussing the whole idea of sexuality, letting the parents talk and say where they were coming from, and helping the kids to understand that the parents were from a different generation. I am making it sound very simple, but I am talking about a process that took eight months of weekly and, most of the time, bi-weekly meetings.

The fourth need of a counselor is the real ability to allow the client, regardless of her age, to make her own decision. That is really hard for many of us. The first thing you think about when you see a 13-year-old child is, "What's she going to do with a baby?" She can not possibly go through labor. The important thing to do for them, though, is to give them the information so that they can make the decision they need to make. Whether or not we believe it, abortion is not always the answer. In fact, it is not always the answer even for the young teenager who is pregnant.

Peggy Hess: Our program is called the Teen Mother program. It is an alternative education program for girls in junior and senior high school who have elected to go through pregnancy. Some are married. About half the girls we have right now are married. The other half are making the decision as to whether they want to be a single parent or relinquish the child. Nationally, only about 15 percent of pregnant teenagers relinquish their children, and 85 percent keep their babies.

The primary reason that any girl drops out of school is pregnancy. For many years, girls have been forced out. It was school board policy which said in effect, "If you are pregnant, you are not going to school here." Maybe they thought it was going to be contagious. I am not sure. They certainly would not allow them in the regular school system. With the new Title IX legislation which says you may not discriminate against any student whether she is married or single, pregnant or not, our school board rewrote the policy. Now the girls have the option of staying in their regular school or coming to school in our alternative education program. We offer academic courses that they need to complete the year of school they are in. They do independent study allowing them to work at their own rate. If they get their work done, they get the grade and the credit. Some of them are able to graduate earlier than they would in the regular school system simply because they work so much harder and do a lot of work at home.

We have physical education classes which our nurse conducts with the girls. These include prenatal exercises, breathing and relaxation techniques. We do a lot of parenting-type classes, and we have group counseling. This provides them with a strong support system for each other. The girls that are planning to relinquish are really very helpful to other girls in making their decisions. We even bring girls that were with us in past years to talk about what their situation is now. Even if they are girls who have decided to keep their children, it is good for them to hear what it is like to have a 4-year-old and be a single parent. We are finding that to have a total, comprehensive program, we need to work with the men, the boyfriends and husbands. We get the parents involved. We're doing this in night classes. If the man is still in school, he gets elective credit for our parenting class, whether it is preparation for parenting or whether it is experience in parenthood. We were very fortunate to get an infant nursery that is right next door to us. It is paid for by Title IV funds, which staffed and equipped this infant nursery. It is licensed by the State Department of Social Services as a large day care center. We have room for ten infants. We place the babies there while the girls go to school. During their child development classes and at other times, they go over for lab experience. If they have not had their children yet and are still pregnant, the lab experience is really good for them. The idea that this little wonderful Cinderella-like thing, this cute baby, is not really going to be that much work is corrected. They actually experience getting up at three, again at four, and then again at five in the morning, having 40,000 dirty diapers to wash, and sometimes smelling like baby barf. The whole reality of motherhood takes a turn when they actually have the baby at home. We do regular weekly group counseling with the girls. The girls that have already delivered take their turn sharing with the still-pregnant girls the experience of having this baby at home. They discuss some real concerns they have; they have unrealistic expectations of their husbands and about sexual intercourse. As soon as they come home from the hospital, they have some real sexual problems, even at their age and having been pregnant. We do a lot of this type of counseling. But we need programs so that the girls do not have to remain in their home school unless they elect to do that. They should have the choice.

Unidentified: In dealing with the myth of motherhood, I don't know how to be realistic without seeming to be against the girl. I have a hard time dealing with that and with keeping a supportive kind of relationship. I want to say, "I'm not trying to tell you not to do this," but I want to make sure that she knows what she's doing and to make sure I'm informing her. It always does seem as though you're against her, her parents are against her, and everybody's against her. Do you have any comments on that?

Fisher: Ask her if she has any friends who have babies. Almost everyone I've talked to does. I say, "Well, how are they making out?" Some of them say, "Oh, just great." Most of them are pretty realistic. They know that they can't go out, they know that they can't find babysitters, and they know that they're lonely. They know that they're not dating. I think that using somebody else's experience may help them.

Unidentified: If given the information and the education and all that you would like to give them, can most 12- or 13-year-olds make a rational decision over something that affects 18 years of their lives?

Fisher: Frequently the answer is no. That's the tragedy.

Werkman: I would just like to emphasize something about figures. More than half of the 400,000 babies born to single parents are born to teenagers. This is a considerable area of preventive work we might consider. One-third of abortions are done on teenagers. They are a very large group of people who are involved or capable of being involved sexually for many years before they've made commitments and decisions about how they'll deal with their lives in a total way.

I would like to speak about the immediate abortion experience of people. As girls and young women become involved in the decision to have an abortion, and even after the abortion, there are many issues that come up. One is the feeling of vulnerability. Someone who is pregnant and trying to decide what to do has a feeling of helplessness, that they are at the mercy of their parents, the man or boyfriend involved. The society and all the forces around them can help or hinder them in trying both to make a decision and to be able to take care of their needs. Secondly, a teenager becomes even more involved in that great issue of dependency. Once a girl is pregnant and is involved in the decision of an abortion, it's often the parents who quickly decide she will or won't. They effectively take away responsibility from her. She may act out and say "I'm going to do this on my own." It seems to me that all of us who work with teenagers need to be negotiators and to work toward a reasonable solution. The solution should not allow parents to make the total decision or a teenager herself to make a total decison. We should ask all the elements.

Third, the issue of guilt, rational or irrational, of feeling that a person's been singled out, is dangerous. "I knew this was going to happen to me," even though she had been on contraception or had planned something. "I knew this was coming, and I couldn't help myself. I knew that something bad was going to happen." There are lots of things that people can feel guilty about throughout adolescence and throughout life. Pregnancy can be one thing that just crystallizes that feeling that there's something wrong, marked, something fatal about their personal life. That speaks a great deal to what kinds of help people need. This is to speak about the experience of abortion itself, which, under good conditions can be a very valuable experience. Under conditions that are less than good, it can be exceedingly frightening and guilt-producing, especially when people within the health care system decide that they're going to take on a role of changing society through the single patient.

All of us have a job in this area. If you can add ideas that help a person who has made a decision for an abortion, to help that experience be more effective or comfortable and acceptable, I hope you'll add that.

One of the issues that Peggy Hess brought up was that, very often, it can be valuable to find out whether a trusted friend can go through the experience with the girl. It's even more so with the young girl. From your experience, do you think that peers or older women might be of help in carrying somebody through such an experience? What about post-abortion counseling? Quite often the feelings don't come up until after a person has had the abortion. Often there's no one to talk with about those feelings. Many times the experience of abortion for a 12-, 13-, or 14-year-old girl has in it an element of coercion. She frequently becomes involved in intercourse by force. To be able to make sense for her out of what has happened is difficult when only a negative experience results from the sexual experience. A person needs a chance to work through that whole thing. If we don't have adequate services now, what kinds of volunteer and supportive activities can we offer throughout the system for a person who is seeking abortion?

One other thing is the problem of teenagers and contraception. There is a myth floating around that it's bad to plan to have sex. If you use contraception or if you start going to Planned Parenthood, you're planning to have sex. Somehow it removes something if it just doesn't happen accidentally, in a moment of passion.

Karen Barquist, Kansas State University, Manhattan, Kansas: You were talking about this feeling of inevitability a girl has that seems to lead toward a guilt reaction. I do pregnancy counseling at Kansas State University. I am Director of Pregnancy Counseling there and Co-Director of a peer sex education program. In our intake and follow-up for pregnancy or emotional referral, we ask, "What methods of contraception are you familiar with?" They know about all of them. "What method were you using?" They aren't using any. Sixty-six percent of them used nothing, 10 percent used withdrawal and 20 percent used foam. "If you aren't using any method, why not?" They say they didn't think about it. Somehow that doesn't fit with the feeling of inevitability, unless we're going to talk about denial or the fact that maybe their value systems aren't well enough developed.

Werkman: I think for all of these issues there are at least two sides of the whole range of experiences people have. When people say they didn't think they'd have to change, it indicates that they had not been given graded responsibility as they went ahead with their lives. Perhaps they had been given so much responsibility for their lives that they said the hell with it.

Unidentified: A person I was counseling said she wasn't sure she wanted the abortion but she thought that's what she wanted. Should she make God punish her further by making herself keep the baby for 18 years? She didn't even realize what she was saying until I repeated her own words to her. I said, "OK, do you want to punish yourself?" She said, "Yes." I said, "Who else would you be punishing if you have a baby?"

When she realized that there was going to be another entity that she would also punish, she wasn't so sure she wanted this punishment trip.

Werkman: You have to go into a good deal of depth with people, if you have the luxury of that, because everyone has layers of views. Often the person who says "I want to carry the baby to term" will have under that a feeling, "Well, I deserve this so I'm going to continue it." If you help the person work through that underview then perhaps abortion will be chosen.

Unidentified: I had two experiences last year that are so similar I'd really like to ask you what you think was happening. I had two 15 year-old girls who were pregnant and had abortions with the support, cooperation and help of their parents. Later, the parents came to me asking for counseling and help because they had such guilt feelings that this had happened to their daughters. In both instances, they complained that the teenager apparently had no remorse. It seemed to bounce off of her like water off a duck's back. Why couldn't she have shown more remorse and repentance for this when they were taking it so heavily? I really didn't know exactly how to handle this except to say that I felt that the young person was probably having more guilt feelings than she was revealing. Can you tell me what you thought was happening?

. *Werkman:* Let's have some comments. Does the teenager feel remorse over becoming pregnant?

Unidentified: I think premarital intercourse is quite an important issue in this. I don't think we have decided as a society whether premarital intercourse is good or bad. We have for many hundreds of years considered it bad. This has been told to us by churches and parents. Now we are at a stage where we can do something practical: avoid the consequences of premarital intercourse. If the consequences (pregnancy), are such that we don't want them, we can do something about it. We have the ways and means now for the first time in history to avoid grave consequences of premarital intercourse. We don't know whether premarital intercourse will make us a better society or happier as individuals.

Werkman: Let's have a little more discussion about it because it brings up the issue of whether one should offer contraceptives to unmarried teenagers.

Unidentified: Can I respond to her question about remorse? At the risk of sounding maybe like a devil's advocate, I think that is an excellent question for all of us involved in counseling with the adults as well as teenagers. At the heart of the question is: do you need guilt in order to make decisions in terms of responsibility? I think that many of us are very mixed up about guilt and conscience and responsibility. When we talk to adults or kids, what is that fine line between trying to explain responsibility and at the same time, trying to eliminate teenagers' pain, which is perhaps another form of guilt or remorse? I'm sure it is. Maybe we do have a problem for ourselves in clarifying the point at which we say, yes, a certain amount of guilt is healthy and a necessary part of any person's development.

Werkman: Any of us who work with teenagers and are concerned about abortion and the availability of contraception have to make a decision about whether we're going to offer rational services to them or leave this issue aside for the time being.

Unidentified: The question it really raises is the dynamics between the teenager and the parents. This is something we have to keep in mind whenever counseling teenagers on this kind of a question. If the parents are very stuck about the whole thing and feeling really bad about what's happening, many teenagers will be very flippant about the abortion. They will go the other way to an extreme. They don't really feel that way. It's just that they haven't been given the space and the opportunity to say, "I really feel bad." Their parents are feeling all the horrible things, and the teenagers are not having a chance to feel bad about it.

Werkman: I think there's a difference between feeling responsibility and feeling guilt. You have to start with whether a person has intercourse or not. After that, you offer services to the people who need them and don't get involved in the question of their remorse or lack of remorse.

Appendix

Remarks by Honored Guests

The Honorable Richard Lamm,
Governor of Colorado

I think it is important that I am here. I think it is important simply because of the fact that abortion is again becoming a political issue. I am very sad that this has come about. It seems unfortunate to me that, in a world which is already at war with its excess fertility, we are continuing to argue issues of abortion in the political marketplace. It is sad that in a world which cannot take care of its unwanted children, some continue to want to force unwilling women to bear unwanted children. It is sad that in a world that needs all the brains it can get, and even then we might not make it, we continue to seem to feel it is good social policy to force some women to become baby machines against their will. It has become a political issue which is particularly interesting to me because I am intrigued with the political process. There is danger within that political process if things are not articulated correctly. It intrigues me that, in spite of the fact that something like 70 percent of the people can be in favor of a given issue, 30 percent of the people can hold political sway if they feel very strongly against that issue. You could solve the inflation problem, you could bring peace between the races, you could solve the cities' crises, you could bring back the land of milk and honey, but if you were against a particular issue, the people would vote against you. I think there is great mischief in that because I do not think the political process then really reflects the majority view.

It is intriguing to me how far the whole issue of fertility has come. I suspect that most of us find its progress in the last ten years to be very important social history. At the same time, one can be both pessimistic and optimistic about how far we have come in the last ten years. I am very sorry that people who are running for the Presidency in trying to find a "moderate" ground are taking positions that I do not find moderate. Probably one of the things that is going to be extremely important in the next year ahead is to try to come up with a thoughtful way to present what I firmly believe and the polls show to be the majority opinion in this country: that it is not good social policy to delude ourselves into thinking that passing a law can eliminate abortion.

Conferences like this are a good step in the right direction. More than that, there has to be some way that people can insert themselves into the political process and show that the rights that were won over the last few years are important rights. They are very basic to humanity, or to at least 51 percent of the population.

That is the only kind of social policy for an intelligent society that literally is at war with excess fertility. When you look at the demographic charts, I think anybody has to be awed. Led by my friend Ruth Steel with her quiet ways, persuading the legislature, using reason, trying to persuade in the very finest ways; I saw here in Colorado that the political process will listen and can listen, if this information is correctly articulated.

There is an interesting demographic aspect to this issue. All you have to do is look at the public opinion polls. It shows that the lower the age group, the higher the percentage of people who really believe that women ought to have the right to control their own reproductive function. I am convinced that the tide of history is with us and the tide of demography is with us. It becomes very important to us to present intelligently in the political marketplace the case of fertility control and the reasoned choice that women ought to have in these matters. We have truly come a startling distance in the last ten years and the question now is to hold the ground that we have won. I am convinced it can be done. I just came out here to say that and symbolically to stand shoulder to shoulder with you. Thank you.

Patricia Schroeder, U.S. Representative

One of the things that I want to do is to read you two things to see if you can guess where they came from. These are two statements that we should all start quoting vigorously. The first is: "This Council declares that the human person has a right to religious freedom. This freedom means that all men are to be immune from coercion on the part of individuals or of social groups or of any human power in such ways that no one can be forced to act in a manner contrary to their own beliefs, whether privately or publicly, whether alone or in association with others within due limits."

I have another one for you that I like even better. "Christian faithful, in common with all other men who possess the civil rights, are not to be hindered in leading their lives in accordance with their consciousness. Therefore a harmony exists between the freedom of the church and all religious freedom, which is to be recognized as the right of all men in the community, sanctioned by constitutional law." Who knows where it came from?

It is the Vatican II. It is a papal encyclical. You keep wondering what happened to this great constitutional religious freedom that we're all talking about? Why do some want to continue dictating to everybody on one issue? I keep saying to people, "Theologians have been arguing about when life begins since the church began and now they want Congress to decide!" I am not sure that Congress is capable of deciding much of anything. Maybe we all ought to pull out Vatican II and quote some of these paragraphs. Some of them are marvelous. They are about religious freedom and allowing the individual to flourish and flowers to bloom.

I think it is so important that you are here. You are saying, "It's part of a bigger issue which is individual freedom," and "How much does government interfere with your lives?" For some reason, we as women have been made to feel terribly inferior about going and asking for our own rights. We are supposed to be apologetic. We are not supposed to be pushy and aggressive. Although the right to control one's body has been one of these very key things that has always been emphasized, we should never ask for that right. This is emphasized in those Planned Parenthood posters of the pregnant male saying, "If it were you . . .," and I think that is very key. I think that that is why we have had so much trouble coming forward. Our culture told us that we should not be pushy, and there we are.

It is nice to see so many men here among us. We commend you for joining us and in discussing some of these things. It is part of the whole picture of individual freedom and where we are going.

The woman who is going to address us tonight is really one of my great heroes. She is a beautiful person. She comes from Marlboro country. She comes from Texas. Nobody believes that there are these kind of women in Texas. This very courageous young woman walks out on the floor of the Supreme Court of the United States to argue the abortion decision. You expect her to be from New York maybe, or from Southern California, but not Texas. When you talk to her she is an amazing, beautiful person who does not fit the stereotype the press would like to imprint upon her. She is soft-spoken, she is articulate, she is educated, and she argued the whole case without crying. She did not pound her shoe on the table. She was rational. She did not scream. It was just incredible. No one could believe it. Washington's still talking about it. Women are not supposed to be able to do those kinds of things. I think you are very fortunate to have her here.

Sarah Weddington is in the State House of Representatives in Texas and that in itself is a scene. One of my favorite Texas clansmen said to me, "You just don't seem to understand politics." He said, "In Texas, it's very simple. It's Chivas Regal, Lear jets, hundred dollar bills and beautiful women." I thought, "No, I guess I don't understand Texas politics." She's been able to survive in that scene also. I do not know how, but I think it is absolutely incredible.

These very rare individuals give us great inspiration. They are terrific role models, and I think it encourages all of us to be a little bit more courageous and to stand up a little more and to say, "The important thing we're talking about is individual rights for everybody." It is so vital that we all feel that we are not just doing our own little narrow thing. The Constitution really means what it says. If we have any limiting Constitutional amendments it will be the first time, except for prohibition, that we have gone backwards. You know how long prohibition lasted.

Our Constitution has tended to be amended to allow more people in, to allow more freedom. What a tragic thing to start retrenching. Once you start retrenching, where does it stop? If the solution to everything is to amend the constitution, we are in real trouble. There go the things that people felt so strongly about in this country and that make this country really terrific. Sarah led the way. She had the courage to walk into that marvelous chamber which is known as one of the last of the great plantations. The Supreme Court is one of the last bastions of male supremacy. She had the courage to walk in and argue the case. Not only that, she won. So if she wins, we win. Here she is, Sarah Weddington.

Banquet address by
THE HONORABLE SARAH WEDDINGTON
28 FEBRUARY, 1976

The Honorable Sarah Weddington

I genuinely appreciate the opportunity of joining you for this very important symposium. Memories of your generous welcome will always warm my heart. But I did not come here to be honored. I came for some very different reasons.

First, I came because I think abortion is the most important issue we could discuss or do something about. It is impossible for people to truly control their lives in any respect when they are unable to control their reproductive capacities. Second, I came because I believe that you are the most important people that I could spend this evening with. Without you and people like you, the successes regarding abortion could not have been won. If we are to continue to win the issue of abortion, you and people exactly like you must forge that victory. I came in tribute to you. Third, I came because of your Governor. In 1971, before I was elected to be a member of the Texas House of Representatives, I was part of a coalition effort working to pass a liberalized abortion bill in Texas. We called Dick Lamm and told him that we needed a legislator from somewhere in the United States to come and testify that a better abortion law should be passed and to tell Texas legislators that they could vote for such a bill and survive politically. We had been unable to get help from even a single legislator from another state. Dick Lamm came. I will forever owe him a debt of gratitude for his help.

I often wonder how all the things mentioned in the introduction have happened to me. I remember so many situations relating to my race for public office. Some of those situations are funny ones.

I was the first woman to win a House seat in my county. Three men and I were in the race. At political meetings early in my race, those attending would discuss one of my opponents and then another of my opponents. Finally one of the women attending would say, "Well, what about Sarah Weddington?" Someone would inevitably say, "Is she a serious candidate?" I got a lot of excellent, dedicated women workers out of that kind of condescending attitude. My main opponent would only refer to me, never by name, as that "sweet little girl." That was a mistake; it made me determined to beat him. When it was announced that he and I were going to be in a run-off, he had a big press conference. He announced to the people of Travis County that sometimes I wore my hair up and sometimes I wore my hair down, and that sometimes I wore short skirts and sometimes I wore long skirts. That showed I was trying to confuse the voters of Travis County. After I beat him, I was told that the bankers in town were giving him a really hard time about how in the world he managed to spend over $30,000 and still be beaten by that "sweet little girl."

After I got to the Legislature, I started receiving invitations to all kinds of meetings. My invitations would always read, "You and your wife are cordially invited . . ." The women in the House (there were five of us) started writing back to point out that times were changing and that more and more women were serving as elected officials. We sometimes suggested the language, "You and your spouse. . . ." Then we realized that there were 30 or more of the members who were not married and that we were making a different, but equally false, assumption about the members. When I get an invitation now, it will most often read, "You and whoever you want to bring. . . ."

After my first session I was one of the members honored by the State Bar of Texas for work done during the session. I was the only woman included. I was called before the Bar at its state convention in Fort Worth, Texas, and presented with a truly beautiful gold and walnut plaque engraved as follows: "With grateful appreciation to the Honorable Sarah Weddington for his service and dedication. . . ."

How I have survived all that I am not sure, but I have and I like public service. I like it in part because I believe that if I had not been in the Texas legislature in 1973 and 1975, a bill severely restricting abortion would have passed. I believe that nothing passed in part because I was there. Today Texas has no laws against abortion. Public involvement is important for me and for each of you.

I also remember various experiences regarding the Supreme Court case, *Roe v. Wade.* I had recently graduated from law school when some friends of mine from the university community in Austin came to me and said they wanted to do abortion counseling. They were afraid they would be prosecuted if they did. That just did not seem right to me. The more I researched, the worse I thought the abortion laws were. In law school they teach that "where there is a wrong, there is a remedy" and what you do is file a law suit. I talked to Linda Coffee, a friend of mine from Dallas who had graduated from law school with me, and we decided to file suit seeking to have the Texas abortion laws declared unconstitutional.

Our main plaintiff, "Jane Roe," is an unmarried woman, slightly younger than I, who does not even have an eighth grade education. When she became pregnant, she had the best job she had ever had, waitressing at a good place where she made good tips. She was afraid that she would be fired if her boss found out she was pregnant. She had gone to many doctors in Dallas but each had refused to do an abortion for her because of the Texas law.

A couple we called "John and Mary Doe" joined in the effort. They had no children. Mary had been advised by her physician not to take the pill and not to get pregnant. They were in a dilemma: if they did not use the best means of birth control (the pill), there was a possibility that Mary would get pregnant and that they then would be faced with the very difficult decision of whether she should go through the pregnancy and risk her health or go through an illegal abortion and risk her health. One night, Linda and I sat up quite late drafting the petition. We put in some wonderful language about how the fear of pregnancy was "hanging as a spectre above the Does' marital bed." When we read it the next day we had better sense and took it out.

The case was filed with those three plaintiffs. A Dallas physician, who was under pending indictment for allegedly having done illegal abortions, intervened as a party plaintiff.

The hearing on the case before the panel of three federal district judges was my first contested case. I was petrified. I remember that Sarah Hughes, the judge who swore in Lyndon Johnson as President, was one of the judges. At one point during the hearing, when my nervousness was obviously showing, Sarah winked at me as if to say, "It's going to be all right." Sure enough, it was.

The three-judge court declared the Texas law to be unconstitutional but denied injunctive relief saying that it assumed state authorities would abide by the decision of a federal court. However, the Dallas District Attorney promptly announced that he would continue to prosecute anyone who performed an abortion pending the appeal of the case to the Supreme Court. The decision was appealed by the Texas Attorney General to the Supreme Court; that Court granted a hearing.

A decision had to be made about whether Jane would continue her pregnancy or whether we would seek funds to send her out-of-state for an abortion. As her lawyers, Linda and I explained to her that, although we could not say for sure, the case might be declared moot and later thrown out if she had an abortion. She decided to carry the pregnancy to term to save the case. At birth the child was placed for adoption.

Linda and I started preparing the Supreme Court brief and for the argument before the Supreme Court. There were all kinds of things we did to get ready. For example, we did numerous moot courts, some with women at the law school and some with law professors. I remember spending hours in front of my bathroom mirror, trying to explain to an imaginary Justice Burger what it would be like to be pregnant and not want to be. I do not think I really ever found a way to convey the proper feeling to him but I certainly spent a great deal of time trying.

The Supreme Court is very formal. For example, all of the court personnel in the courtroom wear cutaway coats and striped pants. About thirteen different types of marble were used in building the courtroom. You cannot take any written materials in unless you are the counsel in a case to be argued; even then you must have a special pass for your materials. Coats and wraps must be left outside. Where you enter the Supreme Court chamber there are church pews for the visitors. There is a five-minute section to seat those who want to stay only a few minutes; there is another section of pews for those people who want to hear the entire case presentation. There was a long line of people wanting to hear the cases the first time we argued. The court has sergeants who come and tell you that you cannot put your arm on the back of the pews, you cannot chew gum, you cannot talk, and you cannot take notes.

There is a gold railing that separates the lay people from chairs where lawyers admitted to practice before the Supreme Court sit. To be admitted to Supreme Court practice you have to be a lawyer, have practiced for about three years, have at least three people say you are of good character, and pay about $25. There are four tables where the people who are arguing the two cases that morning or afternoon sit, a table for each side of each case. The Texas and the Georgia abortion cases were argued the same morning. At my seat were two hand-made goosequill pens, each made by a gentleman in North Carolina who is the only person today who knows how to make the pens. The pens are a long-standing tradition of the court which each counsel can take as a souvenir.

On my left was the press section; on my right was the family section where the friends and family of the judges were sitting. The bench where the judges sat was within inches of where I stood to argue.

At the appointed time, the velvet curtains behind the bench parted. Standing there were the judges, silhouetted in their black robes. They walked out and started peering down at me. I remember an instant reaction of wondering how to react to those men who had so much power over what meant so much to me. Should I smile and wink? Should I look demure? Should I stare back? What should I do?

The argument began. I had given only the introductory remarks about the case when Justice Burger started asking me questions. The first question was about the *Vuitch* case. I remember the great weight of responsibility that I felt, knowing that I was the only person who would ever get to present the basic issues and knowing what a tremendous impact the decision would have on peoples' lives. I remember in particular several humorous questions.

For example, the State of Texas argued that every woman really did have a choice; her choice was whether or not to get pregnant. If she simply refrained from intercourse, she would not get pregnant. We pointed out that in Texas, rape is specifically defined as being carnal knowledge of a woman other than your wife; if it is your wife involved there is no such thing as rape. We pointed out the rate of contraceptive failure. Finally one of the judges said, "It seems to me you are trying to argue that the woman makes her decision when she decides to live down there in Texas." He might have added, "and you can't convince me that Texas women are going to completely abstain."

The state argued that the case was moot because Jane Roe was no longer pregnant when the Supreme Court heard the case. From the time we filed the suit until it was argued before the Supreme Court, almost two years had elapsed. We could not very well argue that Jane Roe was still pregnant; she obviously was not. Another judge responded to the mootness argument by saying, "Well, it just seems to me there will

280

always be unmarried pregnant girls someplace down there in Texas." He might have added, "It's not the woman's fault that the gestation period for a lawsuit is so much longer than that for humans." There was a lot of give and take in the first oral arguments.

Both the Texas and Georgia cases were argued twice. When the Court failed to announce a decision after the first argument, the rumors were that the Court was reluctant to make a decision because the court was "the Nixon court" and Nixon at that time was running for re-election. Also, only seven judges were on the Supreme Court for the first hearing, and several persons speculated that the Court wanted nine judges to participate in the decision.

We argued the case a second time in the fall of 1972. The judges asked fewer questions; Powell and Rehnquist were then on the bench. It is interesting that the decision was announced the first Monday after Nixon was inaugurated.

I was at home that Monday morning when a friend called and said, "You won the case!" I said, "What?" I could not believe it. The Court had read the decision that morning, the press had broadcast the news, and my friend heard about it from somebody who had heard it on the radio. The day of the announcement the Court mailed me a telegram that we'd won and later that day mailed me a copy of the opinion. It was three days after the opinion was announced before I knew what the actual language of the decision was; never have three days seemed so long.

You are all familiar with that decision. As you know, it declared that a state cannot constitutionally prohibit abortion and cannot pass regulations that effectively prevent women from access to abortions. It truly was a landmark decision.

Jane Roe is still in Dallas. I still see her every once in a while. She is so proud that she had a part in the *Roe* v. *Wade* decision. Mary Doe is now a law student who says that she is going to bring other cases for women like the *Roe* case.

Looking back, we really do have reason to celebrate. Had we gathered this same day in 1972 and had someone told us that within a couple of years we would win a Supreme Court decision which would wipe out almost every state law, that three years after that decision no anti-choice constitutional amendment would have passed Congress, that the Senate committeee considering such a constitutional amendment would have turned it down, that we had a good chance of getting such an amendment turned down in the House, and that most major Democratic candidates would be supporting the Supreme Court decision, we would not have believed it. When we think back to what we expected in 1972, we realize that we have accomplished so much and have so much to be grateful for.

The Supreme Court decision was not won by any one person. In fact, I always feel ill at ease when recognized as "the person who won the decision." Although I argued the case, I did not really win it. It was won in part by a great many people like you here in Colorado, who had passed liberalized laws and who, in doing so, had changed public opinion. It was won in part by the people around the country who had been working on other cases and who had set the precedents that we needed for our case. It was won in part by those of you whom I call the front line troops, the ones who had been providing counseling and abortion services (sometimes legal and sometimes illegal), and who had been providing the services that women really needed. It was won by many people.

Some of the people who were very much involved then are also currently involved. One of the things I have enjoyed most about my work has been the people that I have had a chance to meet and to know, the people I have come to love and respect, the people who to me are profiles of courage.

What we have done is great. It is great because of what it has meant to people and their increased ability to decide how they will respond to individual situations. It has meant that a lot of young women have not had to go through the terror their mothers did of knowing that they were pregnant and not wanting to be and yet, not knowing anyone to turn to and not knowing any place to go and perhaps going through an illegal abortion. It has meant that we no longer have to hear about those clandestine meetings with all the horror that you and I have both heard about, about the places and the circumstances and the bad medical consequences that often occurred. It has meant that we do not hear so much about people who are now sterilized, injured in other ways, or dead because of those illegal abortions. It has meant that the woman who has had her family and suddenly discovers that she is pregnant again can make a decision about what her life will be from that time forward. It has meant that the family that suddenly has an unexpected pregnancy can make a decision and, if they so choose, can secure a safe, legal abortion. It has meant that the woman who fears a genetic defect can begin a pregnancy, find out whether or not the fetus is in fact deformed, and then decide whether or not she will carry the pregnancy to term. It has meant that those women in their later reproductive years can make a decision when pregnancy unexpectedly occurs. It has meant that if contraceptives fail, those involved can make a decision. It has meant that the woman who is going through the break-up of marriage can make a decision. It has meant that for a woman, whatever her personal reasons may be, her reproductive nature really is her decision. It has meant that a lot of you are still involved in making it possible for her decision to be translated into action.

Everyone has moments that they go back to and say, "If I had it to do all over again, I'd do it over again and that moment was part of it." At the national NARAL meeting I heard Kenneth Edelin speak. He is such a terrific person, yet he has certainly been through a lot. In his speech, he talked about the trial that he had been through in Boston and all the different aspects of it and the appeal. His closing remarks involved his grandmother who had an abortion in the woods of Washington, D.C. many years ago. He shared with us that part of what he was doing was seeing that no woman ever had to go through what his grandmother went through so long ago. I think that is what we are about: trying to see that women do not have to go through what women have had to go through in the past. That is important. It is a good thing we have done.

Now that we have accomplished so much, I think all of us tend sometimes to get a little tired. We think about all the years and all the effort we have spent on abortion, and we hope we can move on to some new issues. Every time we start feeling that way, the opposition starts a new push to impose their wishes on the rest of us. It is happening again. It is especially important that we react this time because I am firmly convinced that every year, every month, every day, that we hold the line we have already drawn the chances are improved it will never go back again. Each day longer we hold the line, the chances are that much less that the situation will ever be changed. The opposition knows that. That is why I think this year is a crucial year. It is a year when we are seeing an all-out attack on the work we have done and the accomplishments we have achieved.

The opposition is attacking in several ways. We see their attack on public opinion which is favorable to us through misleading ads. They are attacking the Supreme Court decision. Through the anti-choice movement, through the Catholic pastoral plan in which they say they are going to organize down to every local parish level—a tremendous potential for organization and opposition—and through things like the march on Congress, they are attacking Congress and state legislatures. We now have House hearings in progress on the subject of an anti-choice constitutional amendment. We are in the process of an election, and we see all the pressures they are putting on candidates.

The states' rights argument they are making is such a wonderful argument to make to anyone in Congress because he or she can then say "We're not deciding; we're just giving it back to the local people to decide." If a states' right amendment ever passes, it would mean we would have to fight the battle not just in Congress, but in every one of the fifty states. That would be an even more difficult battle for every one of us and would take a lot more time.

We have "what's-her-name" running for President. Have any of you seen her ads? If not, let me tell you about them. They say, "You can help put pro-life ads on national TV, and the federal government will match your every dollar. Send your money to pro-life committee of such and such." Sometimes it will say, "What's-her-name, Pres." A lot of times it does not even say "candidate for president" or "President of the United States." In fact, she was the vice-president of the National Right-to-Life Organization. The whole campaign has focused on saying to people "you can do something; you can put ads on national TV to see that abortion is no longer safe and no longer legal." Some ads have her saying, "Hello, I'm what's-her-name, candidate for president and now I want you to meet

Mildred Jefferson." You all know of Mildred Jefferson and her usual tirade. That's what your federal campaign dollars are going to be paying to put on TV.

NARAL has filed a complaint with the Federal Elections Commission, first saying that giving matching funds to her is a violation of the spirit of the federal law on matching funds, and that there are also technical violations of the law. The complaint is still pending, but she is getting federal matching money. We are going to have to combat public opinion regarding what those ads are saying. We really are going to have to be on the defensive.

Regarding members of Congress and candidates for Congress, you in Colorado are so lucky to have people in Congress with the positive stands that they have. Do not let them think that just because you talked to them last year, that is the last contact you are going to have, because the other side is talking to them. One of the things that we have got to do is keep that contact up and keep saying, "We appreciate your stand, we are for you and we'll help you in the political arena," to encourage them to maintain that kind of positive stand.

We talk about the availability of safe, legal abortions. Yet Planned Parenthood studies show that in many areas of the country, women do not have abortion facilities close to where they live. We have got the problem of trying to make abortions available to those people who have fewer resources. The opposition is making a constant effort to prevent federal and state money from going to pay for Medicaid abortions, to deny eligible women that particular kind of medical care. We are now discovering that many insurance policies do not cover all reproductive services. We have work to do to make abortion services truly available.

We have to make information on abortion available. We have to get the word out constantly that there are safe, legal abortions available, where they can be obtained, and all the information about the importance of getting them early.

We need to be alert to maintain favorable public opinion. Each time someone does a straw poll like the one conducted last year by *The National Observer,* we have got to be sure that we send in many favorable answers; you know the other side is going to be sending unfavorable ones. NARAL and Planned Parenthood have produced some TV spots you might consider sponsoring in your area.

I would like to suggest two final things we need to do. The first thing is that everyone here should join NARAL. NARAL is the only national organization that has as its one goal maintaining the Supreme Court abortion decision and preventing unfavorable legislation from passing in Congress. Many of the women's organizations are involved on our side and it is good if you support them, but I hope you will all also consider joining NARAL. Another suggestion is that perhaps the organization that you had, which had such an important role in getting a better law passed in Colorado, needs to be rejuvenated. I know some of are already thinking about that. Everybody here should be thinking about how to see that the decision is maintained through the election process, through public opinion, and through all the kinds of things that we were doing three years ago.

We need to talk more about working together. I get so frustrated with the time that some spend fighting people who believe as we do when we have the enemy out there to fight. Please, let us beat our opposition first and then work out our own problems.

I think every one of us has had to be involved in who is elected president and to see that we support those who have supported us, like Dick Lamm and Pat Schroeder. I personally have made a pledge that I will not support any candidate who does not agree with me on abortion. That is the kind of commitment it is going to take this year. I hope you will all consider making that kind of commitment until we really have it won.

Let me just share a closing thought. Every individual wants to leave a legacy. History will not remember our names, but I am convinced that history will remember what we have done and will record it as having been a valuable contribution that made lives better. The only thing that bothers me is the fear that history might record that we were successful for several years, that we became complacent and gave up the fight, and that finally we lost the fight. Let us each pledge to do whatever it takes for us to be recorded by history as the winners. That is what we are today.

SPECIAL PRESENTATION
TO
HON. SARAH WEDDINGTON
BY
Colorado Women's Political Caucus
and
Colorado National Organization for Women

The Colorado Women's Political Caucus and Colorado National Organization for Women wish to honor Ms. Weddington. She is an example to all of us of what women can achieve. Soon there will be more of us able to get into the places and do these kinds of things. She has worked hard in many areas: in education, legal protection for rape victims, credit, in family law and increasing participation for women and minorities in the Bar. We would like to thank her again for her work on behalf of all of us.

Ms. Weddington: I really had a thing against roses when "Right-to-Life" started using them. I just overcame it. I love yellow roses. Thank you.

Dr. Hern: Thank you very much, Sarah. We appreciated your remarks and will remember them for a long time. We will take an example from your idealism and hard work and excellent results.

A Pregnant Woman's Bill of Rights

All who believe in the right to choose are being depicted as the butchers of the innocent. A deliberate, well-funded and well organized attempt is being made to cast those who believe in the right of a woman to a safe, .legal abortion as proponents of an unethical pro-death movement. The time has come to make a clear, concise defense of the effort to increase and undergird the dignity of *all* human life.

It is a great contemporary American tragedy that a woman who wants to terminate her pregnancy is the object of a bicentennial witch-hunt by self-appointed moralists. Restrictive legislation introduced in the state and in the national legislatures is designed to make her the victim of this persecution.

Therefore, the Executive Committee of The National Abortion Rights Action League, at a meeting in Denver, Colorado, February 28-29, 1976, affirms the following:

BILL OF RIGHTS FOR A PREGNANT WOMAN

1. She has the right to choose what is best for her life.
2. She is free to deliver a wanted child or to terminate a disastrous pregnancy.
3. Her choice must be implemented by safe, legal, adequate and available medical care in approved facilities.
4. Laws affecting her choice must be equitable, intelligible and enforceable.
5. In exercising her right to choose, she must be loyal to her own conscience.
6. She should be supported in her decision by society and defended from persecution by any who disagree.

We urge all people of good will and all branches of government to support these rights.

Dr. Jesse Lyons
The Riverside Church
New York, New York

INDEX

INDEX

Abortion services
evaluation, 89; 99-102; 95-98
facilities and services, 91; 121-123
fees, 101
objectives, 93
team care, 118; 119; 114

Adolescents
counseling, 263; 264
special problems, 131; 247; 261-269

Allergic reaction
to prostaglandin, 28

Amenorrhea
post-abortion, 38

Amniocentesis
technique, 29

Amniotic fluid
bloody, 29

Anesthesia
complications, 47; 34; 37
general vs. local, 47; 34
with tenaculum, 22

Antibiotics
prophylactic, 23-25

Anomalies, uterine
abortion in, 35
diagnosis of, 35

Aspiration
vacuum, 168; 169; 33
technique, 35

Bicornuate uterus
abortion in, 35
diagnosis of, 35

Birth control
risks compared to abortion, 57-67
information in counseling, 139; 143; 144; 145; 146

Bishops, Catholic
action against abortion, 250; 231

Bleeding
management of, 36; 37

Blue Cross-Blue Shield
in Colorado, 173
policies on abortion, 173

Catholic church
position on abortion, 247; 248; 232

Cannulas
Karmann, 21
motion during procedure, 35
perforation with, 21; 35
plastic vs metal, 20; 21

Center for Disease Control
goals, 80
methods, 79; 80
number of abortions 1970-72, 78
preliminary report with JPSA, 81
role in abortion surveillance, 77

Cervical dilators
Hanks, 49
Hawkins-Ambler, 35
Hegar, 19; 34
perforation with, 35
Pratt, 19; 33

Cervix
application of tenaculum, 21; 22; 36
cervicovaginal fistula, 28
dilatation of, 52; 19; 35
injury to, 28; 36
internal os, 35
mechanical ripening in second trimester abortion, 52; 19; 28

Church, Catholic
position on abortion, 247; 248; 232

Clinics, abortion
evaluation of, 89; 95-98
safety of abortion in, 90; 92; 34
structure of, 95; 96; 34; 85
role of, 103; 57

Coagulopathy
in saline abortion, 27

Colorado
abortion law, 211; 212; 175-177
health impact of abortion, 77
political process in, 77-79;
sex education in, 153-155

Hypertonic saline
complications of, 27
use of in second trimester abortion, 27

Hysterogram
use of in diagnosis of anomalies, 35

Infections
causes of, 37
management of, 37
prevention of, 23-25

Instillation techniques
prostaglandin, 29
safety compared to D & E abortion, 44; 45

Instruments
comparative advantages of, 19-21; 35
proper use of, 35; 36

Insurance
actuarial considerations, 172
risk-spreading principle, 172

Intrauterine devices
safety compared to other methods, 65; 66
removal of in pregnancy, 49; 53; 54; 22

Intravenous therapy
use of in prevention of water intoxication, 37

Joint Program for the Study of Abortion
results of, 81; 41; 42; 33

Judicial decisions
discussion of, 187-198

Labor
in prostaglandin abortion, 28; 29

Laminaria treatment
control of, 53
in first trimester abortion, 53; 54; 19
in prostaglandin abortion, 28; 29
in second trimester abortion, 48; 52; 19; 28; 29
perforation rate, 54

Legislation
federal, 233; 234
state, 175-177; ?; 229; 230
tactics, 175-177; 235

Major complication
definition, 43

Marital status
in pregnant teenagers, 264; 266; 63

Mechanical techniques
of ripening cervix in second trimester abortion, 48; 52; 28-29

Medicaid
South Dakota case, 167-169; 212

Menstrual regulation
experience with, 100; 53

Minors
feeling toward, 164
legal aspects of treatment, 215; 216; 211

Missouri
acceptance of abortion, 113
case before Supreme Court, 191

Mole, hydatidiform
illustration of, **36D**

Moral issues
discussion of, 247-259

Morbidity of abortion
compared with risk of contraception, 65-67
difference in stage of gestation, 44
difference in technique, 44-46

Mortality in abortion
compared with risks of contraception, 65-67
in legal vs. illegal, 78; 60
in the United States, 77

New York City
impact of legal abortion, 74-76
number and rate of abortion, 69; 70; 62